RES
PUBLICA
CONQUASSATA

RES PUBLICA

CLASSICAL STUDIES PEDAGOGY SERIES

GENERAL EDITOR
Norma Goldman
Wayne State University

ADVISORY EDITORS
Herbert W. Benario
Emeritus, Emory University
Sally Davis
*Wakefield High School
Arlington, Virginia*
Judith Lynn Sebesta
University of South Dakota
Meyer Reinhold
Boston University

BOOKS IN THIS SERIES

Caesaris Augusti Res Gestae et Fragmenta, second edition, revised and enlarged by Herbert W. Benario, 1990

Roman Letters: History from a Personal Point of View, by Finley Hooper and Matthew Schwartz, 1990

Cicero's Verrine Oration II.4: With Notes and Vocabulary, by Sheila K. Dickison, 1992

Res Publica Conquassata: Readings on the Fall of the Roman Republic, selected and edited by James K. Finn and Frank J. Groten, Jr., 1997

CONQUASSATA

Readings on the Fall of the
Roman Republic

EDITED BY JAMES K. FINN AND
FRANK J. GROTEN, JR.

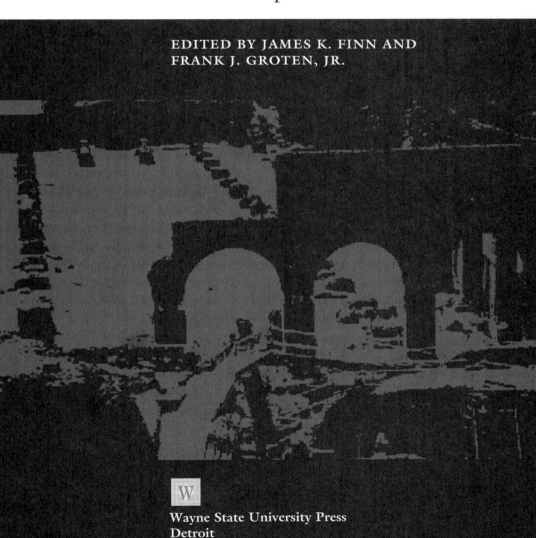

Wayne State University Press
Detroit

Library of Congress Cataloging-in-Publication Data

Res publica conquassata : readings on the fall of the Roman Republic /
    edited by James K. Finn and Frank J. Groten, Jr.
        p.   cm.—(Classical studies pedagogy series)
    Fifty-five texts in Latin from the last fifty years of the
Roman Republic, with critical matter in English.
    Includes bibliographical references.
    ISBN 0-8143-2678-1 (pbk. : alk. paper)
    1. Latin language—Readers—Rome. 2. Rome—History—Republic,
265-30 B.C.—Problems, exercises, etc.   I. Finn, James K.
II. Groten, Frank J.   III. Series.
PA2095.R38 1998
478.6′421—dc21   97-20631

**To Captain Curtiss Cummings,
MC USNR (Ret.)**

*semper honōs nōmenque
tuum laudēsque manēbunt*

Contents

Preface

This book consists of seven parts: historical introduction, chronology of key dates, Latin texts, critical commentary, list of personal names, glossary of key terms, and a Latin-English vocabulary. It has thus been designed as a self-contained edition for students of intermediate or advanced Latin.

The text describes the outbreak and some of the effects of the civil war between Caesar and Pompey in 49 B.C. Caesar's continuous narrative (from *Bellum Cīvīle*) has been interspersed with appropriate selections from Cicero's personal correspondence that recount, discuss, and elucidate—from a different and often opposing point of view—the very events related by Caesar. Because Caesar's writings present his deeds as he wishes them to be seen, his real motives and aims can be inferred only by informed conjecture based on the facts, which can often be gleaned from other sources, especially Cicero's *Letters*. This correspondence of Cicero contrasts with Caesar's narrative in that the letters record Cicero's intimate thoughts, usually sincerely expressed without the suppressions and distortions often required for personal justification before the public.

The critical commentary provides aids to translating and grammatical explanations for a wide range of important Latin constructions, historical information about many details of the readings, and information about Roman magistracies, assemblies, and electioneering practices in an authoritative, meaningful context. To assist those who prefer not to approach the readings sequentially, we have repeated or cross-referenced many historical and grammatical notes. These notes have been furnished with references to J. H. Allen and James B. Greenough's *New Latin Grammar* (New Rochelle, NY: Caratzas, 1988), which is cited as an authority for the grammatical explanations. In cases where the treatment of a particular point in *New Latin Grammar* seems insufficient for the student, we have referred to Basil L. Gildersleeve and Gonzalez Lodge's *Gildersleeve's Latin Grammar* (New York: St. Martin's Press, 1971).

The division of Latin words in the Latin-English vocabulary follows that of the *Oxford Latin Dictionary* (Oxford: Clarendon Press, 1982).

A reference map has been included to enable the student to locate quickly the place names cited in the Latin text and to follow Caesar's line of march down through Italy. There is also a short bibliography.

The title *Res Publica Conquassata* originates from a letter (Text 53) of Cicero's friend Servius Sulpicius Rufus, who describes the devastation caused by the civil war. Sulpicius was an eminent jurist who had remained neutral throughout that bloody conflict.

In addition to the works of such eminent historians as T. Robert S. Broughton, P. A. Brunt, Matthias Gelzer, Erich S. Gruen, Ronald Syme, and Lily Ross Taylor, frequent use has been made of D. R. Shackleton Bailey's *Cicero's Letters to Atticus* (Cambridge: Cambridge University Press, 1965–70); Robert Y. Tyrrell and Louis C. Purser's *The Correspondence of Cicero* (Dublin: Hodges, Foster, & Figgis, 1885–1901); W. W. How's *Cicero: Select Letters* (Oxford: Clarendon Press, 1959); David Stockton's *Thirty-Five Letters of Cicero* (Oxford: Oxford University Press, 1969); and J. M. Carter's *Julius Caesar: The Civil War, Books I and II* (Warminster: Aris & Phillips, 1990). James S. Ruebel's *Caesar and the Crisis of the Roman Aristocracy* (Norman: University of Oklahoma Press, 1994) came to our attention too late for us to profit significantly from his stimulating treatment of some of the same material.

We owe a special debt of gratitude to Professor John T. Ramsey of the University of Illinois at Chicago, who read portions of an early draft of this edition with a scholarly eye and offered numerous improvements with a keen sensitivity to the needs of students. In addition, we appreciate the contributions of our colleagues Robert J. Iorillo and Wayne N. Bell, who, in teaching from earlier versions of the manuscript, made constructive suggestions and criticisms. Finally, special recognition is due to our editor at Wayne State University Press, Janet Witalec, for her constant vigilance in correcting matters of format and style. All infelicities that remain may be attributed to our own recalcitrance.

James K. Finn
Frank J. Groten, Jr.

The Roman senate house as it appears today, a restoration by the emperor Diocletian during the years 284–305 A.D. It stands in the northwest corner of the forum near the location of an earlier senate house begun by Julius Caesar in 44 B.C. Caesar's building replaced the senate house that had been erected by Sulla's son Faustus. The interior of the senate house has, on either side, three low broad steps for chairs of the more important senators (with standing room for the others on the top step) and, at the far end, a raised platform for the presiding magistrate.

The east façade of the Roman record office, in which the Romans kept the official archives of the city. The building was erected by Quintus Lutatius Catulus during his consulship in 78 B.C. Sitting at the foot of the eastern slope of the Capitoline Hill, it formed a backdrop for the northwest corner of the forum, where it overlooked the temple of Concord, the senate house, the *comitium*, and the *clīvus Capitōlīnus*. The upper portion of the building was destroyed by Michelangelo, who built on top of the ancient construction the Palazzo del Senatore, here visible above the remains of Catulus's building.

Historical Introduction

From an ode of the lyric poet Horace (*Odes* 2.1), we learn that the historian Gaius Asinius Pollio chose as the starting point of his narrative of the Roman civil war the year 60. Pollio's choice was judicious: that year saw the formation of a political coalition which was to dominate Roman politics for years and which, with its final collapse, was to produce a bloody conflict persisting intermittently for nearly two decades. The coalition, known by modern historians as the "First Triumvirate," consisted of three of the most influential men in Rome: Gnaeus Pompeius Magnus (Pompey), Marcus Licinius Crassus, and Gaius Julius Caesar.

Pompey, upon returning gloriously from a five-year eastern campaign against Mithridates, king of Pontus in Asia Minor, had enjoyed at Rome a splendid triumph in recognition of his greatest achievement in an already illustrious career as a military commander. He had been awaiting the ratification by the senate of his reorganization of the province of Asia and the approval of a land grant for his veteran soldiers.

After a visit to the province of Asia for his own financial interests, Crassus had found himself approached by a number of tax collectors. Upon overestimating the amount collectable in that war-weary province, these tax collectors or "publicans" had wanted the senate to revise their tax contracts so that they would not have to empty their own pockets to meet the total stipulated by the original agreements.

Led by the uncompromising conservative Marcus Porcius Cato,

the senate first refused to revise the tax contracts and then, with the support of Crassus, blocked the ratification of Pompey's eastern settlement.

Caesar, returning to Rome from a tour of duty in the province of Further Spain, had been seeking political and financial support in his campaign to be elected consul. A much detested man in some political circles, Caesar had hoped to stand *in absentiā* for the consulship. But the senate, with Cato again in the forefront, denied his request.

Annoyed by the senatorial slight to their public standing, Pompey and Crassus, long-standing rivals who continued to distrust each other, sought other ways to achieve their separate goals. They both knew well of Caesar's opposition to the senatorial majority on various issues in earlier times. Caesar, in turn, had realized that with their support he might secure his election to the consulship, where he could repay them by sponsoring legislation for Pompey and his soldiers as well as for Crassus's friends in the tax companies. The resulting "Triumvirate," an informal personal alliance, appeared to satisfy the ambitions of all three partners.

Aware of the need for effective support in the senate, Pompey invited Marcus Tullius Cicero, late in 60, to join the new coalition. Cicero had long ago established himself as one of the finest orators and most effective politicians in Rome. As consul in 63, while Pompey was still campaigning in Asia Minor, Cicero had convinced many fellow senators of a conspiracy in their midst. His forceful actions had exposed a clique of desperate nobles and thwarted the plot organized by L. Sergius Catilina. In addition, Cicero had supported the proposed revision of the tax contract even though, as he wrote to his confidant Titus Pomponius Atticus, he knew that it was "a scandalous business, a disgraceful proposal, an admission of recklessness" (*Ad Att.* 1.17.9). But Cicero feared a rupture in the political harmony of the upper classes (*concordia ōrdinum*) in Rome if the request for a revision were denied. Nevertheless, he declined an invitation to join the "Triumvirs," whose desire to concentrate power among themselves violated his republican ideals. They would have to find another mouthpiece.

As one of the consuls for the year 59, Caesar proceeded to reconcile Pompey and Crassus and to repay their support. When his land bill for Pompey's veterans met with obstruction by his consular colleague Marcus Calpurnius Bibulus (Cato's son-in-law) and by many other senators, Caesar presented a revised version of the bill directly to the popular assembly. Such a tactic would provoke angry criticism from conservative oligarchs in the senate, who espoused the status quo and liked to refer to themselves as *optimātēs* ("best men") while attacking as *populārēs* their political opponents, who sought to legislate without consulting them. The new bill, sponsored by a tribune of the people, contained an additional clause requiring that each senator swear an oath to support all its provisions. Caesar also persuaded Pompey and Crassus to support the bill publicly and to promise force against any attempt to block it. He threatened Bibulus and the opposing tribunes by warning them of the violence of the Roman mob and of Pompey's veterans. Support for the bill by Cicero, as he wrote to his friend Atticus, might have brought the orator "a very close connection with Pompey and also with Caesar, a return to favor with my enemies, peace with the common people, and security in my old age" (*Ad Att.* 2.3.4). Aligning himself, however, with the conservative aristocrats whose favor he had long tried to cultivate, Cicero unsuccessfully opposed the bill. After it was passed, Caesar never again presented any legislative proposals to the senate. Instead, he used the office of tribune and the assembly to pass measures to ratify Pompey's eastern settlement and, for Crassus, to grant concessions to the tax companies.

The "Triumvirs" would remember how Cicero had disappointed them again. When his oratory began to swell with complaints about their political machinations, Caesar and Pompey expedited the eligibility of Cicero's deadliest enemy, Publius Clodius, for the office of tribune. Despite assurances to Cicero of their support, and even after an offer from Caesar of a staff position in Gaul for the following year, Cicero was justifiably anxious about Clodius's threats. For the new tribune would pass, in December of 59, a series of bills to pave the way for the banishment of Cicero a few months later.

To invalidate further legislation by Caesar, Bibulus resorted to an unorthodox form of religious obstruction: each day, from his house, he claimed to be observing omens, which would automatically invalidate Caesar's legislation. Caesar, however, ignored this activity and proceeded to secure, through a tribune named Vatinius, a five-year command (proconsulship) in Cisalpine Gaul and Illyricum. The position in Gaul would keep him close to Italy when not compaigning in the province. Illyricum would afford him the opportunity to establish an overland route through the Balkans to draw Pompey's eastern acquisitions more tightly under Roman control. With the help of Pompey, who became Caesar's son-in-law in 59 by marrying his daughter Julia, Caesar also obtained for his proconsulship the additional province of Transalpine Gaul.

In February of 58, the tribune Clodius passed a bill calling for the banishment of anyone who had put Roman citizens to death without a

15

trial. The measure was aimed at Cicero, who had so acted to crush the conspiracy during his consulship by interpreting an emergency decree of the senate (*senātūs cōnsultum ultimum*) as the authorization to take such extreme steps to protect the state. Caesar publicly stated that, in his opinion, Cicero had violated the law in dealing with the apprehended conspirators. Pompey, too, offered no support but only referred the appealing Cicero to the consuls, who had already indicated their hostility to him. Despite expressions of support and sympathy from numerous other fellow senators, Cicero had to leave Italy. His fifteen months in exile comprised the darkest period in his life. The former hero was now being treated like a condemned criminal without a country. Degraded, disillusioned, his ego shattered, Cicero poured out a stream of letters bemoaning his misfortune. "No one," he declared to Atticus, "has ever been afflicted by so great a disaster, and no one has ever had more right to long for death" (*Ad Att.* 3.7.2). That Cicero felt betrayed is made clear in a letter to his younger brother Quintus: "There is no wrongdoing on my part except that I trusted those by whom I had considered it outrageous that I be deceived; I thought that ⟨my exile⟩ was not even in their interest. Each close, nearest, dearest friend feared for himself or was jealous of me" (*Ad Q.F.* 1.4.1). Cicero's self-pity obscured the facts: almost immediately after his exile, many fellow senators would exert their efforts for a decree to recall him.

In March of 58, just after Cicero left Rome for exile, Caesar assumed his provincial command in Gaul, where he would spend a large part of the next nine years in subjugating the Gauls and in developing the finest army in the Roman world, excellently trained and remarkably loyal to him. Pompey and Crassus remained in Rome, where Pompey bore the brunt of senatorial resentment of the "Triumvirate," which had never been sanctioned by law. Pompey, as Caesar must have realized, remained uncomfortable not only with the loss of respectability which the coalition had cost him in the eyes of the senate but also with the humiliation of dependence on his younger partner for the ratification of his Asian settlement. Crassus, who had receded to the background during Caesar's consulship, now tried to drive a wedge between Caesar and Pompey and break their domination of politics at Rome.

In August of 57, after a year of turmoil unleashed by the political gangsterism of Clodius, a Roman assembly voted nearly unanimously to recall Cicero. The orator arrived in Rome early in September to find a spectacular welcome. Cicero wrote to Atticus that near the gate through which he reentered the city, "the steps of the temples were mobbed with the common people. Their joy was displayed with the loudest applause. A similar crowd and applause escorted me to the Capitoline hill, and in the forum as well as on the Capitoline itself there was an amazing throng" (*Ad Att.* 4.1.5). Cicero, who had since the glorious days of his consulship identified himself with the republic that he had saved, was again ready to aid an ailing state.

Merely days after his return, however, Cicero aggravated the disease. Mindful of the widespread urban unrest that a sudden food shortage would provoke, he heightened tension among the "Triumvirs" by making a motion that Pompey be granted another special commission—supervision of the grain supply—with extraordinary powers for five years. This proposal must have shocked, if not enraged, many senators who had worked for the recall of Cicero while strenuously opposing Pompey and his two partners. It certainly displeased Caesar and Crassus, who were already resentful of each other. And yet opposition of the conservative aristocracy that had so often confronted them in the past kept the unsteady alliance intact, especially after Caesar intervened to bring his two partners closer together. In April of 56, a meeting at Luca, a town in southwestern Cisalpine Gaul, produced a renewal of the coalition after a candidate for the consulship of 55, Lucius Domitius Ahenobarbus (Cato's brother-in-law), announced that he would replace Caesar in Gaul and attacked, in the senate, the legislation of Caesar's consulship. Pompey and Crassus returned to Rome to stand together for the consulship of 55, and their political victory in Rome probably owed much to the presence of a large number of Caesar's troops on leave. Once in office, the two colleagues promptly renewed Caesar's command in Gaul for another five years and secured for themselves five-year proconsulships—in Spain for Pompey and in Syria for Crassus. Each would again have an army of his own.

The following year, Domitius finally reached the consulship, much to the embarrassment of the "Triumvirate," which had actively supported other candidates. Crassus departed for his command in Syria, but Pompey, contrary to established procedures, remained in the suburban vicinity of Rome and governed Spain through two of his legates, Lucius Afranius and Marcus Petreius. To Pompey's political discomfort was added deep personal grief: his wife Julia died in childbirth, and the infant followed her only days later. Dissolved at once was both a happy marriage and a personal bond between Pompey and Caesar, both of whom keenly felt the loss of Julia.

But in his province Caesar had other problems. The recalcitrant Gauls were threatening to throw off Roman attempts to control them. Rebellions seemed imminent, and during the winter of 54–53 Caesar needed additional troops. When recruitments in Cisalpine Gaul failed to produce enough men, he requested, and obtained, a legion from Pompey.

The coalition suffered a serious blow in 53 when Crassus left Syria to invade the Parthian Empire, the only major power on the frontiers of the Roman world. He was hoping to achieve a triumph to rival Pompey's in Asia and Caesar's successes in Gaul. Victory over the Parthians would also have ingratiated Crassus with many powerful senators and businessmen, who for years had been reaping large profits from financial investments in Asia. But at Carrhae in Mesopotamia, Crassus, his son Publius, and the bulk of his eight legions were defeated and killed, with the humiliating loss of legionary standards which would not be recovered for thirty-three years. Now there were no longer three partners but two.

By this time the political corruption and disorder in Rome erupted in riots, with gangs of slaves and freedmen roaming the streets in support of political candidates as directed by their masters or patrons. This street violence terrorized actual or suspected political rivals and their supporters. So much disorder shook Rome that public business was often suspended, and the consular candidates themselves contended in the violence and rioting. When the year 52 opened without consuls and with continued gang fighting in the city, claiming among others the life of Cicero's enemy Clodius, the senate issued an emergency decree (*senātūs cōnsultum ultimum*) and instructed Pompey to recruit soldiers throughout Italy. At the proposal of Caesar's former colleague Bibulus, a conservative bloc of senators offered Pompey the consulship without a colleague (a constitutional contradiction in terms) with a special mandate to heal the battered state. With the support of armed forces, Pompey restored order and secured the conviction of the most notorious disturbers of the peace.

Pompey's second consulship in three years strained political precedent and violated a long-standing law requiring a gap of ten years between consulships. He was now simultaneously proconsul of Spain and chief executive magistrate in Rome. As often in the past, the senate had suspended normal constitutional procedures to deal with a crisis in the city, and Pompey had seemed the best man for the job. At once he turned to the task of creating smoother and more efficient government. He brought about the passage of a measure to stop the manipulation of provincial assignments by means of tribunitial action. The new law (*lēx Pompēia dē prōvinciīs*) prescribed that provincial duties be granted to an ex-consul or ex-praetor only when a five-year interval had elapsed after his magistracy instead of before or during it. This would prevent subsequent praetors or consuls from doing what Caesar had done in 59 and what Crassus and Pompey had done in 55. From now on, the senate would allot new provincial assignments to ex-consuls and ex-praetors whose year in office had long ago concluded.

Many conservative aristocrats must have seen, in Julia's death, prospects for weakening the partnership of Pompey and Caesar. An attractive opportunity developed when the death of Crassus's son at Carrhae had made a widow of Cornelia, the daughter of Quintus Metellus Scipio. But for Pompey, always watching for new alliances, this was a chance to join one of the most illustrious families in Rome. And for Scipio, the new father-in-law, it meant another magistracy: Pompey chose him, with the approval of the senate, as his consular colleague for the remaining half of the year 52. As a consul whose wife boasted one of the most distinguished families in Italy and whose former father-in-law and political ally commanded the most powerful army in the Mediterranean world, Pompey seemed to have returned to the stage of his former dignity and power.

An unwilling beneficiary of Pompey's *lēx Pompēia dē prōvinciīs* was Cicero himself, who was named to serve as governor of the province of Cilicia along the southeastern coast of Asia Minor. The orator, who had declined a similar appointment after his consulship in 63, could not refuse this time. En route to his province, Cicero revealed his attitude toward the new assignment in a letter to Atticus. "Don't think," he wrote, "that I have any consolation for this tremendous nuisance except to hope that it will not last longer than a year" (*Ad Att.* 5.2.3). But before leaving Rome, Cicero had arranged to be kept informed of the political developments in the city during his absence by securing from a talented and observant former student, Marcus Caelius Rufus, the promise to send periodic reports to him in his province.

Meanwhile, in Gaul, though his conquests were far from complete, Caesar was already envisioning a second consulship upon his glorious return to Rome as soon as his five-year extension of command finally expired. With the privilege of standing as a candidate *in absentiā*, he would be able to step directly from his provincial command into the consulship. Once again, however, Cato represented an obstacle, as he had in 60. Caesar needed a tribunitial bill to exempt him from the standard practice of declaring one's candidacy at Rome in person, and Pompey provided the means by exerting his influence upon the current tribunes. The groundwork had been laid during the winter of 53–52 while Caesar was staying in winter quarters at Ravenna; despite resistance from Cato and his supporters, the tribunes unanimously passed in the assembly a law known as the "law of the ten tribunes" (*lēx decem tribūnōrum*), which permitted Caesar to stand *in absentiā*, before the expiration of his provincial command, for the office of consul. Thanks to the strenuous efforts of Pompey, Caesar now obtained what Cato had, years earlier, succeeded in denying him. Resentment in the senate, which traditionally considered itself the arbiter of provincial arrangements, must have run deep.

Despite his enormous prestige, Pompey exerted little influence upon the consular elections for the year 51. The new officers, Servius Sulpicius Rufus and Marcus Claudius Marcellus, could hardly be counted among his friends, and Marcellus was well known as a bitter enemy of Caesar. He had opposed Caesar's request to campaign *in absentiā* for the consulship. And he was determined to remove Caesar from his command and his army in Gaul. Months before he stepped into office, his efforts to recall Caesar had dominated discussion and debate in the senate. Late in the summer of 51, Marcellus was actively soliciting support for a proposal to terminate Caesar's command as of March of the following year. Opposition by Pompey contributed to the rejection of Marcellus's motion, but Metellus Scipio successfully proposed that a debate on the reassignment of Caesar's province should commence on March 1 of 50. Though the motion found no favor with Caesar, it need not have provoked alarm: he had friends among the tribunes who could use their powers to veto any senatorial decree hostile to his interests. In addition, a continuous stream of Gallic gold, which had already found its way into the hands of many an agent in Rome for personal use as well as to finance public spectacles and building programs, would ensure their loyalty. For the moment, at least, Caesar's options remained open. If the political situation in Rome improved, he would stand for the consulship; if not, he would find enough support for a pretext not to be recalled immediately from Gaul.

On March 1, 50, when the scheduled debate on the provinces was to be held, the tribune Gaius Scribonius Curio interposed his veto of any legislation designed to abbreviate or terminate Caesar's command in Gaul. Curio's motives remain unclear, though he is alleged to have received from Caesar enormous bribes to help finance his extravagant lifestyle. Perhaps he sought priority for his own program of agrarian reforms and grain laws. At any rate, the postponement of the provincial debate enraged Caesar's opponents in the senate. When Pompey, under intense pressure from other senators, proposed that Caesar remain in Gaul only until November, Curio blocked the proposal and verbally abused Pompey himself. Yet Curio was no Caesarian puppet. The tribune may have been trying to dissolve the coalition of Caesar and Pompey to serve his own political interests. Caesar's enemies in the senate, however, were concerned less with Curio's motives than with the effect of his veto. The consul Gaius Claudius Marcellus, cousin of the consul of 51, proposed that Curio be formally censured, but the motion was soundly defeated. Despite vehement opposition by such extremists as Cato and the Marcelli, most senators had no interest in provoking a crisis that might engulf them. Curio had gambled on that attitude among the majority of senators, and he was right.

By late summer of 51, the disgraceful defeat of Crassus in the east had created new worries in the senate. From his province of Cilicia, Cicero had himself sent a dispatch about the precarious situation there. Responding, in October, to hostile activity on the border between his province and Syria, Cicero captured some fortified outposts and was hailed as *imperātor* by his troops. That gesture qualified him to apply to the senate for a triumph. Such a special honor, if granted, would place his name in the official list of distinguished generals, which already included the name of Pompey.

Concern about a Parthian invasion of Roman provinces provoked discussion at every level of society. Pompey himself had seemed willing to accept the mission of securing Roman borders, but the majority of senators, partly from fear of another outbreak of urban violence and partly from unwillingness to advance Pompey's prestige or military strength, had refused him the command. Now, in late summer of 50, to meet the need for troops in Parthia, the senate decreed that Caesar and Pompey should each contribute a legion. Pompey volunteered his legion of recruits from Cisalpine Gaul, which he had lent to Caesar in the winter of 54–53. Caesar, therefore, had to surrender two legions: the borrowed one and another of his own choosing. Uncomfortable and suspicious, he complied nevertheless. Two legions set out for Italy to be billeted in Campania, south of Rome, in preparation for departure to the east.

Meanwhile, senatorial recognition of Caesar's *in absentiā* candidacy for the consulship—a privilege granted by tribunitial law—left Pompey, who had been absent from the session because of illness, in an embarrassing position since he had supported a termination to Caesar's command in November. This meant that Caesar would have to give up his provinces and army before standing for consul again. And although the Marcelli had been overwhelmingly outvoted by their fellow senators, they had at least succeeded in escalating tensions in the same way (though for different motives) as had Curio. Both they and Curio had been trying to split apart the coalition; the Marcelli hoped to use Pompey against Caesar, and Curio sought to employ Caesar against Pompey. Caesar himself saw Pompey's position as a sign that his former partner had joined the ranks of the anti-Caesarians in the senate. Rumors of an armed conflict saturated Rome.

In December, Curio made a proposal which offered hope of defusing an increasingly volatile situation: that both Pompey and Caesar resign their commands. The measure found favor among 370 of the 392 votes recorded in the senate. To the twenty-two dissenting voters, however, the proposal severely curtailed Pompey's five-year renewal of command, legislated in 52. And that, to Pompey, was unacceptable, as Curio and Caesar would have anticipated; perhaps they even publicized their own version of Pompey's reaction to exploit his intransigence. Caesar, on the other hand, had no intention of becoming a *prīvātus* while his enemies held so much power in Rome.

To Gaius Marcellus, the consul, Curio's proposal was equally unacceptable. Ignoring the expressed will of the senatorial majority, he left the inner city with his cousin of the same name (now elected for the consulship of 49) and his cousin's future colleague, Lucius Cornelius Lentulus Crus. Acting on his own initiative, Marcellus charged Pompey to defend Rome. Pompey was to deploy the two legions sent down into Italy by Caesar and now under his command, and he was to recruit additional legions as needed to protect the city. When Pompey accepted the command, the tattered threads of the bond between him and Caesar, which had been worn thin by the tribune Curio as well as by the Marcelli, Metellus Scipio, Cato, and a small but vehement clique of their conservative supporters, were finally severed. That further negotiations were likely to fail and result in war was foreseen by Caelius, who in his faithful correspondence to his mentor Cicero realistically summarized the situation in Rome (Text 1).

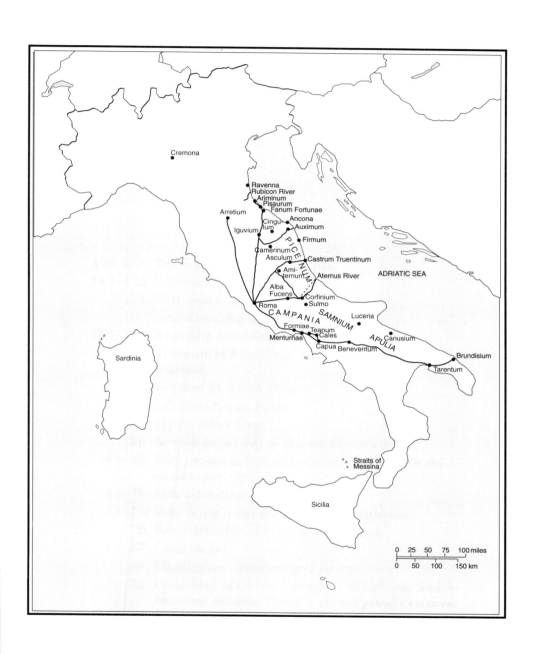

Cremona

Ravenna
Rubicon River
Ariminum
Pisaurum
Fanum Fortunae
Arretium
Ancona
Cingu-
lum
Auximum
Iguvium
Firmum
Camerinum
Asculum
Castrum Truentium
Ami-
ternum
Aternus River
ADRIATIC SEA
Alba
Fucens
Corfinium
Roma
Sulmo
CAMPANIA
SAMNIUM
Luceria
Formiae
Teanum
Cales
Canusium
Menturnae
APULIA
Capua
Beneventum
Brundisium
Tarentum

PICENUM

Sardinia

Straits of
Messina

Sicilia

| 0 | 25 | 50 | 75 | 100 miles |
| 0 | 50 | 100 | 150 km |

61 Caesar's propraetorship in Spain.

60 "First triumvirate" formed by Caesar, Pompey, and Crassus.

59 Consulship of Caesar. Pompey marries Julia, Caesar's daughter.

58–49 Caesar's proconsulship in Gaul.

58 Tribunate of Clodius. Cicero is exiled.

57 Cicero returns from exile.

56 (Apr.) Conference at Luca.

55 Second consulship of Pompey and Crassus.

54 Death of Julia.

53 Crassus is killed at Carrhae.

52 Sole consulship of Pompey. Law of the ten tribunes.

51–50 Cicero's proconsulship in Cilicia. Parthian invasion of Syria.

50 (spring) Senate decrees that Pompey and Caesar each send one legion to fight the Parthians.

50 (Dec. 1) Senate approves a motion by a vote of 370 to 22 that both Caesar and Pompey give up their respective commands. Motion is vetoed by tribunes.

50 (Dec. 2) C. Marcellus, the consul, asks Pompey to save the republic and assume command of all forces in Italy. Pompey accepts.

49 (Jan. 1) Caesar's letter to the senate in Rome delivered by Curio.

Jan. 4 Cicero reaches Rome upon returning from his proconsulship in Cilicia.

Jan. 7 *senātūs cōnsultum ultimum* is passed.

Jan. 10–11 Caesar crosses the Rubicon and seizes Ariminum.

Jan. 13–14 Caesar secures Pisaurum, Fanum, and Ancona.

Jan. 17–18 Pompey and the government flee from Rome.

Jan. 20–21 Iguvium falls to Caesar's forces, commanded by Curio.

Jan. 23 L. Caesar and Roscius meet Pompey and the consuls at Teanum Sidicinum.

Jan. 25 Senate meets at Capua.

Jan. 28 Caesar advances to Auximum from Ancona.

Jan. 29–
Feb. 1 Caesar leaves Auximum to occupy Picenum.

Feb. 1–7 Caesar overruns Picenum.

Feb. 4 Caesar takes Asculum in Picenum.

Feb. 14–17 Caesar begins to besiege Corfinium.

Feb. 19 Pompey leaves Luceria for Canusium and Brundisium.

Feb. 21 Caesar accepts the surrender of Corfinium and departs.

Feb. 25 Pompey arrives in Brundisium.

Mar. 4 Consuls depart for Dyrrachium in Greece.

Mar. 9 Caesar reaches Brundisium.

Mar. 17 Pompey sets sail from Brundisium.

Mar. 28 Cicero meets with Caesar at Formiae.

Apr. 1 Caesar meets with the senate in Rome.

Apr. 16 Caesar departs for Massilia and Spain.

Apr. 19 Caesar besieges Massilia.

June 7 Cicero embarks to join Pompey.

June 22 Caesar arrives in Spain.

Aug. 2 Pompey's forces surrender to Caesar in Spain.

48 (Jan. 4) Caesar departs from Brundisium for Epirus in Greece.

Aug. 9 Battle of Pharsalus.

Sept. 28 Pompey is assassinated in Egypt.

Oct. 2 Caesar arrives in Egypt.

47 (June) Caesar leaves Egypt.

Oct. Caesar returns to Rome.

Dec. 28 Caesar lands in Africa.

46 (Apr. 6) Battle of Thapsus.

July Caesar returns to Rome.

Nov. Caesar sets out for Spain.

45 (Feb.) Death of Tullia, Cicero's daughter.

Mar. 17 Battle of Munda.

Oct. Caesar returns to Rome.

44 (Mar. 15) Caesar is assassinated.

43 (Dec. 7) Cicero is assassinated.

List of Abbreviations

A. Terms

abl.	ablative	loc.	locative
absol.	absolute	m.	masculine
acc.	accusative	n.	note/neuter
adj.	adjective	nom.	nominative
adv.	adverb	p.	page
cf.	compare (Lat. *cōnfer*)	partic.	participle
conj.	conjunction	pass.	passive
dat.	dative	pf.	perfect
e.g.	for example (Lat. *exemplī grātiā*)	pl.	plural
gen.	genitive	plupf.	pluperfect
f.	feminine	prep.	preposition
fut.	future	pres.	present
i.e.	that is (Lat. *id est*)	pron.	pronoun
impers.	impersonal	sc.	supply (Lat. *scīlicet*)
impf.	imperfect	sing.	singular
indic.	indicative	subjn.	subjunctive
inf.	infinitive	subst.	substantive
lit.	literally	s.v.	under the word (Lat. *sub verbō*)

B. Personal Names

C.	Gaius	P.	Publius
Cn.	Gnaeus	Q.	Quintus
L.	Lucius	Sex.	Sextus
M.	Marcus	T.	Titus

28

C. Works Cited

Ad Att.   *Ad Atticum* (Cicero's letters to Atticus)

Ad Fam.   *Ad Familiārēs* (Cicero's letters to his friends)

Ad Q.F.   *Ad Quintum Frātrem* (Cicero's letters to his brother Quintus)

AG   J. H. Allen and James B. Greenough, *New Latin Grammar* (New Rochelle, NY: Caratzas, 1988)

GL   Basil L. Gildersleeve and Gonzalez Lodge, *Gildersleeve's Latin Grammar* (New York: St. Martin's Press, 1971)

JRS   *Journal of Roman Studies*

SB   D. R. Shackleton Bailey, *Cicero's Letters to Atticus* (Cambridge: Cambridge University Press, 1965)

D. Textual Signs

. . .   indicates an omitted portion of a text or citation

[ ]   encloses text of doubtful authenticity

⟨ ⟩   encloses missing text to be restored or supplied

Although construction of the legionary fort at Chester, England, did not begin until the late 70s A.D., in its characteristic "playing card" shape, with a gate on each side, it typifies the Roman military outposts in the provinces. This model of the fortress, which served as headquarters of the Twentieth Legion, shows parallel barrack blocks flanking a central facility for the commanding officer. Provincial outposts in Caesar's time would not have been significantly different. Note the amphitheater (lower left), a feature of "permanent" legionary fortresses, which provided space for weapons training and drill but also for entertainment (such as wild beast hunts and gladiatorial shows), executions, and other public activities.

A reconstructed gate of a Roman fort at South Shields, England, showing earthworks running along the interior wall. Such gates also functioned as defense turrets. Around many Roman military outposts sprang up civilian settlements including colonies of discharged veterans.

LATIN TEXTS ON
THE FALL OF THE
ROMAN REPUBLIC

1

*During Cicero's tenure as governor of the province of Cilicia from August of
51 to July of 50, he receives frequent letters from his friend Caelius, who has
been informing him of events in Rome during a turbulent period of political
unrest. The following letter, written early in August 50, is not received by
Cicero until October at Piraeus, the seaport of Athens. At this time Cicero is
returning home to Italy from Cilicia.*

Caelius Cicerōnī s.

　　Dē summā rē pūblicā saepe tibi scrīpsī mē in annum
pācem nōn vidēre, et quō propius ea contentiō, quam fierī
necesse est, accēdit, eō clārius id perīculum appāret. Prō-
5　positum hoc est, dē quō quī rērum potiuntur sunt dīmicātūrī:
quod Cn. Pompēius cōnstituit nōn patī C. Caesarem cōnsulem
aliter fierī nisi exercitum et prōvinciās trādiderit; Caesarī
autem persuāsum est sē salvum esse nōn posse sī ab exercitū
recesserit. Fert illam tamen condiciōnem, ut ambō exercitūs
10　trādant.
　　Sīc illī amōrēs et invidiōsa coniūnctiō nōn ad occultam
recidit obtrectātiōnem, sed ad bellum sē ērūpit. Neque
meārum rērum quid cōnsilī capiam reperiō; quod nōn dubitō
quīn tē quoque haec dēlīberātiō sit perturbātūra. Nam mihi

31

15 cum hominibus hīs et grātiae et necessitūdinēs sunt: causam
illam amō unde hominēs ōdī.

Illud tē nōn arbitror fugere quīn hominēs in dissēnsiōne domesticā dēbeant, quam diū cīvīliter sine armīs certētur, honestiōrem sequī partem; ubī ad belllum et castra
20 ventum sit, firmiōrem et id melius statuere quod tūtius sit.
In hāc discordiā videō Cn. Pompēium senātum quīque rēs iūdicant sēcum habitūrum, ad Caesarem omnīs quī cum timōre aut
malā spē vīvant accessūrōs; exercitum cōnferendum nōn esse.
Omnīnō satis spatī est ad cōnsīderandās utrīusque cōpiās et
25 ēligendam partem. . . .

Ad summam, quaeris quid putem futūrum. Sī alter uter
eōrum ad Parthicum bellum nōn eat, videō magnās impendēre
discordiās, quās ferrum et vīs iūdicābit; uterque et animō et
cōpiīs est parātus. Sī sine summō perīculō fierī posset,
30 magnum et iūcundum tibi Fortūna spectāculum parābat.

(*Ad Familiārēs* 8.14.2–4)

2

These final two chapters of Book VIII of the Bellum Gallicum, *written by
Aulus Hirtius, one of Caesar's officers, summarize Caesar's maneuvers in the
closing months of the year 50.*

Fit deinde senātūs cōnsultum, ut ad bellum Parthicum
legiō ūna ā Cn. Pompēiō, altera ā C. Caesare mitterētur;
neque obscūrē hae duae legiōnēs ūnī dētrahuntur. Nam Cn. Pompēius legiōnem prīmam, quam ad Caesarem mīserat, cōnfectam
5 ex dīlectū prōvinciae Caesaris, eam tamquam ex suō numerō
dedit. Caesar tamen, cum dē voluntāte minimē dubium esset
adversāriōrum suōrum, Pompēiō legiōnem remīsit et suō nōmine
quintam decimam, quam in Galliā citeriōre habuerat, ex
senātūs cōnsultō iubet trādī.
10 In eius locum tertiam decimam legiōnem in Ītaliam
mittit quae praesidia tuērētur, ex quibus praesidiīs quinta
decima dēdūcēbatur. Ipse exercituī distribuit hīberna:
C. Trebōnium cum legiōnibus quattuor in Belgiō collocat,
C. Fabium cum totidem in Aeduōs dēdūcit. Sīc enim exīstimā-
15 bat tūtissimam fore Galliam, sī Belgae, quōrum maxima virtūs, et Aeduī, quōrum auctōritās summa esset, exercitibus
continērentur. Ipse in Ītaliam profectus est.

Quō cum vēnisset, cognōscit per C. Mārcellum cōnsulem
legiōnēs duās ab sē missās, quae ex senātūs cōnsultō
20 dēbērent ad Parthicum bellum dūcī, Cn. Pompēiō trāditās atque
in Ītaliā retentās esse. Hōc factō, quamquam nūllī erat
dubium quidnam contrā Caesarem parārētur, tamen Caesar omnia
patienda esse statuit, quoad sibi spēs aliqua relinquerētur
iūre potius disceptandī quam belligerandī. Contendit ⟨per
25 litterās ā senātū ut etiam Pompēius sē imperiō abdicāret,
sēque idem factūrum prōmittit; sīn minus, sē neque sibi neque
patriae dēfutūrum⟩.

(*Bellum Gallicum* 8.54–55)

3

*The narrative of Hirtius is resumed by Caesar himself in the opening chapters
of his* Bellum Cīvīle, *where the reactions to Caesar's dispatch are summarized in a description of the senate meeting on January 1, 49.*

Litterīs C. Caesaris cōnsulibus redditīs, aegrē ab hīs
impetrātum est summā tribūnōrum plēbis contentiōne ut in
senātū recitārentur; ut vērō ex litterīs ad senātum referrētur, impetrārī nōn potuit. Referunt cōnsulēs dē rē pūblicā
5 īnfīnītē. L. Lentulus cōnsul senātuī reī pūblicae sē nōn
dēfutūrum pollicētur, sī audācter ac fortiter sententiās
dīcere velint; sīn Caesarem respiciant atque eius grātiam
sequantur, ut superiōribus fēcerint temporibus, sē sibi
cōnsilium captūrum neque senātūs auctōritātī obtemperātūrum;
10 habēre sē quoque ad Caesaris grātiam atque amīcitiam receptum. In eandem sententiam loquitur Scipiō: Pompēiō esse
in animō reī pūblicae nōn dēesse, sī senātus sequātur; sī
cūnctētur atque agat lēnius, nēquīquam eius auxilium, sī
posteā velit, senātum implorātūrum.
15 Haec Scipiōnis ōrātiō, quod senātus in urbe habēbātur
Pompēiusque aberat, ex ipsīus ōre Pompēī mittī vidēbātur.
Dīxerat aliquis lēniōrem sententiam, ut prīmō M. Mārcellus,
ingressus in eam ōrātiōnem, nōn oportēre ante dē eā rē ad
senātum referrī quam dīlectūs tōtā Ītaliā habitī et exer-
20 citūs cōnscrīptī essent, quō praesidiō tūtō et līberē
senātus quae vellet dēcernere audēret; ut M. Calidius, quī

33

cēnsēbat ut Pompēius in suās prōvinciās proficīscerētur, nē
qua esset armōrum causa: timēre Caesarem ēreptīs ab eō
duābus legiōnibus, nē ad eius perīculum reservāre et retinēre
25 eās ad urbem Pompēius vidērētur; ut M. Rūfus, quī sententiam
Calidī paucīs ferē mūtātīs rēbus sequēbātur. Hī omnēs, convīciō L. Lentulī cōnsulis correptī, exagitābantur. Lentulus
sententiam Calidī prōnūntiātūrum sē omnīnō negāvit, Mārcellus
perterritus convīciīs ā suā sententiā discessit. Sīc vōcibus
30 cōnsulis, terrōre praesentis exercitūs, minīs amīcōrum Pompēī
plērīque compulsī, invītī et coāctī, Scipiōnis sententiam
sequuntur: utī ante certam diem Caesar exercitum dīmittat;
sī nōn faciat, eum adversus rem pūblicam factūrum vidērī.
Intercēdit M. Antōnius, Q. Cassius, tribūnī plēbis. Refertur
35 cōnfestim dē intercessiōne tribūnōrum. Dīcuntur sententiae
gravēs; ut quisque acerbissimē crūdēlissimēque dīxit, ita
quam maximē ab inimīcīs Caesaris collaudātur.

(Bellum Cīvīle 1.1–2)

4

Pompey calls a meeting. Unrest in Rome continues.

   Missō ad vesperum senātū omnēs quī sunt eius ōrdinis
ā Pompēiō ēvocantur. Laudat promptōs atque in posterum
cōnfirmat, sēgniōrēs castīgat atque incitat. Multī undique
ex veteribus Pompēī exercitibus spē praemiōrum atque ōrdinum
5 ēvocantur, multī ex duābus legiōnibus quae sunt trāditae ā
Caesare arcessuntur. Complētur urbs, clīvus, comitium
tribūnīs, centuriōnibus, ēvocātīs. Omnēs amīcī cōnsulum,
necessāriī Pompēī atque eōrum quī veterēs inimīcitiās cum
Caesare gerēbant in senātum cōguntur; quōrum vōcibus et
10 concursū terrentur īnfirmiōrēs, dubiī cōnfirmantur, plērīsque
vērō līberē dēcernendī potestās ēripitur. Pollicētur L. Pīsō
cēnsor sēsē itūrum ad Caesarem, item L. Roscius praetor, quī
dē hīs rēbus eum doceant; sex diēs ad eam rem cōnficiendam
spatī postulant. Dīcuntur etiam ab nōnnūllīs sententiae,
15 ut lēgātī ad Caesarem mittantur quī voluntātem senātūs eī
prōpōnant.

(Bellum Cīvīle 1.3)

5

Caesar analyzes the motives of his enemies.

Omnibus hīs resistitur omnibusque ōrātiō cōnsulis,
Scipiōnis, Catōnis oppōnitur. Catōnem veterēs inimīcitiae
Caesaris incitant et dolor repulsae. Lentulus aeris aliēnī
magnitūdine et spē exercitūs ac prōvinciārum et rēgum
5　appellandōrum largītiōnibus movētur sēque alterum fore
Sullam inter suōs glōriātur, ad quem summa imperī redeat.
Scipiōnem eadem spēs prōvinciae atque exercituum impellit,
quōs sē prō necessitūdine partītūrum cum Pompēiō arbitrātur,
simul iūdiciōrum metus, adulātiō atque ostentātiō suī et
10　potentium, quī in rē pūblicā iūdiciīsque tum plūrimum
pollēbant. Ipse Pompēius, ab inimīcīs Caesaris incitātus
et quod nēminem dignitāte sēcum exaequārī volēbat, tōtum sē
ab eius amīcitiā averterat et cum commūnibus inimīcīs in
grātiam redierat, quōrum ipse maximam partem illō adfīnitā-
15　tis tempore iniūnxerat Caesarī; simul infāmiā duārum
legiōnum permōtus, quās ab itinere Āsiae Syriaeque ad suam
potentiam dominātumque converterat, rem ad arma dēdūcī
studēbat.

(Bellum Cīvīle 1.4)

6

January 7, 49: the senātūs cōnsultum ultimum *is passed.*

Hīs dē causīs aguntur omnia raptim atque turbātē. Nec
docendī Caesaris prōpinquīs eius spatium datur nec tribūnīs
plēbis suī perīculī dēprecandī neque etiam extrēmī iūris
intercessiōne retinendī, quod L. Sulla relīquerat, facultās
5　tribuitur, sed dē suā salūte septimō diē cōgitāre cōguntur,
quod illī turbulentissimī superiōribus temporibus tribūnī
plēbis post octō dēnique mēnsīs variārum actiōnum respicere
ac timēre cōnsuerant. Dēcurritur ad illud extrēmum atque
ultimum senātūs cōnsultum, quō nisi paene in ipsō urbis
10　incendiō atque in dēspērātiōne omnium salūtis lātōrum audāciā numquam ante discessum est: dent operam cōnsulēs, praetōrēs, tribūnī plēbis, quīque prō cōnsulibus sunt ad urbem,
nē quid rēs pūblica dētrīmentī capiat. Haec senātūs cōn-

sultō perscrībuntur a. d. vii Id. Iān. Itaque v prīmīs
15 diēbus quibus habērī senātus potuit, quā ex diē cōnsulātum
iniit Lentulus, biduō exceptō comitiālī et dē imperiō
Caesaris et dē amplissimīs virīs, tribūnīs plēbis, gravissimē acerbissimēque dēcernitur. Prōfugiunt statim ex urbe
tribūnī plēbis sēsēque ad Caesarem cōnferunt. Is eō tempore
20 erat Ravennae exspectābatque suīs lēnissimīs postulātīs
respōnsa, sī quā hominum aequitāte rēs ad ōtium dēdūcī
posset.

(*Bellum Cīvīle* 1.5)

7

The government reacts and prepares for war.

Proximīs diēbus habētur extrā urbem senātus. Pompēius
eadem illa quae per Scipiōnem ostenderat agit; senātūs vir-
tūtem cōnstantiamque collaudat; cōpiās suās expōnit: legiōnēs habēre sēsē parātās x; praetereā cognitum compertumque
5 sibi aliēnō esse animō in Caesarem mīlitēs neque eīs posse
persuādērī utī eum dēfendant aut sequantur. Statim dē
reliquīs rēbus ad senātum refertur: tōtā Ītaliā dīlectus
habeātur; Faustus Sulla properē in Mauretāniam mittātur;
pecūnia utī ex aerāriō Pompēiō dētur; refertur etiam dē rēge
10 Iubā, ut socius sit atque amīcus. Marcellus cōnsul passūrum
in praesentiā negat; dē Faustō impedit Philippus, tribūnus
plēbis. Dē reliquīs rēbus senātūs cōnsulta perscrībuntur.
Prōvinciae prīvātīs dēcernuntur, duae cōnsulārēs, reliquae
praetōriae. Scipiōnī obvenit Syria, L. Domitiō Gallia.
15 Philippus et Cotta prīvātō cōnsiliō praetereuntur, neque
eōrum sortēs dēiciuntur. In reliquās prōvinciās praetōrēs
mittuntur. Neque exspectant, quod superiōribus annīs ac-
ciderat, ut dē eōrum imperiō ad populum ferātur, palūdātīque
vōtīs nuncupātīs exeunt. Cōnsulēs, quod ante id tempus
20 accidit numquam, ex urbe prōficīscuntur lictōrēsque habent
in urbe et Capitōliō prīvātī contrā omnia vetustātis exempla. Tōtā Ītaliā dīlectūs habentur, arma imperantur,
pecūniae ā mūnicipiīs exiguntur, ē fānīs tolluntur, omnia
dīvīna hūmānaque iūra permiscentur.

(*Bellum Cīvīle* 1.6)

36

8

The following letter was written by Cicero from the vicinity of Rome on January 12, 49, the day after Caesar crossed the Rubicon. The recipient, his secretary Tiro, had remained in Greece because of illness and so could not accompany Cicero on his homeward journey from Cilicia. Cicero offers Tiro his reaction to the critical situation developing in Rome during the first few days of the new year.

Tullius et Cicerō, Terentia, Tullia, QQ. Tīrōnī s. p. d.

Ego ad urbem accessī pr. Nōn. Iān. Obviam mihi sīc est prōditum, ut nihil possit fierī ōrnātius; sed incidī in ipsam flammam cīvīlis discordiae vel potius bellī. Cui cum
5 cuperem medērī et, ut arbitror, possem, cupiditātēs certōrum hominum (nam ex utrāque parte sunt quī pugnāre cupiant) impedimentō mihi fuērunt. Omnīnō et ipse Caesar, amīcus noster, minācīs ad senātum et acerbās litterās mīserat et erat adhūc impudens quī exercitum et prōvinciam invītō
10 senātū tenēret, et Curiō meus illum incitābat. Antōnius quidem noster et Q. Cassius nūllā vī expulsī ad Caesarem cum Curiōne profectī erant, posteāquam senātus cōnsulibus, praetōribus, tribūnīs plēbis et nōbīs, quī prō cōnsulibus sumus, negōtium dederat ut cūrārēmus nē quid rēs pūblica
15 dētrimentī caperet. Numquam māiōre in perīculō cīvitās fuit, numquam improbī cīvēs habuērunt parātiōrem ducem. Omnīnō ex hāc quoque parte dīligentissimē comparātur. Id fit auctōritāte et studiō Pompēī nostrī, quī Caesarem sērō coepit timēre.
20 Nōbīs inter hās turbās senātus tamen frequēns flāgitāvit triumphum; sed Lentulus cōnsul, quō māius suum beneficium faceret, simul atque expedisset quae essent necessāria dē rē pūblicā, dīxit sē relātūrum. Nōs agimus nihil cupidē eōque est nostra plūris auctōritās. Ītaliae
25 regiōnēs discrīptae sunt, quam quisque partem tuerētur. Nōs Capuam sūmpsimus.
Haec tē scīre voluī. Tū etiam atque etiam cūrā ut valeās litterāsque ad mē mittās, quotiēnscumque habēbis cui dēs. Etiam atque etiam valē. D. pr. Īdūs Iān.

(*Ad Familiārēs* 16.11.2–3)

9

Meanwhile, Caesar addresses his soldiers in Ravenna.

Quibus rēbus cognitīs Caesar apud mīlitēs contiōnātur.
Omnium temporum iniūriās inimīcōrum in sē commemorat; ā
quibus dēductum ac dēprāvātum Pompēium queritur invidiā
atque obtrectātiōne laudis suae, cuius ipse honōrī et dig-
5 nitātī semper fāverit adiūtorque fuerit. Novum in rem
pūblicam intrōductum exemplum queritur, ut tribūnicia
intercessiō armīs notārētur atque opprimerētur [quae superiōribus annīs armīs esset restitūta.] Sullam nūdātā omnibus
rēbus tribūniciā potestāte tamen intercessiōnem līberam
10 relīquisse; Pompēium, quī āmissa restituisse videātur bona,
etiam quae ante habuerint adēmisse. Quotiēnscumque sit
dēcrētum, darent operam magistrātūs nē quid rēs pūblica
dētrīmentī caperet, quā vōce et quō senātūs cōnsultō
populus Rōmānus ad arma sit vocātus, factum in perniciōsīs
15 lēgibus, in vī tribūniciā, in sēcessiōne populī, templīs
locīsque ēditiōribus occupātīs; atque haec superiōris
aetātis exempla expiāta Sāturnīnī atque Gracchōrum cāsibus
docet; quārum rērum illō tempore nihil factum, nē cōgitātum
quidem. Hortātur, cuius imperātōris ductū viiii annīs rem
20 pūblicam fēlicissimē gesserint plūrimaque proelia secunda
fēcerint, omnem Galliam Germāniamque pācāverint, ut eius
existimātiōnem dignitātemque ab inimīcīs dēfendant. Con-
clāmant legiōnis xiii, quae aderat, mīlitēs—hanc enim
initiō tumultūs ēvocāverat, reliquae nōndum convēnerant—
25 sēsē parātos esse imperātōris suī tribūnōrumque plēbis
iniūriās dēfendere.   (*Bellum Cīvīle* 1.7)

10

*Suetonius, a political biographer born in the last half of the first century A.D.
and author of* The Lives of the Caesars, *describes in his biography of Julius
Caesar one of the most critical moments in all Roman history: the crossing of
the Rubicon River.*

Cum ergō sublātam tribūnōrum intercessiōnem ipsōsque
urbe cessisse nūntiātum esset, praemissīs cōnfestim clam
cohortibus, nē qua suspiciō mōvērētur, et spectāculō

pūblicō per dissimulātiōnem interfuit et fōrmam quā lūdum
5 gladiātōrium erat aedificātūrus cōnsīderāvit et ex cōn-
suētūdine convīviō sē frequentī dedit.

Dein post sōlis occāsum, mūlīs ē proximō pistrīnō ad
vehiculum iūnctīs, occultissimum iter modicō comitātū ingressus est; et cum lūminibus extinctīs dēcessisset viā, diū
10 errābundus, tandem ad lūcem duce repertō, per angustissimōs
trāmitēs pedibus ēvāsit, cōnsecūtusque cohortīs ad Rubicōnem
flūmen, quī prōvinciae eius fīnis erat, paulum cōnstitit, ac
reputāns quantum mōlīrētur, conversus ad proximōs, "Etiam
nunc," inquit, "regredī possumus; quod sī ponticulum trānsi-
15 erimus, omnia armīs agenda erunt."

Cūnctantī ostentum tāle factum est. Quīdam eximiā
magnitūdine et fōrmā in proximō sedēns repente appāruit,
harundine canēns; ad quem audiendum cum praeter pāstōrēs
plūrimī etiam ex statiōnibus mīlitēs concurrissent interque
20 eōs et aeneātōrēs, raptā ab ūnō tubā prōsiliuit ad flūmen
et ingentī spiritū classicum exōrsus pertendit ad alteram
rīpam. Tunc Caesar, "Eātur," inquit, "quō deōrum ostenta
et inimīcōrum inīquitās vocat. Iacta ālea est," inquit.

Atque ita trāiectō exercitū, adhibitīs tribūnīs plēbis,
25 quī pulsī supervēnerant, prō contiōne fidem mīlitum flēns
ac veste ā pectore discissā invocāvit.

(Divus Iūlius 31–33)

11

Caesar describes his meetings with Lucius Caesar and Roscius.

Cognitā mīlitum voluntāte Arīminum cum eā legiōne
proficīscitur ibique tribūnōs plēbis quī ad eum cōnfūgerant
convenit; reliquās legiōnēs ex hibernīs ēvocat et subsequī
iubet. Eō L. Caesar adulēscēns venit, cuius pater Caesaris
5 erat lēgātus. Is, reliquō sermōne cōnfectō, cuius reī causā
vēnerat habēre sē ā Pompēiō ad eum prīvātī officī mandāta
dēmōnstrat: velle Pompēium sē Caesarī pūrgātum, nē ea quae
reī pūblicae causā ēgerit in suam contumēliam vertat. Semper
sē reī pūblicae commoda prīvātīs necessitūdinibus habuisse
10 potiōra. Caesarem quoque prō suā dignitāte dēbēre et studium
et īrācundiam suam reī pūblicae dimittere neque adeō graviter
īrāscī inimīcīs, ut cum illīs nocēre sē spēret reī pūblicae

39

noceat. Pauca eiusdem generis addit cum excūsātiōne Pompēī
coniūncta. Eadem ferē atque eīsdem verbīs praetor Roscius
15 agit cum Caesare sibīque Pompēium commemorāsse dēmōnstrat.

(*Bellum Cīvīle* 1.8)

12

Caesar formulates a reply.

Quae rēs etsī nihil ad levandās iniūriās pertinēre
vidēbantur, tamen idōneōs nactus hominēs per quōs ea quae
vellet ad eum perferrentur, petit ab utrōque, quoniam
Pompēī mandāta ad sē dētulerint, nē graventur sua quoque ad
5 eum postulāta dēferre, sī parvō labōre magnās contrōversiās
tollere atque omnem Ītaliam metū līberāre possint. Sibi
semper prīmam fuisse dignitātem vītāque potiōrem. Doluisse
sē quod populī Rōmānī beneficium sibi per contumēliam ab
inimīcīs extorquērētur ēreptōque sēmestrī imperiō in urbem
10 retraherētur, cuius absentis ratiōnem habērī proximīs
comitiīs populus iussisset. Tamen hanc iactūram honōris suī
reī pūblicae causā aequō animō tulisse; cum litterās ad
senātum mīserit, ut omnēs ab exercitibus discēderent, nē id
quidem impetrāvisse. Tōta Ītaliā dīlectūs habērī, retinērī
15 legiōnēs ii, quae ab sē simulātiōne Parthicī bellī sint
abductae, cīvitātem esse in armīs. Quōnam haec omnia nisi ad
suam perniciem pertinēre? Sed tamen ad omnia sē dēscendere
parātum atque omnia patī reī pūblicae causā. Proficīscātur
Pompēius in suās prōvinciās, ipsī exercitūs dīmittant, dis-
20 cēdant in Ītaliā omnēs ab armīs, metus ē cīvitāte tollātur,
lībera comitia atque omnis rēs pūblica senātuī populōque
Rōmānō permittātur. Haec quō facilius certīsque condiciōnibus fiant et iūre iūrandō sanciantur, aut ipse propius
accēdat aut sē patiātur accēdere; fore utī per colloquia
25 omnēs contrōversiae compōnantur.

(*Bellum Cīvīle* 1.9)

13

The ambassadors depart. Caesar continues his advance.

Acceptīs mandātīs Roscius cum Caesare Capuam pervenit
ibique cōnsulēs Pompēiumque invenit; postulāta Caesaris

renūntiat. Illī dēlīberātā rē respondent scrīptaque ad eum
mandāta per eōsdem remittunt, quōrum haec erat summa: Caesar
5 in Galliam reverterētur, Arīminō excēderet, exercitūs
dīmitteret; quae sī fēcisset, Pompēium in Hispāniās itūrum.
Intereā, quoad fidēs esset data Caesarem factūrum quae
pollicērētur, nōn intermissūrōs cōnsulēs Pompēiumque
dīlectūs.

10   Erat inīqua condiciō postulāre, ut Caesar Arīminō
excēderet atque in prōvinciam reverterētur, ipsum et
prōvinciās et legiōnēs aliēnās tenēre; exercitum Caesaris
velle dīmittī, dīlectūs habēre; pollicērī sē in prōvinciam
itūrum neque ante quem diem itūrus sit dēfīnīre, ut, sī
15 perāctō cōnsulātū Caesaris nōn profectus esset, nūllā tamen
mendācī religiōne obstrictus vidērētur; tempus vērō colloquiō
nōn dare neque accessūrum pollicērī magnam pācis dēspērātiōnem adferēbat. Itaque ab Arīminō M. Antōnium cum cohortibus
v Arretium mittit; ipse Arīminī cum duābus subsistit ibique
20 dīlectum habēre īnstituit; Pisaurum, Fānum, Ancōnam singulīs
cohortibus occupat.

(*Bellum Cīvīle* 1.10–11)

14

Iguvium and Auximum fall to Caesar.

    Intereā certior factus Iguvium Thermum praetōrem
cohortibus v tenēre, oppidum mūnīre, omniumque esse
Iguvīnōrum optimam ergā sē voluntātem, Curiōnem cum tribus
cohortibus quās Pisaurī et Arīminī habēbat mittit. Cuius
5 adventū cognitō diffīsus mūnicipī voluntātī Thermus cohortīs
ex urbe redūcit et profugit. Mīlitēs in itinere ab eō
discēdunt ac domum revertuntur. Curiō summā omnium voluntāte
Iguvium recipit. Quibus rēbus cognitīs cōnfīsus mūnicipiōrum
voluntātibus Caesar cohortīs legiōnis xiii ex praesidiīs
10 dēdūcit Auximumque proficīscitur; quod oppidum Attius
cohortibus intrōductīs tenēbat dīlectumque tōtō Pīcēnō
circummissīs senātōribus habēbat.

    Adventū Caesaris cognitō decuriōnēs Auximī ad Attium
Vārum frequentēs conveniunt; docent suī iūdicī rem nōn esse;
15 neque sē neque reliquōs mūnicipēs patī posse C. Caesarem
imperātōrem, bene dē rē pūblicā meritum, tantīs rēbus gestīs,

41

abl. of separation

oppidō moenibusque prohibērī: proinde habeat ratiōnem
posteritātis et perīculī suī. Quōrum ōrātiōne permōtus
Vārus praesidium quod intrōdūxerat ex oppidō ēdūcit ac
20 prōfugit. Hunc ex prīmō ōrdine paucī Caesaris cōnsecūtī
mīlitēs cōnsistere coēgērunt. Commissō proeliō dēseritur
ā suīs Vārus; nōnnūlla pars mīlitum domum discēdit; reliquī
ad Caesarem perveniunt, atque ūnā cum eīs dēprēnsus L.
Pupius, prīmī pīlī centuriō, addūcitur quī hunc eundem
25 ōrdinem in exercitū Cn. Pompēī antea dūxerat. Caesar mīlitēs
Attiānōs collaudat, Pūpium dīmittit, Auximātibus agit grātiās
sēque eōrum factī memorem fore pollicētur.

(*Bellum Cīvīle* 1.12–13)

15

The government abandons Rome.

Quibus rēbus Rōmam nūntiātīs tantus repente terror
invāsit ut, cum Lentulus cōnsul ad aperiendum aerārium
vēnisset ad pecūniamque Pompēiō ex senātūs cōnsultō prō-
ferendam, protinus apertō sanctiōre aerāriō ex urbe
5 prōfugeret. Caesar enim adventāre iam iamque et adesse
eius equitēs falsō nūntiābantur. Hunc Mārcellus collēga et
plērīque magistrātūs cōnsecūtī sunt. Cn. Pompēius prīdiē
eius diēī ex urbe profectus iter ad legiōnēs habēbat, quās
ā Caesare acceptās in Āpūliā hībernōrum causā disposuerat.
10 Dīlectūs circā urbem intermittuntur; nihil citrā Capuam tūtum
esse vidētur. Capuae prīmum sēsē cōnfirmant et colligunt
dīlectumque colōnōrum quī lēge Iūliā Capuam dēductī erant
habēre īnstituunt; gladiātōrēsque, quōs ibi Caesar in lūdō
habēbat, ad forum prōductōs Lentulus lībertātis spē cōn-
15 firmat atque hīs equōs attribuit et sē sequī iussit; quōs
posteā monitus ab suīs, quod ea rēs omnium iūdiciō reprehendēbātur, circum familiārīs conventūs Campāniae custōdiae
causā distribuit.

(*Bellum Cīvīle* 1.14)

16

*On or about January 17, Cicero, in the vicinity of Rome, writes to his intimate
friend and confidant Titus Pomponius Atticus, a prosperous* eques *residing in
Rome. Cicero notes that he has decided to leave the area and is deliberating
about what should be done concerning Pompey's apparent indecisiveness.*

42

Cicerō Atticō sal.

Subitō cōnsilium cēpī ut, antequam lūcēret, exīrem,
nē quī cōnspectus fieret aut sermō, lictōribus praesertim
laureātīs. Dē reliquō neque hercule quid agam nec quid
5 āctūrus sim sciō; ita sum perturbātus temeritāte nostrī
āmentissimī cōnsilī. Tibi vērō quid suādeam, cuius ipse
cōnsilium exspectō? Gnaeus noster quid cōnsilī cēperit
capiatve nesciō adhūc, in oppidīs coartātus et stupēns.
Omnēs, sī in Ītaliā cōnsistet, erimus ūnā; sīn cēdet, cōn-
10 silī rēs est. Adhūc certē, nisi ego insāniō, stultē omnia
et incautē. Tū, quaesō, crēbrō ad mē scrībe vel quod in
buccam vēnerit.

(*Ad Atticum* 7.10)

17

In a letter to Atticus written about January 21, Cicero reacts to Caesar's
maneuvers against the legitimate government.

Cicerō Atticō sal.

Quaesō, quid est hoc? Aut quid agitur? Mihi enim
tenebrae sunt. "Cingulum," inquit, "nōs tenēmus, Ancōnem
āmīsimus. Labiēnus discessit ā Caesare." Utrum dē imperā-
5 tōre pōpulī Rōmānī an dē Hannibale loquimur? Ō hominem
āmentem et miserum quī nē umbram quidem umquam τοῦ καλοῦ
vīderit! Atque haec āit omnia facere sē dignitātis causā.
Ubi est autem dignitās nisi ubi honestās? Honestum igitur
habēre exercitum nūllō pūblicō cōnsiliō, occupāre urbīs
10 cīvium, quō facilior sit aditūs ad patriam . . . ?
Mālim . . . potius morī mīliēns quam semel istīus modī
quicquam cōgitāre.

(*Ad Atticum* 7.11.1)

18

January 23: from Menturnae in Campania, where he had gone to supervise
local recruiting at the request of the government, Cicero perceptively com-
ments on the nature of the impending civil war, the motives of Caesar,
the ineptitude of Pompey, and the hopelessness of the whole situation.

43

Cicerō Atticō sal.

Labiēnum ἥρωα iūdicō. Facinus iam diū nūllum cīvīle
praeclārius; quī, ut aliud nihil, hoc tamen prōfēcit: dedit
illī dolōrem. Sed etiam ad summam prōfectum aliquid putō.
5 Amō etiam Pīsōnem. Cuius iūdicium dē generō suspicor vīsum
īrī grave. Quamquam genus bellī quod sit vidēs. Ita cīvīle
est ut nōn ex cīvium dissēnsiōne sed ex ūnīus perditī cīvis
audāciā nātum sit. Is autem valet exercitū, tenet multōs spē
et prōmissīs, omnia omnium concupīvit. Huic trādita urbs est
10 nūda praesidiō, referta cōpiīs. Quid est quod ab eō nōn
metuās, quī illa templa et tecta nōn patriam sed praedam
putet? Quid autem sit āctūrus aut quō modō nesciō, sine
senātū, sine magistrātibus. Nē simulāre quidem poterit
quicquam πολιτικῶς. Nōs autem ubi exsurgere poterimus aut
15 quandō? Quōrum dux quam ἀστρατήγητος tu quoque animadvertis,
cui nē Pīcēna quidem nōta fuerint; quam autem sine cōnsiliō
rēs testis. Ut enim alia ōmittam decem annōrum peccāta,
quae condiciō nōn huic fugae praestitit? Nec vērō nunc
quid cōgitet sciō, ac nōn dēsinō per litterās scīscitārī.
20 Nihil esse timidius cōnstat, nihil perturbātius. Itaque
nec praesidium, cuius parāndī causā ad urbem retentus est,
nec locum ac sēdem praesidī ūllam videō. Spēs omnis in
duābus insidiōsē retentīs, paene aliēnīs legiōnibus. Nam
dīlectus adhūc quidem invītōrum est et ā pugnandō abhor-
25 rentium; condiciōnum autem āmissum tempus est. Quid futūrum
sit nōn videō; commissum quidem ā nōbīs certē est sīve ā
nostrō duce ut ē portū sine gubernāculīs ēgressī tempestātī
nōs trāderēmus.

(*Ad Atticum* 7.13.1–2)

19

*On the same day, Cicero writes to his family members in Rome to advise them
about the situation described in the previous letter to Atticus.*

Tullius Terentiae et pater Tulliae, duābus animīs suīs,
et Cicerō mātrī optimae, suāvissimae sorōrī s. p. d.

Sī vōs valētis, nōs valēmus. Vestrum iam cōnsilium est,
nōn sōlum meum, quid sit vōbīs faciendum. Sī ille Rōmam
5 modestē ventūrus est, rēctē in praesentiā domī esse potestis;

sīn homō āmēns dīripiendam urbem datūrus est, vereor ut
Dolabella ipse satis nōbīs prōdesse possit. Etiam illud
metuō nē iam interclūdāmur, ut cum velītis exīre nōn
liceat. Reliquum est, quod ipsae optimē cōnsīderābitis,
10 vestrī similēs fēminae sintne Rōmae. Sī enim nōn sunt,
videndum est ut honestē vōs esse possītis. Quō modō quidem
nunc sē rēs habet, modo ut haec nōbīs loca tenēre liceat,
bellissimē vel mēcum vel in nostrīs praediīs esse poteritis.
Etiam illud verendum est nē brevī tempore famēs in urbe sit.
15 Hīs dē rēbus velim cum Pompōniō, cum Camillō, cum quibus
vōbīs vidēbitur, cōnsīderētis; ad summam, animō fortī sītis.
Labiēnus rem meliōrem fēcit. Adiuvat etiam Pīsō, quod ab
urbe discēdit et sceleris condemnat generum suum. Vōs, meae
cārissimae animae, quam saepissimē ad mē scrībite et vōs
20 quid agātis et quid istīc agātur. Quintus pater et fīlius
et Rūfus vōbīs s. d. Valēte. viii K. Menturnīs.

(Ad Familiārēs 14.14)

20

*On January 26, the day after his arrival in Capua, Cicero sends Atticus one
of his many reports about the local situation. He also comments on the meeting of the senators the previous day, when they reacted skeptically to Caesar's
proposals.*

Cicerō Atticō sal.

    Ut ab urbe discessī, nūllum adhūc intermīsī diem quīn
aliquid ad tē litterārum darem, nōn quō habērem magnō opere
quod scrīberem sed ut loquerer tēcum absēns; quō mihi, cum
5 cōram id nōn licet, nihil est iūcundius.
    Capuam cum vēnissem a. d. vi Kal. prīdiē quam hās
litterās dedī, cōnsulēs convēnī multōsque nostrī ōrdinis.
Omnēs cupiēbant Caesarem abductīs praesidiīs stāre condiciōnibus iīs, quās tulisset. Ūnī Favōniō lēgēs ab illō nōbīs
10 impōnī nōn placēbat, sed is haud audītus in cōnsiliō. Catō
enim ipse iam servīre quam pugnāre māvult; sed tamen āit in
senātū sē adesse velle cum dē condiciōnibus agātur, sī Caesar
adductus sit ut praesidia dēdūcat. . . . In disputātiōnibus
nostrīs summa varietās est. Plērīque negant Caesarem in
15 condiciōne mānsūrum postulātaque haec ab eō interposita esse
quōminus quod opus esset ad bellum ā nōbīs parārētur. Ego

45

autem eum putō factūrum ut praesidia dēdūcat. Vīcerit enim,
sī cōnsul factus erit, et minōre scelere vīcerit quam quō
ingressus est. Sed accipienda plāga est. Sumus enim
20 flāgitiōsē imparātī cum ā mīlitibus tum ā pecūniā; quam
quidem omnem nōn modo prīvātam, quae in urbe est, sed etiam
pūblicam, quae in aerāriō est, illī relīquimus. Pompēius ad
legiōnēs Appiānās est profectus. Labiēnum sēcum habet. Ego
tuās opīniōnēs dē hīs rēbus exspectō. Fōrmiās mē continuō
25 recipere cōgitābam.

(Ad Atticum 7.15)

21

On January 27, Cicero apprises Tiro of recent events in the developing civil
strife between Caesar and the government. After a one-day sojourn in Cales,
Cicero has reached Capua on January 25 in accordance with instructions
from Pompey to assist with the recruiting.

Tullius s. d. Tīrōnī suō

    Quō in discrīmine versētur salūs mea et bonōrum omnium
atque ūniversae reī pūblicae ex eō scīre potes quod domōs
nostrās et patriam ipsam vel dīripiendam vel īnflammandam
5 relīquimus. In eum locum rēs dēducta est ut, nisi quī deus
vel cāsus aliquis subvēnerit, salvī esse nequeāmus.

    Equidem ut vēnī ad urbem, nōn dēstitī omnia et sentīre
et dīcere et facere quae ad concordiam pertinērent. Sed
mīrus invāserat furor nōn sōlum improbīs, sed etiam iīs quī
10 bonī habentur, ut pugnāre cuperent, mē clāmante nihil esse
bellō cīvīlī miserius. Itaque, cum Caesar āmentiā quādam
raperētur et oblītus nōminis atque honōrum suōrum Arīminum,
Pisaurum, Ancōnam, Arretium occupāvisset, urbem relīquimus:
quam sapienter aut quam fortiter nihil attinet disputārī.
15 Quō quidem in cāsū sīmus vidēs. Feruntur omnīnō condiciōnēs
ab illō, ut Pompēius eat in Hispāniam, dīlectūs quī sunt
habitī et praesidia nostra dīmittantur; sē ulteriōrem Galliam
Domitiō, citeriōrem Cōnsidiō Noniānō—hīs enim obtigērunt
—trāditūrum; ad cōnsulātūs petitiōnem sē ventūrum, neque
20 sē iam velle absente sē ratiōnem habērī suam; sē praesentem
trīnum nūndinum petitūrum. Accēpimus condiciōnēs, sed ita ut
removeat praesidia ex iīs locīs quae occupāvit, ut sine metū
dē hīs ipsīs condiciōnibus Rōmae senātus habērī possit. Id

46

ille sī fēcerit, spēs est pācis, nōn honestae—lēgēs enim
25 impōnuntur—sed quidvīs est melius quam sīc esse ut sumus.
Sīn autem ille suīs condiciōnibus stāre nōluerit, bellum
parātum est, eius modī tamen quod sustinēre ille nōn possit,
praesertim cum ā suīs condiciōnibus ipse fūgerit, tantum modo
ut eum interclūdāmus nē ad urbem possit accēdere; quod
30 spērābāmus fierī posse. Dīlectūs enim magnōs habēbāmus
putābāmusque illum metuere, sī ad urbem īre coepisset, nē
Galliās āmitteret, quās ambās habet inimīcissimās praeter
Trānspadānōs; ex Hispāniāque sex legiōnēs et magna auxilia
Āfrāniō et Petreiō ducibus habet ā tergō. Vidētur, sī
35 insāniet, posse opprimī, modo ut urbe salvā. Maximam autem
plāgam accēpit quod, is quī summam auctōritātem in illīus
exercitū habēbat, T. Labiēnus, socius sceleris esse nōluit.
Relīquit illum et est nōbīscum, multīque idem factūrī esse
dīcuntur.
40   Ego adhūc ōrae maritimae praesum ā Formiīs. Nūllum
māius negōtium suscipere voluī, quō plūs apud illum meae
litterae cohortātiōnēsque ad pācem valērent. Sīn autem erit
bellum, videō mē castrīs et certīs legiōnibus praefutūrum.
Habeō etiam illam molestiam, quod Dolabella noster apud
45 Caesarem est.
      Haec tibi nōta esse voluī; quae cavē nē tē perturbent
et impediant valētūdinem tuam. . . . Sed dā operam ut valeās
et, sī valēbis, cum rectē navigārī poterit, tum navigēs.
Cicerō meus in Fōrmiānō erat, Terentia et Tullia Rōmae.
50 Cūrā ut valeās. iiii K. Febr. Capuā.

(*Ad Familiārēs* 16.12)

22

After receiving the news that negotiations have collapsed, Cicero expresses to
Atticus his despondency in a brief note written on February 3.

Cicerō Atticō sal.

      Nihil habeō quod ad tē scrībam quī etiam eam epistulam
quam eram ēlūcubrātus ad tē nōn dederim. Erat enim plēna
speī bonae, quod et contiōnis voluntātem audieram et illum
5 condiciōnibus ūsūrum putābam, praesertim suīs. Ecce tibi
iii Nōnās Febr. māne accēpī litterās tuās, Philotimī, Furnī,
Curiōnis ad Furnium, quibus inrīdet L. Caesaris lēgātiōnem.

47

Plānē oppressī vidēmur, nec quid cōnsilī capiam sciō. Nec
mēhercule dē mē labōrō, dē puerīs quid agam nōn habeō.
10 Capuam tamen proficīscēbar haec scrībēns quō facilius dē
Pompēī rēbus cognōscerem.

(*Ad Atticum* 7.19)

23

Caesar occupies Picenum.

Auximō Caesar prōgressus omnem agrum Pīcēnum percurrit. Cūnctae eārum regiōnum praefectūrae libentissimīs
animīs eum recipiunt exercitumque eius omnibus rēbus iuvant.
Etiam Cingulō, quod oppidum Labiēnus cōnstituerat suāque
5 pecūniā exaedificāverat, ad eum lēgātī veniunt quaeque
imperāverit sē cupidissimē factūrōs pollicentur. Mīlitēs
imperat: mittunt. Intereā legiō xii Caesarem cōnsequitur.
Cum hīs duābus Āsculum Pīcēnum proficīscitur. Id oppidum
Lentulus Spinther x cohortibus tenēbat; quī Caesaris adventū
10 cognitō profugit ex oppidō cohortīsque sēcum abdūcere cōnātus magnā parte mīlitum dēseritur. Relictus in itinere cum
paucīs incidit in Vibullium Rūfum missum ā Pompēiō in agrum
Pīcēnum cōnfirmandōrum hominum causā. Ā quō factus Vibullius certior quae rēs in Pīcēnō gererentur mīlitēs ab eō
15 accipit, ipsum dīmittit. Item ex fīnitimīs regiōnibus quās
potest contrahit cohortīs ex dīlectibus Pompēiānīs; in hīs
Camerīnō fugientem Lucilium Hirrum cum sex cohortibus, quās
ibi in praesidiō habuerat, excipit; quibus coāctīs xiii
efficit. Cum hīs ad Domitium Ahēnobarbum Corfinium magnīs
20 itineribus pervenit Caesaremque adesse cum legiōnibus duābus
nūntiat. Domitius per sē circiter xx cohortīs Albā, ex
Marsīs et Paelignīs, fīnitimīs ab regiōnibus coēgerat.

(*Bellum Cīvīle* 1.15)

24

*On February 8, Cicero anticipates Caesar's advance into Apulia and com-
plains of the total inactivity of Pompey and the consuls.*

Cicerō Atticō sal.

Dē malīs nostrīs tū prius audīs quam ego. Istim enim
ēmānant. Bonī autem hinc quod exspectēs nihil est. Vēnī

Capuam ad Nōnās Febr. ita ut iusserant cōnsulēs. Eō diē
5 Lentulus vēnit sērō. Alter cōnsul omnīnō nōn vēnerat vii
Īdūs. Eō enim diē ego Capuā discessī et mānsī Calibus.
Inde hās litterās postrīdiē ante lūcem dedī. Haec Capuae
dum fuī cognōvī, nihil in cōnsulibus, nūllum usquam
dīlectum. Nec enim conquīsītōrēs φαινοπροσωπεῖν audent cum
10 ille adsit, contrāque noster dux nusquam sit, nihil agat,
nec nōmina dant. Dēficit enim nōn voluntās sed spēs.
Gnaeus autem noster—ō rem miseram et incrēdibilem!—ut
tōtus iacet! Nōn animus est, nōn cōnsilium, nōn cōpiae, nōn
dīligentia. Mittam illa, fugam ab urbe turpissimam, timi-
15 dissimās in oppidīs contiōnēs, ignōrātiōnem nōn sōlum adversārī sed etiam suārum cōpiārum; hoc cuius modī est? vii
Īdūs Febr. Capuam C. Cassius tribūnus plēbis vēnit, adtulit
mandāta ad cōnsulēs ut Rōmam venīrent, pecūniam dē sanctiōre
aerāriō auferrent, statim exīrent. Urbe relictā redeant;
20 quō praesidiō? deinde exeant; quis sinat? Cōnsul eī rescrīpsit ut prius ipse in Pīcēnum. At illud tōtum erat
āmissum; sciēbat nēmō praeter mē ex litterīs Dolabellae.
Mihi dubium nōn erat quīn ille iam iamque foret in Āpūliā,
Gnaeus noster in nāvī.
25   Ego quid agam σκέμμα magnum—neque mēhercule mihi
quidem ūllum, nisi omnia essent ācta turpissimē, neque ego
ūllīus cōnsilī particeps—sed tamen, quid mē deceat. Ipse
mē Caesar ad pācem hortātur; sed antīquiōrēs litterae quam
ruere coepit. Dolabella, Caelius mē illī valdē satis
30 facere. Mīra mē ἀπορία torquet. Iuvā mē cōnsiliō sī potes,
et tamen ista quantum potes prōvidē. Nihil habeō tantā
rērum perturbātiōne quod scrībam. Tuās litterās exspectō.

(*Ad Atticum* 7.21)

25

*In a brief note written on February 10, Pompey gives Cicero a situation
report and urges him to come to his headquarters in Luceria, where he hopes
to consolidate his forces with those of Domitius.*

Cn. Magnus prōcōs. s. d. M. Cicerōnī imp.

Q. Fabius ad mē vēnit a. d. iiii. Īdūs Febr. Is nūntiat
L. Domitium cum suīs cohortibus xii et cum cohortibus xiiii
quās Vibullius addūxit ad mē iter habēre; habuisse in animō

5 proficīscī Corfīniō a. d. v Īdūs Febr.; C. Hirrum cum v cohortibus subsequī. Cēnseō ad nōs Lūceriam veniās. Nam tē
hīc tūtissimē putō fore.

(*Ad Atticum* 8.11A)

26

*Surprised by the lack of direct information from Domitius Ahenobarbus,
commander of the troops at Corfinium, Pompey writes Domitius on February
11 or 12 to outline the tactical situation as well as to ask his proconsular
colleague to join forces with him at Luceria.*

Cn. Magnus prōcōs. s. d. L. Domitiō prōcōs.

Valdē mīror tē ad mē nihil scrībere et potius ab aliīs
quam ā tē dē rē pūblicā mē certiōrem fierī. Nōs disiectā
manū parēs adversāriō esse nōn possumus; contractīs nostrīs
5 cōpiīs spērō nōs et reī pūblicae et commūnī salūtī prōdesse
posse. Quam ob rem cum cōnstituissēs, ut Vibullius mihi
scrīpserat, a. d. v Īd. Febr. Corfīniō proficīscī cum exercitū et ad mē venīre, mīror quid causae fuerit quā rē
cōnsilium mūtārīs. Nam illa causa quam mihi Vibullius
10 scrībit levis est, tē proptereā morātum esse quod audierīs
Caesarem Firmō prōgressum in Castrum Truentīnum vēnisse.
Quantō enim magis appropinquāre adversārius coepit eō tibi
celerius agendum erat ut tē mēcum coniungerēs, priusquam
Caesar aut tuum iter impedīre aut mē abs tē exclūdere
15 posset.
Quam ob rem etiam atque etiam tē rogō et hortor, id
quod nōn dēstitī superiōribus litterīs ā tē petere, ut
prīmō quōque diē Lūceriam advenīrēs, antequam cōpiae quās
īnstituit Caesar contrahere in ūnum locum coāctae vōs ā
20 nōbīs distrahant. Sed sī erunt quī tē impediant ut vīllās
suās servent, aequum est mē ā tē impetrāre ut cohortīs quae
ex Pīcēnō et Camerīnō vēnērunt, quae fortūnās suās relīquē-
runt, ad mē missum faciās.

(*Ad Atticum* 8.12B)

27

Caesar reaches Corfinium.

Receptō Firmō expulsōque Lentulō Caesar conquīrī mīlitēs
quī ab eō discesserant, dīlectumque īnstituī iubet; ipse ūnum

diem ibi reī frūmentāriae causā morātus Corfīnium contendit.
Eō cum vēnisset, cohortēs v praemissae ā Domitiō ex oppidō
5 pontem flūminis interrumpēbant, quī erat ab oppidō mīlia passuum circiter iii. Ibi cum antecursōribus Caesaris proeliō
commissō celeriter Domitiānī ā ponte repulsī sē in oppidum
recēpērunt. Caesar legiōnibus trāductīs ad oppidum cōnstitit
iuxtāque mūrum castra posuit.
10   Rē cognitā Domitius ad Pompēium in Āpūliam perītōs
regiōnum magnō prōpositō praemiō cum litterīs mittit quī
petant atque ōrent ut sibi subveniat: Caesarem duōbus
exercitibus et locōrum angustiīs facile interclūdī posse
frūmentōque prohibērī. Quod nisi fēcerit, sē cohortīsque
15 amplius xxx magnumque numerum senātōrum atque equitum
Rōmānōrum in perīculum esse ventūrum. Interim suōs cohor-
tātus tormenta in mūrīs dispōnit certāsque cuique partīs ad
custōdiam urbis attribuit; mīlitibus in contiōne agrōs ex
suīs possessiōnibus pollicētur, xl in singulōs iūgera et prō
20 ratā parte centuriōnibus ēvocātīsque.

(*Bellum Cīvīle* 1.16–17)

28

The town of Sulmo surrenders while Caesar besieges Corfinium.

Interim Caesarī nūntiātur Sulmōnensēs, quod oppidum ā
Corfīniō vii mīlium intervallō abest, cupere ea facere quae
vellet, sed ā Q. Lucrētiō senātōre et Attiō Paelignō prohibērī, quī id oppidum vii cohortium praesidiō tenēbant.
5 Mittit eō M. Antōnium cum legiōnis xiii cohortibus v. Sulmōnensēs simul atque signa nostra vīdērunt, portās aperuērunt
ūniversīque, et oppidānī et mīlitēs, obviam grātulantēs
Antōniō exiērunt. Lucrētius et Attius dē mūrō sē dēiēcērunt.
Attius ad Antōnium dēductus petit ut ad Caesarem mitterētur.
10 Antōnius cum cohortibus et Attiō eōdem diē quō profectus erat
revertitur. Caesar eās cohortīs cum exercitū suō coniunxit
Attiumque incolumem dīmīsit.
     Caesar prīmīs diēbus castra magnīs operibus mūnīre et
ex fīnitimīs mūnicipiīs frūmentum comportāre reliquāsque
15 cōpiās exspectāre īnstituit. Eō trīduō legiō viii ad eum
vēnit cohortēsque ex nōvīs Galliae dīlectibus xxii equitēsque
ab rēge Nōricō circiter ccc. Quōrum adventū altera castra ad

alteram oppidī partem pōnit; hīs castrīs Curiōnem praefēcit.
Reliquīs diēbus oppidum vallō castellīsque circumvenīre īn-
20 stituit. Cuius operis maximā parte effectā eōdem ferē tempore missī ad Pompēium revertuntur.

(Bellum Cīvīle 1.18)

29

*On February 17, Pompey writes for the last time from Luceria to Domitius,
now surrounded, exhorting him to escape.*

Cn. Magnus prōcōs. s. d. L. Domitiō prōcōs.

Litterae mihi ā tē redditae sunt a. d. xiii Kal. Mārtiās
in quibus scrībis Caesarem apud Corfīnium castra posuisse.
Quod putāvī et praemonuī fit, ut nec in praesentiā committere
5 tēcum proelium velit et omnibus cōpiīs conductīs tē implicet,
nē ad mē iter tibi expedītum sit atque istās cōpiās coniun-
gere optimōrum cīvium possīs cum hīs legiōnibus dē quārum
voluntāte dubitāmus. Quō etiam magis tuīs litterīs sum
commōtus. Neque enim eōrum mīlitum quōs mēcum habeō volun-
10 tāte satis cōnfīdō ut dē omnibus fortūnīs reī pūblicae
dīmicem neque etiam quī ex dīlectibus cōnscriptī sunt cōnsulibus convēnērunt.
Quā rē dā operam, sī ūllā ratiōne etiam nunc efficere
potes, ut tē explicēs, hōc quam prīmum veniās, antequam
15 omnēs cōpiae adversārium conveniant. Neque enim celeriter ex dīlectibus hōc hominēs convenīre possunt et, sī
convenīrent, quantum iīs committendum sit quī inter sē nē
nōtī quidem sunt contrā veterānās legiōnēs nōn tē praeterit.

(Ad Atticum 8.12D)

30

The surrender of Corfinium.

Litterīs perlectīs Domitius dissimulāns in cōnsiliō
prōnuntiat Pompēium celeriter subsidiō ventūrum hortāturque
eōs nē animō dēficiant quaeque ūsuī ad dēfendendum oppidum
sint parent. Ipse arcānō cum paucīs familiāribus suīs
5 colloquitur cōnsiliumque fugae capere cōnstituit. Cum
vultus Domitī cum ōrātiōne nōn cōnsentīret atque omnia
trepidantius timidiusque ageret quam superiōribus diēbus

cōnsuēsset multumque cum suīs cōnsiliandī causā secrētō
praeter cōnsuētūdinem colloquerētur, concilia conventūsque
10 hominum fugeret, rēs diūtius tegī dissimulārīque nōn potuit.
Pompēius enim rescrīpserat sēsē rem in summum perīculum dē-
ductūrum nōn esse, neque suō cōnsiliō aut voluntāte Domitium
sē in oppidum Corfīnium contulisse: proinde, sī qua fuisset
facultās, ad sē cum omnibus cōpiīs venīret. Id nē fierī
15 posset, obsidiōne atque oppidī circummunitiōne fiēbat.

Dīvulgātō Domitī cōnsiliō mīlitēs quī erant Corfīnī
prīmō vesperī sēcessiōnem faciunt atque ita inter sē per
tribūnōs mīlitum centuriōnēsque atque honestissimōs suī
generis colloquuntur: obsiderī sē ā Caesare; opera mūnitiō-
20 nēsque prope esse perfectās; ducem suum Domitium, cuius spē
atque fīdūciā permānserint, prōiectīs omnibus fugae cōnsilium capere; dēbēre sē suae salūtis ratiōnem habēre. Ab
hīs prīmō Marsī dissentīre incipiunt eamque oppidī partem
quae mūnītissima vidērētur occupant, tantaque inter eōs
25 dissensiō exsistit ut manum cōnserere atque armīs dīmicāre
cōnentur; post paulō tamen internūntiīs ultrō citrōque
missīs, quae ignōrābant dē L. Domitī fugā cognōscunt. Itaque omnēs ūnō cōnsiliō Domitium prōductum in pūblicum
circumsistunt et custōdiunt lēgātōsque ex suō numerō ad
30 Caesarem mittunt: sēsē parātōs esse portās aperīre quaeque
imperāverit facere et L. Domitium vīvum in eius potestātem
trādere.

(*Bellum Cīvīle* 1.19–20)

31

*Upon learning from Domitius of Caesar's arrival at Corfinium, Pompey
apprised the consuls, on February 18 or 19, of his plans to proceed south from
Luceria to Brundisium, where he asked them to meet him. Since, however, the
consuls were in Apulia by February 20, they were probably en route when this
letter was written and therefore may never have received it.*

Cn. Magnus prōcōs. s. d. C. Mārcellō L. Lentulō cōss.

Ego quod existimābam dispersōs nōs neque reī pūblicae
ūtilīs neque nōbīs praesidiō esse posse, idcircō ad L.
Domitium litterās mīsī, prīmum utī ipse cum omnī cōpiā ad
5 nōs venīret; sī dē sē dubitāret, ut cohortīs xviiii quae ex
Pīcēnō ad mē iter habēbant ad nōs mitteret. Quod veritus

sum factum est, ut Domitius implicārētur et neque ipse satis
firmus esset ad castra facienda, quod meās xviiii et suās
xii cohortīs tribus in oppidīs distribūtās habēret (nam
10 partim Albae, partim Sulmōne conlocāvit) neque sē, sī
vellet, expedīre posset.

Nunc scītōte mē esse in summā sollicitūdine. Nam et tot
et tālīs virōs perīculō obsidiōnis līberāre cupiō neque subsidiō īre possum, quod hīs duābus legiōnibus nōn putō esse
15 committendum ut illūc dūcantur, ex quibus tamen nōn amplius
xiiii cohortīs contrahere potuī, quod Brundisium praesidium mīsī
neque Canusium sine praesidiō, dum abessem, putāvī esse
dīmittendum.

D. Laeliō mandāram, quod māiōrēs cōpiās spērābam nōs
20 habitūrōs, ut, sī vōbīs vidērētur, alter uter vestrum ad mē
venīret, alter in Siciliam cum eā cōpiā quam Capuae et circum
Capuam comparāstis et cum iīs mīlitibus quōs Faustus lēgit
proficīscerētur, Domitius cum xii suīs cohortibus eōdem adiungerētur, reliquae cōpiae omnēs Brundisium cōgerentur et
25 inde nāvibus Dyrrachium trānsportārentur. Nunc cum hōc
tempore nihilō magis ego quam vōs subsidiō Domitiō īre possim
⟨neque ipse possit⟩ sē per montīs explicāre, nōn est nōbīs
committendum ut ad hās xiiii cohortīs quās dubiō animō habeō
hostis accēdere aut in itinere mē cōnsequī possit.
30 Quam ob rem placitum est mihi (tālia videō cēnsērī
M. Mārcellō et cēterīs nostrī ōrdinis quī hīc sunt), ut
Brundisium dūcerem hanc cōpiam quam mēcum habeō. Vōs hortor
ut quodcumque mīlitum contrahere poteritis contrahātis et
eōdem Brundisium veniātis quam prīmum. Arma quae ad mē
35 missūrī erātis, iīs cēnseō armētis mīlitēs quōs vōbīscum
habētis. Quae arma superābunt, ea sī Brundisium iūmentīs
dēportāritis, vehementer reī pūblicae prōfueritis. Dē hāc
rē velim nostrōs certiōrēs faciātis. Ego ad P. Lupum et
C. Copōnium praetōrēs mīsī sē vōbīs coniungerent et
40 mīlitum quod habērent ad vōs dēdūcerent.

(*Ad Atticum* 8.12A)

32

*In this introspective letter, written on the night of February 18 in his
lodging at Cales, Cicero consults with Atticus about what he should do if
Pompey abandons Italy. To help Atticus advise him, Cicero sets forth the*

qui tum erat aut quī mihi esse vidēbātur; cum hōc vērō quī
ante fugit quam scit aut quem fugiat aut quō, quī nostra
trādidit, quī patriam relīquit, Ītaliam relinquit, sī māluī,
15 contigit: victus sum. Quod superest, nec ista vidēre possum
quae numquam timuī nē vidērem nec mēhercule istum propter
quem mihi nōn modo meīs sed mēmet ipsō carendum est.

(*Ad Atticum* 8.7.1–2)

37

Caesar receives the conquered at Corfinium.

Caesar, ubi lūxit, omnīs senātōrēs senātōrumque līberōs,
tribūnōs mīlitum equitēsque Rōmānōs ad sē prōdūcī iubet.
Erant quinque senātōriī ōrdinis, L. Domitius, P. Lentulus
Spinther, L. Caecilius Rūfus, Sex. Quintilius Vārus quaestor,
5 L. Rubrius; praetereā fīlius Domitī aliīque complūrēs adulēs-
centēs et magnus numerus equitum Rōmānōrum et decuriōnum,
quōs ex mūnicipiīs Domitius ēvocāverat. Hōs omnīs prōductōs
ā contumēliīs mīlitum conviciīsque prohibet; pauca apud eōs
loquitur, quod sibi ā parte eōrum grātia relāta nōn sit prō
10 suīs in eōs maximīs beneficiīs; dīmittit omnīs incolumīs.
HS |lx|, quod advexerat Domitius atque in pūblicō dēposuerat,
allātum ad sē ab iiiivirīs Corfīniensibus Domitiō reddit, nē
continentior in vītā hominum quam in pecūniā fuisse videātur,
etsī eam pecūniam pūblicam esse cōnstābat datamque ā Pompēiō
15 in stipendium. Mīlitēs Domitiānōs sacrāmentum apud sē dīcere
iubet atque eō diē castra movet iūstumque iter cōnficit, vii
omnīnō diēs ad Corfinium commorātus, et per fīnīs Marrūcīnōrum, Frentānōrum, Lārīnātium in Āpūliam pervenit.

(*Bellum Cīvīle* 1.23)

38

Pompey withdraws to Brundisium.

Pompēius, hīs rēbus cognitīs quae erant ad Corfīnium
gestae, Lūceriā proficīscitur Canusium atque inde Brundisium.
Cōpiās undique omnīs ex novīs dīlectibus ad sē cōgī iubet;
servōs, pāstōrēs armat atque eīs equōs attribuit; ex hīs
5 circiter ccc equitēs cōnficit. L. Manlius praetor Albā cum
cohortibus sex prōfugit, Rutilius Lupus praetor Tarracīnā

cum tribus; quae procul equitātum Caesaris cōnspicātae, cui
praeerat Vibius Curius, relictō praetōre signa ad Curium
trānsferunt atque ad eum trānseunt. Item reliquīs itineribus
10 nōnnūllae cohortēs in agmen Caesaris, aliae in equitēs in-
cidunt. Redūcitur ad eum dēprensus ex itinere N. Magius
Cremōnā, praefectus fabrum Cn. Pompēī. Quem Caesar ad eum
remittit cum mandātīs: quoniam ad id tempus facultās col-
loquendī nōn fuerit atque ipse Brundisium sit ventūrus,
15 interesse reī pūblicae et commūnis salūtis sē cum Pompēiō
colloquī; neque vērō idem prōficī longō itineris spatiō, cum
per aliōs condiciōnēs ferantur, ac sī cōram dē omnibus condiciōnibus disceptētur.

(*Bellum Cīvīle* 1.24)

39

*At the end of February, L. Cornelius Balbus, who had close ties of friendship
with Caesar, Pompey, and Cicero, writes to Cicero urging him to use his
influence to bring about a reconciliation between Caesar and Pompey.*

Balbus Cicerōnī imp. sal.

Obsecrō tē, Cicerō, suscipe cūram et cōgitātiōnem
dignissimam tuae virtūtis ut Caesarem et Pompēium perfidiā
hominum distractōs rursus in pristinam concordiam redūcās.
5 Crēde mihi Caesarem nōn sōlum fore in tuā potestāte sed
etiam maximum beneficium tē sibi dedisse iūdicātūrum, sī
hōc tē rēicis. Velim idem Pompēius faciat. Quī ut addūcī
tālī tempore ad ūllam condiciōnem possit magis optō quam
spērō. Sed cum cōnstiterit et timēre dēsierit, tum
10 incipiam nōn dēspērāre tuam auctōritātem plūrimum apud eum
valitūram.
Quod Lentulum cōnsulem meum voluistī hīc remanēre,
Caesarī grātum, mihi vērō grātissimum medius fidius fēcistī.
Nam illum tantī faciō ut nōn Caesarem magis dīligam. Quī sī
15 passus esset nōs sēcum, ut cōnsuēverāmus, loquī et nōn sē
tōtum etiam atque etiam ab sermōne nostrō āvertisset, minus
miser quam sum essem. Nam cavē putēs hōc tempore plūs mē
quemquam cruciārī, quod eum quem ante mē dīligō videō in
cōnsulātū quidvīs potius esse quam cōnsulem. Quod sī vol-
20 uerit tibi obtemperāre et nōbīs dē Caesare crēdere et
cōnsulātum reliquum Rōmae peragere, incipiam spērāre etiam

cōnsiliō senātūs, auctōre tē, illō relātōre, Pompēium et
Caesarem coniungī posse. Quod sī factum erit, mē satis
vīxisse putābō.

25   Factum Caesaris dē Corfīniō tōtum tē probātūrum sciō
et, quō modō in eius modī rē, commodius cadere nōn potuit
quam ut rēs sine sanguine cōnfieret.

    Balbī meī tuīque adventū dēlectātum tē valdē gaudeō.
Is quaecumque tibi dē Caesare dīxit quaeque Caesar scrīpsit,
30 sciō, rē tibi probābit, quaecumque fortūna eius fuerit,
vērissimē scrīpsisse.

(Ad Atticum 8.15A)

40

Writing to Atticus from Formiae on February 27, Cicero speculates about the
"guardian of the state," moderātor reī pūblicae, and contrasts him with the
two antagonists, Pompey and Caesar, in their quest for absolute power.

Cicerō Atticō sal.

    Cōnsumō igitur omne tempus cōnsīderāns quanta vīs sit
illīus virī quem nostrīs librīs satis dīligenter, ut tibi
quidem vidēmur, expressimus. Tenēsne igitur moderātōrem illum
5 reī pūblicae quō referre velimus omnia? Nam sīc quīntō, ut
opīnor, in librō loquitur Scīpiō, "Ut enim gubernātōrī cursus
secundus, medicō salūs, imperātōrī victōria, sīc huic moderā-
tōrī reī pūblicae beāta cīvium vīta prōposita est, ut opibus
firma, cōpiīs locuplēs, glōriā ampla, virtūte honesta sit.
10 Huius enim operis maximī inter hominēs atque optimī illum
esse perfectōrem volō." Hoc Gnaeus noster cum anteā numquam
tum in hāc causā minimē cōgitāvit. Dominātiō quaesīta ab
utrōque est, nōn id āctum beāta et honesta cīvitās ut esset.
Nec vērō ille urbem relīquit quod eam tuērī nōn posset nec
15 Ītaliam quod eā pellerētur, sed hoc ā prīmō cōgitāvit, omnīs
terrās, omnia maria movēre, rēgēs barbarōs incitāre, gentīs
ferās armātās in Ītaliam addūcere, exercitūs cōnficere
maximōs. Genus illud Sullānī rēgnī iam prīdem appetitur
multīs quī ūnā sunt cupientibus. An cēnsēs nihil inter eōs
20 convenīre, nūllam pactiōnem fierī potuisse? Hodiē potest.
Sed neutrī σκοπὸς est ille ut nōs beātī sīmus; uterque
rēgnāre vult.

(Ad Atticum 8.11.1–2)

61

41

On March 1, Cicero, now sending letters to Atticus from Formiae on a daily basis, contrasts the decisiveness and foresight of Caesar with the indecisiveness and inertia of many aristocrats who remain selfishly uncommitted.

Cicerō Atticō sal.

Lippitūdinis meae signum tibi sit librārī manus et
eadem causa brevitātis; etsī nunc quidem quod scrīberem
nihil erat. Omnis exspectātiō nostra erat in nūntiīs
5   Brundisīnīs. Sī nactus hic esset Gnaeum nostrum, spēs
dubia pācis, sīn ille ante trāmīsisset, exitiōsī bellī
metus. Sed vidēsne in quem hominem inciderit rēs pūblica,
quam acūtum, quam vigilantem, quam parātum? Sī mēhercule
nēminem occīderit nec cuiquam quicquam adēmerit, ab iīs
10   quī eum maximē timuerant maximē dīligētur.

Multum mēcum mūnicipālēs hominēs loquuntur, multum
rusticānī; nihil prorsus aliud cūrant nisi agrōs, nisi
vīllulās, nisi nummulōs suōs. Et vidē quam conversa rēs
sit; illum quō anteā cōnfīdēbant metuunt, hunc amant quem
15   timēbant. Id quantīs nostrīs peccātīs vitiīsque ēvēnerit
nōn possum sine molestiā cōgitāre. Quae autem impendēre
putārem, scrīpseram ad tē et iam tuās litterās exspectābam.

(Ad Atticum 8.13)

42

En route to Brundisium early in March, Caesar forwards to Oppius and Balbus, two of his agents, a letter intended for widespread distribution as propaganda.

Caesar Oppiō, Cornēliō sal.

Gaudeō mēhercule vōs significāre litterīs quam valdē
probētis ea quae apud Corfīnium sunt gesta. Cōnsiliō vestrō
ūtar libenter et hōc libentius quod meā sponte facere cōn-
5   stitueram ut quam lēnissimum mē praebērem et Pompēium darem
operam ut reconciliārem. Temptēmus hōc modō sī possīmus
omnium voluntātēs reciperāre et diuturnā victōriā ūtī,
quoniam reliquī crūdēlitāte odium effugere nōn potuērunt
neque victōriam diutius tenēre praeter ūnum L. Sullam, quem
10   imitātūrus nōn sum. Haec nova sit ratiō vincendī ut

misericordiā et līberālitāte nōs mūniāmus. Id quem ad modum
fierī possit nōnnūlla mī in mentem veniunt et multa reperīrī
possunt. Dē hīs rēbus rogō vōs ut cōgitātiōnem suscipiātis.

    N. Magium Pompēī praefectum dēprehendī. Scīlicet meō
15 īnstitūtō ūsus sum et eum statim missum fēcī. Iam duo praefectī fabrum Pompēī in meam potestātem vēnērunt et ā mē
missī sunt. Sī volent grātī esse, dēbēbunt Pompēium hortārī
ut mālit mihi esse amīcus quam iīs quī et illī et mihi
semper fuērunt inimīcissimī, quōrum artificiīs effectum est
20 ut rēs pūblica in hunc statum pervenīret.

(Ad Atticum 9.7C)

43

*During the first week of March, Caesar, still on the march to Brundisium,
forwards in haste a brief note to Cicero to request a meeting in Rome.*

Caesar imp. s. d. Cicerōnī imp.

    Cum Furnium nostrum tantum vīdissem neque loquī neque
audīre meō commodō potuissem, properārem atque essem in
itinere praemissīs iam legiōnibus, praeterīre tamen nōn potuī
5 quīn et scrīberem ad tē et illum mitterem grātiāsque agerem,
etsī hoc et fēcī saepe et saepius mihi factūrus videor; ita
dē mē merēris. In prīmīs ā tē petō, quoniam cōnfīdō mē
celeriter ad urbem ventūrum, ut tē ibi videam, ut tuō cōnsiliō, grātiā, dignitāte, ope omnium rērum ūtī possim. Ad
10 prōpositum revertar; festīnātiōnī meae brevitātīque litterārum ignōscēs. Reliqua ex Furniō cognōscēs.

(Ad Atticum 9.6A)

44

*After sending Magius to Pompey with a request for a conference, Caesar
presses on to Brundisium, hoping to find Pompey and the consuls there. But
nothing happens to fulfill his expectations. A great disappointment awaits
Caesar when he learns of the departure of the consuls for Dyrrachium in
Greece on March 4 since their absence makes it difficult to bring matters
before the senate. Nevertheless, when Caesar arrives on March 9 and finds
Pompey still in Brundisium, he decides to mount a blockade, which Pompey
counters with his own preparations.*

63

His datīs mandātīs Brundisium cum legiōnibus vi
pervēnit, veterānīs iii et reliquīs, quās ex novō dīlectū
cōnfēcerat atque in itinere complēverat; Domitiānās enim
cohortīs prōtinus ā Corfīniō in Siciliam mīserat. Repperit

5 cōnsulēs Dyrrachium profectōs cum magnā parte exercitūs,
Pompēium remanēre Brundisī cum cohortibus xx; neque certum
invenīrī poterat, obtinendīne Brundisī causā ibi remānsisset,
quō facilius omne Hadriāticum mare ex ultimīs Ītaliae
partibus regiōnibusque Graeciae in potestāte habēret atque

10 ex utrāque parte bellum administrāre posset, an inopiā
nāvium ibi restitisset; veritusque nē ille Ītaliam dīmittendam nōn existimāret, exitūs administrātiōnēsque Brundisīnī
portūs impedīre īnstituit. . . .

Atque haec Caesar ita administrābat, ut condiciōnēs

15 pācis dīmittendās nōn existimāret; ac tametsī magnopere ad-
mīrābātur Magium, quem ad Pompēium cum mandātīs mīserat, ad
sē nōn remittī, atque ea rēs saepe temptāta etsī impetūs
eius cōnsiliaque tardābat, tamen omnibus rēbus in eō
perseverandum putābat. Itaque Canīnium Rebilum lēgātum,

20 familiārem necessāriumque Scrībōnī Libōnis, mittit ad eum
colloquī causā; mandat ut Libōnem dē conciliandā pāce hortētur; in prīmīs ut ipse cum Pompēiō colloquerētur postulat;
magnopere sēsē cōnfīdere dēmōnstrat, sī eius reī sit potestās
facta, fore ut aequīs condiciōnibus ab armīs discēdātur;

25 cuius reī magnam partem laudis atque existimātiōnis ad
Libōnem perventūram sī illō auctōre atque agente ab armīs
sit discessum. Libō ā colloquiō Canīnī dīgressus ad Pompēium
proficīscitur. Paulō post renūntiat, quod cōnsulēs absint,
sine illīs nōn posse agī dē compositiōne. Ita saepius rem

30 frūstrā temptātam Caesar aliquandō dīmittendam sibi iūdicat
et dē bellō agendum.

Prope dīmidiā parte operis ā Caesare effectā diēbusque
in eā rē cōnsumptīs viiii, nāvēs ā cōnsulibus Dyrrachiō
remissae, quae priōrem partem exercitūs eō dēportāverant,

35 Brundisium revertuntur. Pompēius, sīve operibus Caesaris
permōtus sīve etiam quod ab initiō Ītaliā excēdere cōnstituerat, adventū nāvium profectiōnem parāre incipit. . . .
Hīs parātīs rēbus mīlitēs silentiō nāvīs cōnscendere iubet. . . .
Brundisīnī Pompēiānōrum mīlitum iniūriīs atque ipsīus

40 Pompēī contumēliīs permōtī Caesaris rēbus favēbant. Itaque
cognitā Pompēī profectiōne concursantibus illīs atque in eā rē

occupātīs vulgō ex tectīs significābant. Per quōs rē cognitā
Caesar scālās parārī mīlitēsque armārī iubet, nē quam reī gerendae
facultātem dīmittat. Pompēius sub noctem nāvēs solvit. . . .

45 Caesar, etsī ad spem cōnficiendī negōtī maximē probābat
coāctīs nāvibus mare trānsīre et Pompēium sequī priusquam
ille sēsē trānsmarīnīs auxiliīs cōnfirmāret, tamen eius reī
moram temporisque longinquitātem timēbat, quod omnibus
coāctīs nāvibus Pompēius praesentem facultātem īnsequendī suī
50 adēmerat. Relinquēbātur ut ex longinquiōribus regiōnibus
Galliae Pīcēnīque et ā frētō nāvēs essent exspectandae. Id
propter annī tempus longum atque impedītum vidēbātur. Intereā veterem exercitum, duās Hispāniās cōnfirmārī, quārum
erat altera maximīs beneficiīs Pompēī dēvincta, auxilia,
55 equitātum parārī, Galliam Ītaliamque temptārī sē absente
nōlēbat. Itaque in praesentiā Pompēī sequendī ratiōnem
ōmittit, in Hispāniam proficīscī cōnstituit.

(Bellum Cīvīle 1.25–30.1)

45

*Replying from Formiae on March 19 or 20 to Caesar's note (Text 43), Cicero
explains his own position. This letter satisfies Caesar enough to publish it at
once, much to the displeasure of the anti-Caesarians and to the personal
discomfort of Cicero himself.*

Cicerō imp. s. d. Caesarī imp.

Ut lēgī tuās litterās quās ā Furniō nostrō accēperam
quibus mēcum agēbās ut ad urbem essem, tē velle ūtī "cōnsiliō et
dignitāte meā" minus sum admīrātus; dē "grātiā" et dē "ope"
5 quid significārēs mēcum ipse quaerēbam, spē tamen dēdūcēbar
ad eam cōgitātiōnem ut tē prō tuā admīrābilī ac singulārī
sapientiā dē ōtiō, dē pāce, dē concordiā cīvium agī velle
arbitrārer, et ad eam ratiōnem existimābam satis aptam esse
et nātūram et persōnam meam.

10 Quod sī ita est et sī qua dē Pompēiō nostrō tuendō et
tibi ac reī pūblicae reconciliandō cūra tē attingit, magis
idōneum quam ego sum ad eam causam profectō reperiēs nēminem
quī et illī semper et senātuī, cum prīmum potuī, pācis auctor
fuī, nec sūmptīs armīs bellī ūllam partem attigī, iūdicāvīque
15 eō bellō tē violārī contrā cuius honōrem populī Rōmānī beneficiō concessum inimīcī atque invidī nīterentur. Sed ut eō

tempore nōn modo ipse fautor dignitātis tuae fuī vērum etiam
cēterīs auctor ad tē adiuvandum, sīc mē nunc Pompēī dignitās
vehementer movet. Aliquot enim sunt annī cum vōs duo dēlēgī
20 quōs praecipuē colerem et quibus essem, sīcut sum, amīcis-
simus.

Quam ob rem ā tē petō vel potius omnibus tē precibus ōrō
et obtestor ut in tuīs maximīs cūrīs aliquid impertiās temporis huic quoque cōgitātiōnī ut tuō beneficiō bonus vir,
25 grātus, pius, dēnique esse in maximī beneficī memōriā possim.
Quae sī tantum ad mē ipsum pertinērent, spērārem mē ā tē
tamen impetrātūrum, sed, ut arbitror, et ad tuam fidem et ad
rem pūblicam pertinet mē, et pācis et utriusque vestrum
⟨amīcum, et ad vestram⟩ et ad cīvium concordiam per tē quam
30 accommodātissimum cōnservārī.

Ego cum anteā tibi dē Lentulō grātiās ēgissem, cum eī
salūtī quī mihi fuerat fuissēs, tamen lectīs eius litterīs
quās ad mē grātissimō animō dē tuā līberālitāte beneficiōque
mīsit, eandem mē salūtem ā tē accēpisse ⟨putāvī⟩ quam ille. In
35 quem sī mē intellegis esse grātum, cūrā, obsecrō, ut etiam in
Pompēium esse possim.

(Ad Atticum 9.11A)

46

On March 25 a letter from Gaius Matius, a close friend of Cicero and
partisan of Caesar, and Gaius Trebatius Testa, formerly a protégé of Cicero,
furnishes news about Caesar's movements to prepare Cicero for a meeting
with Caesar.

Matius et Trebātius Cicerōnī imp. sal.

Cum Capuā exīssēmus, in itinere audīvimus Pompēium
Brundisiō a. d. xvi K. Aprīlīs cum omnibus cōpiīs quās
habuerit profectum esse; Caesarem posterō diē in oppidum
5 introīsse, contiōnātum esse, inde Rōmam contendisse, velle
ante K. esse ad urbem et pauculōs diēs ibi commorārī, deinde
in Hispāniās proficīscī. Nōbīs nōn aliēnum vīsum est,
quoniam dē adventū Caesaris prō certō habēbāmus, puerōs tuōs
ad tē remittere, ut id tū quam prīmum scīrēs. Mandāta tua
10 nōbīs cūrae sunt eaque ut tempus postulārit agēmus. Trebātius sēdulō facit ut antecēdat.

Epistulā cōnscrīptā nūntiātum est nōbīs Caesarem a. d.

viii K. Aprīlīs Beneventī mānsūrum, a. d. vii Capuae, a. d.
vi Sinuessae. Hoc prō certō putāmus.

(Ad Atticum 9.15.6)

47

*In reply to his praise of Caesar's clemency at Corfinium, Cicero receives a note
from Caesar, which he includes in a letter to Atticus written no earlier than
March 26.*

Cicerō Atticō sal.

Cum quod scrīberem ad tē nihil habērem, tamen nē quem
diem intermitterem hās dedī litterās. A. d. vi K. Caesarem
Sinuessae mānsūrum nūntiābant. Ab eō mihi litterae
5 redditae sunt a. d. vii K. quibus iam "opēs" meās, nōn ut
superiōribus litterīs "opem," exspectat. Cum eius clēmentiam
Corfīniensem illam per litterās collaudāvissem, rescrīpsit
hōc exemplō:
Caesar imp. Cicerōnī imp. sal. dīc.
10 Rectē augurāris dē mē (bene enim tibi cognitus sum)
nihil ā mē abesse longius crūdēlitāte. Atque ego cum ex
ipsā rē magnam capiō voluptātem tum meum factum probārī abs
tē triumphō gaudiō. Neque illud mē movet quod iī quī ā mē
dīmissī sunt discessisse dīcuntur ut mihi rursus bellum
15 īnferrent. Nihil enim mālō quam et mē meī similem esse et
illōs suī. Tū velim mihi ad urbem praestō sīs ut tuīs
cōnsiliīs atque opibus, ut cōnsuēvī, in omnibus rēbus ūtar.
Dolabellā tuō nihil scītō mihi esse iūcundius. Hanc adeō
habēbō grātiam illī; neque enim aliter facere poterit.
20 Tanta eius hūmānitās, is sēnsus, ea in mē est benevolentia.

(Ad Atticum 9.16)

48

*When Cicero fails to accede to Caesar's wish for a meeting in Rome, Caesar
comes to him at Formiae, conveniently situated on Caesar's route back to the
capital, on March 28. After the conference—perhaps the same day or the next
one—Cicero sends his confidant an account of the highlights.*

Cicerō Atticō sal.

Utrumque ex tuō cōnsiliō; nam et ōrātiō fuit ea nostra
ut bene potius ille dē nōbīs existimāret quam grātiās ageret,

67

et in eō mānsimus, nē ad urbem. Illa fefellērunt, facilem
5 quod putārāmus: nihil vīdī minus. Damnārī sē nostrō iūdiciō,
tardiōrēs fore reliquōs, sī nōs nōn venīrēmus, dīcere. Ego
dissimilem illōrum esse causam. Cum multa, "Venī igitur et
age dē pāce." "Meōne," inquam, "arbitrātū?" "An tibi,"
inquit, "ego praescrībam?" "Sīc," inquam, "agam: senātuī nōn
10 placēre in Hispāniās īrī nec exercitūs in Graeciam trānspor-
tārī, multaque," inquam, "dē Gnaeō dēplōrābō." Tum ille,
"Ego vērō ista dīcī nōlō." "Ita putābam," inquam; "sed ego
eō nōlō adesse quod aut sīc mihi dīcendum est multaque quae
nūllō modō possem silēre sī adessem aut nōn veniendum."
15 Summa fuit ut ille ⟨rogāret⟩, quasi exitum quaerēns, ut
dēlīberārem. Nōn fuit negandum. Ita discessimus. Crēdō
igitur hunc mē nōn amāre. At ego mē amāvī, quod mihi iam
prīdem ūsū nōn venit.

(*Ad Atticum* 9.18.1)

49

*En route to Arpinum after his interview with Caesar, Cicero learns from
Atticus about the publication of his letter to Caesar (Text 45), which caused
much displeasure among the* optimātēs. *In the following letter, written to
Atticus on March 29 or 30, Cicero attempts to answer their criticism.*

Cicerō Atticō sal.

Epistulam meam quod pervulgātam scrībis esse nōn ferō
molestē; quīn etiam ipse multīs dedī dēscrībendam. Ea enim
et accidērunt iam et impendent, ut testātum esse velim dē
5 pāce quid sēnserim. Cum autem ad eam hortārer eum praesertim hominem, nōn vidēbar ūllō modō facilius mōtūrus quam
sī id quod eum hortārer convenīre eius sapientiae dīcerem.
Eam sī "admīrābilem" dīxī cum eum ad salūtem patriae hortābar, nōn sum veritus nē vidērer adsentārī cui tālī in rē
10 libenter mē ad pedēs abiēcissem. Quā autem est "aliquid
impertiās temporis;" nōn est dē pāce sed dē mē ipsō et dē
meō officiō ut aliquid cōgitet. Nam quod testificor mē
expertem bellī fuisse, etsī id rē perspectum est, tamen eō
scrīpsī quō in suādendō plūs auctōritātis habērem; eōdemque
15 pertinet quod causam eius probō.

Sed quid haec nunc? Utinam aliquid prōfectum esset!
Ne ego istās litterās in contiōne recitārī velim, sī quidem

30   Vibullius, sēdātō tumultū quem repentīnus adventus
Caesaris concitāverat, ubi prīmum ē rē vīsum est, adhibitō
Libōne et L. Lucceiō et Theophane, quibuscum communicāre dē
maximīs rēbus Pompēius cōnsuēverat, de mandātīs Caesaris
agere īnstituit. Quem ingressum in sermōnem Pompēius inter-
35 pellāvit et loquī plūra prohibuit. "Quid mihi," inquit, "aut
vītā aut cīvitāte opus est, quam beneficiō Caesaris habēre
vidēbor? Cuius reī opiniō tollī nōn poterit, cum in Ītaliam
ex quā profectus sum reductus existimābor." Bellō perfectō,
ab eīs Caesar haec facta cognōvit quī sermōnī interfuērunt;
40 cōnātus tamen nihilō minus est aliīs ratiōnibus per colloquia
dē pāce agere.

(*Bellum Cīvīle* 3.18.3–5)

53

Several months of maneuvering allow Caesar time to consolidate reinforce-
ments from Greece and Italy. Finally, after numerous minor skirmishes,
Pompey deploys for an all-out assault near Pharsalus on August 9 of 48.
Confident in his vastly superior manpower, Pompey aims the spearhead of his
attack at Caesar's right flank by concentrating his cavalry on his own left.
With typical acumen, however, Caesar recognizes the tactic and draws up a
special reserve behind the third line of his right wing. As a result, Pompey's
attacking left wing is routed, and its dispersal exposes the entire flank. Whole
legions are smashed from their unprotected left, and their camp is captured.
The next morning the bulk of Pompey's army surrenders, while their com-
mander escapes and flees eastward. Caesar pursues him along much of the
seaboard of Asia Minor and from there to Egypt, where he arrives on October
2. But after more than eight years since he last saw Pompey's face, he receives a
ghastly trophy—a severed human head and a signet ring, brought to him to
confirm the news that his adversary had been assassinated on the beach.
    There follows a whirlwind campaign against King Ptolemy XIII and
the Alexandrians, resulting in the installment of Cleopatra as queen of
Egypt, and against Pharnaces in Asia, which is said to have inspired his now
famous boast: "vēnī, vīdī, vīcī" (Suetonius, Dīvus Iūlius 37.2). Another
sojourn in Rome provides a brief respite from his next campaign, launched
against the Pompeian army under Scipio in Africa, in December of 47.
Within four months, he overwhelms the Pompeians at Thapsus and returns
again to Rome to celebrate a fourfold triumph over Gaul, Alexandria, Pontus
in Asia, and Africa. One final pocket of resistance remains—in Spain under
the command of Pompey's sons and Caesar's former lieutenant Titus

Labienus—but by the middle of March 45, the last remnants of the once great Pompeian forces are crushed at Munda in the most gruelling battle of the entire civil war.

Meanwhile, in Rome, another severe personal blow strikes Cicero with the death of his daughter Tullia in childbirth. Aware of his friend's intense grief, Servius Sulpicius Rufus, a longtime friend, prominent jurist, and former consular colleague of the anti-Caesarian M. Marcellus in 51, writes the following letter to Cicero in March 45 from Greece, where he has been serving as Caesar's governor. Sulpicius, politically a moderate republican, has remained neutral throughout the civil war. In this letter he reminds his friend that Cicero has already been suffering a far greater loss than the demise of his only daughter.

Servius Cicerōnī s.

Posteāquam mihi renūntiātum est dē obitū Tulliae,
fīliae tuae, sānē quam prō eō ac dēbuī graviter molestēque
tulī commūnemque eam calamitātem existimāvī, quī sī istīc
5 adfuissem, neque tibi dēfuissem cōramque meum dolōrem tibi
dēclārāssem. . . .
   Quid est quod tantō opere tē commoveat tuus dolor
intestīnus? Cōgitā, quem ad modum adhūc fortūna nōbīscum
ēgerit; ea nōbīs ērepta esse, quae hominibus nōn minus quam
10 līberī cāra esse dēbent—patriam, honestātem, dignitātem,
honōrēs omnīs. Hōc ūnō incommodō additō, quid ad dolōrem
adiungī potuit? . . .
   Quae rēs mihi nōn mediocrem cōnsōlātiōnem attulit, volō
tibi commemorāre, sī forte eadem rēs tibi dolōrem minuere
15 possit. Ex Āsiā rediēns cum ab Aegīnā Megaram versus
nāvigārem, coepī regiōnēs circumcircā prōspicere. Post mē
erat Aegīna, ante mē Megara, dextrā Pīraeus, sinistrā
Corinthus, quae oppida quōdam tempore flōrentissima fuērunt,
nunc prōstrāta et dīruta ante oculōs iacent. Coepī egomet
20 mēcum sīc cōgitāre: "Hem! Nōs homunculī indignāmur, sī quis
nostrum interiit aut occīsus est, quōrum vīta brevior esse
dēbet, cum ūnō locō tot oppidum cadāvera prōiecta iacent?
Vīsne tū tē, Servī, cohibēre et meminisse hominem tē esse
nātum?" Crēde mihi, cōgitātiōne eā nōn mediocriter sum
25 cōnfirmātus. Hoc idem, sī tibi vidētur, fac ante oculōs
tibi prōpōnās. Modo ūnō tempore tot virī clārissimī interiērunt; dē imperiō populī Rōmānī tanta dēminūtiō facta est;

omnēs prōvinciae conquassātae sunt; in ūnīus mulierculae
animulā sī iactūra facta est, tantō opere commovēris? Quae
30 sī hōc tempore nōn diem suum obīsset, paucīs post annīs
tamen eī moriendum fuit, quoniam homō nāta fuerat. Etiam tū
ab hīsce rēbus animum ac cōgitātiōnem tuam āvocā atque ea
potius reminīscere, quae digna tuā persōnā sunt: illam,
quam diū eī opus fuerit, vīxisse; ūnā cum rē pūblicā fuisse;
35 tē, patrem suum, praetōrem, cōnsulem, augurem vīdisse;
adulēscentibus prīmāriīs nuptam fuisse; omnibus bonīs prope
perfunctam esse; cum rēs pūblica occideret, vītā excessisse.
Quid est quod tū aut illa cum fortūnā hōc nōmine querī
possītis?

(*Ad Familiārēs* 4.5.1–5)

54

*With the defeat of the Pompeians at Munda, more than three years of conflict
with the* optimātēs *and their supporters come to a bloody end. Caesar returns
to Rome to inaugurate a political settlement with the same extraordinary
energy and the same speed in making and acting upon decisions as had so
often distinguished his military career. Republican institutions are preserved
intact as far as possible, for Caesar remains acutely aware of the emotional
significance of the term* rēs pūblica; *in reality, however, his basis of power rests
not within the framework of any constitution but upon the shoulders of a
victorious army. For Caesar may well have believed that* nihil esse rem
pūblicam, appellātiōnem modo sine corpore ac speciē *(Suetonius,* Dīvus
Iūlius *77), words which T. Ampius Balbus, a political enemy, attributes to
him. Nonetheless, from the senate he accepts new and unprecedented honors—
among these, the dictatorship for ten years; the right of speaking first on all
questions debated in the senate, where he would sit between the consuls at all
meetings; the right to designate magistrates for popular election; a statue of
himself upon a triumphal chariot, with the globe at his feet and an inscription
designating him as a demigod, in the Capitoline Temple; the right to signal
the opening of all games; and a forty-day thanksgiving for his victory. His
ready acceptance of these and other honors disappointed many of the*
optimātēs *who had survived the civil war and still entertained hopes of a
restored republic. In a letter of January 44, Cicero describes to Manius Curius
an incident which took place in December 45 and must have deeply insulted
many* optimātēs, *who cherished the dignity and prestige of the highest magistracy in the land. This incident produced the briefest consulship in Roman
history.*

Cicerō Curiō s. d.

Ego vērō iam tē nec hortor nec rogō ut domum redeās;
quīn hinc ipse ēvolāre cupiō et aliquō pervenīre, "ubi nec
Pelopidārum nōmen nec facta audiam." Incrēdibile est quam
5 turpiter mihi facere videar, quī hīs rēbus intersim. Ne tū
vidēris multō ante prōvīdisse quid impendēret, tum cum hinc
prōfūgistī. Quamquam haec etiam audītū acerba sunt, tamen
audīre tolerābilius est quam vidēre. In Campō certē nōn
fuistī, cum hōrā secundā comitiīs quaestōriīs īnstitūtīs
10 sella Q. Maximī, quem illī cōnsulem esse dīcēbant, posita
esset; quō mortuō nūntiātō sella sublāta est. Ille autem,
quī comitiīs tribūtīs esset auspicātus, centuriāta habuit;
cōnsulem hōrā septimā renūntiāvit quī usque ad K. Iān. esset,
quae erant futūrae māne postrīdiē. Ita Canīniō cōnsule
15 scītō nēminem prandisse. Nihil tamen eō cōnsule malī factum
est. Fuit enim mīrificā vigilantiā, quī suō tōtō cōnsulātū
somnum nōn vīderit. Haec tibi rīdicula videntur; nōn enim
ades. Quae sī vidērēs, lacrimās nōn tenērēs. Quid, sī
cētera scrībam? Sunt enim innumerābilia generis eiusdem;
20 quae quidem ego nōn ferrem, nisi mē in philosophiae portum
contulissem et nisi habērem socium studiōrum meōrum Atticum
nostrum.

(Ad Familiārēs 7.30.1–2)

55

*As the year 44 opens, the senate continues to heap honors upon Caesar, among
them the title of* pater patriae, *the renaming of the month of his birth
(formerly* Quintīlis, *now to be called* Iūlius*), statues of himself to be set up in
all temples and in the* forum *at Rome as well as in the* mūnicipia, *and the
extension of his dictatorial powers for life (*dictātor perpetuus*), which he
officially bears on February 15. The rift between Caesar and the old Roman
aristocracy increases despite his professed policies of reconciliation, and he no
longer tries to bridge this widening gap. Although the Roman political setting
remains a stage on which many aspire to play a leading role, Caesar's drive to
sustain the gratification of his* dignitās *seems to leave little room for others to
realize their own ambitions. To many conservative Romans the title* dictātor
perpetuus *means "monarchy" as much as the hated word* rēx. *Their reaction
unites some sixty men whose leaders have, since swearing an oath of allegiance
to Caesar, been enjoying his highest favor; indeed, several of them number the
praetorship or consulship among the honors already received or soon to be*

granted. These men recall the glorious beginnings of the republic, brought about when their ancestors, whose names some of them now bear, removed a tyrant; is this not their civic duty as well? A plot is formed for March 15, when a meeting of the senate has been planned. That morning the senate assembles in a hall of Pompey's theater to await Caesar, who is not feeling well and must be persuaded by Decimus Brutus to disregard the premonitions of his wife Calpurnia and attend the meeting. As Caesar takes his seat he is surrounded by the conspirators, who pretend to have personal requests. As they press upon him they draw daggers. Caesar first raises his arms to ward off the blows, then wraps himself in his toga and collapses, stabbed some twenty-three times.

At this point, the plans of the conspirators go awry. Numb with panic, the senate fails to assume control of the government. The resulting political vacuum foments only another civil war, for not all Romans align themselves beneath the standards of the assassins. Many, like Caesar's loyal friend Matius, believe that the conspirators are mere brigands who have succeeded only in removing the one viable prospect of a solution to the problems of political reconciliation after a civil war, when the surviving enemies must somehow be led to embrace and partake of the new regime. In a letter to Cicero written late in the summer or early in the autumn of 44, Matius demonstrates that grief over Caesar's death is not incompatible with true patriotism.

Matius Cicerōnī s.

    Nōta enim mihi sunt quae in mē post Caesaris mortem contulerint. Vitiō mihi dant quod mortem hominis necessārī graviter ferō atque eum quem dīlēxī perīsse indignor; aiunt
5 enim patriam amīcitiae praepōnendam esse, proinde ac sī iam vīcerint obitum eius reī pūblicae fuisse ūtilem. Sed nōn agam astūtē; fateor mē ad istum gradum sapientiae nōn per-vēnisse. Neque enim Caesarem in dissēnsiōne cīvīlī sum secūtus, sed amīcum, quamquam rē offendēbar, tamen nōn
10 dēseruī; neque bellum umquam cīvīle aut etiam causam dis-sēnsiōnis probāvī, quam etiam nāscentem exstinguī summē studuī. Itaque in victōriā hominis necessārī . . . cīvibus victīs ut parcerētur aequē ac prō meā salūte labōrāvī.
    Possum igitur, quī omnīs voluerim incolumīs, eum ā quō
15 id impetrātum est perīsse nōn indignārī, cum praesertim īdem hominēs illī et invidiae et exitiō fuerint? "Plectēris ergō," inquiunt, "quoniam factum nostrum improbāre audēs." Ō superbiam inaudītam, aliōs in facinore glōriārī, aliīs

77

nē dolēre quidem impūnītē licēre! At haec etiam servīs
20 semper lībera fuērunt, ut timērent, gaudērent, dolērent suō
potius quam alterius arbitriō; quae nunc, ut quidem istī
dictitant, "lībertātis auctōrēs" metū nōbīs extorquēre
cōnantur. Sed nihil agunt. Nūllīus umquam perīculī
terrōribus ab officiō aut ab hūmānitāte dēscīscam; numquam
25 enim honestam mortem fugiendam, saepe etiam oppetendam
putāvī. Sed quid mihi suscēnsent sī id optō ut paeniteat
eōs suī factī? Cupiō enim Caesaris mortem omnibus esse
acerbam.

    "At dēbeō prō cīvīlī parte rem pūblicam velle salvam."
30 Id quidem mē cupere, nisi et ante ācta vīta et reliqua mea
spēs, tacente mē, probat, dīcendō vincere nōn postulō. Quā
rē māiōrem in modum tē rogō ut rem potiōrem ōrātiōne dūcās
mihique, sī sentīs expedīre rectē fierī, crēdās nūllam
commūniōnem cum improbīs esse posse.

                          (*Ad Familiārēs* 11.28.2–5)

In the foreground stand three columns of the marble temple of Venus Genetrix, the ancestress of the *gēns Iūlia*, in Rome's first privately financed forum, the *Forum Iūlium*, also known as the *Forum Caesaris*. In 54 B.C., Caesar purchased the land for his building site at enormous cost through the agency of Cicero. The rectangular *Forum Iūlium* stood along the northeast base of the Capitoline Hill, behind and perpendicular to the axis of the senate house.

At the southwest corner of the Roman forum, behind the excavations in the base of the temple of Saturn (which also housed the state treasury), lie the remains of the Basilica Julia, a hall for business, banking tables, and perhaps some government offices. Its construction began in the 50s B.C. and was financed by spoils from Caesar's wars in Gaul. It replaced the Basilica Sempronia built by the censor Tiberius Sempronius Gracchus in 170 B.C. The Basilica Julia stood across the forum from the senate house.

CRITICAL
COMMENTARY

1.1. **Caelius Cicerōnī s(alūtem dīcit):** "Caelius sends greetings to Cicero." The Roman custom was to combine the name of the sender and the addressee in the heading (*salūtātiō*) of a letter. For Caelius, see list of personal names.

2. **Dē summā rē pūblicā:** "concerning the welfare of the state."—**in annum:** "(lasting) for a year."

3. **quō propius . . . eō clārius:** "the nearer . . . the more obvious" (AG 414a). The abl. *quō* and *eō* express degree of difference. — **quam:** acc. relative pron. used as subject of the inf. *fierī*, which is governed by the impers. *necesse est.*

5. **rērum:** *potior* always takes the gen. (instead of the abl.) in the phrase *rērum potīrī* (AG 357a).

6. **quod:** "the fact that." The subst. clause introduced by *quod* with the indic. is in apposition to *prōpositum* (4); see AG 572 and n. — **Cn.:** = *Gnaeus*, Pompey's *praenōmen.* —**cōnstituit:** "has made up his mind" (pres. pf. indic.) —**patī:** complementary pres. inf. governed by *cōnstituit.* —**Cn. Pompēius . . . trādiderit:** Caelius implies that Pompey is repudiating the so-called "law of the ten tribunes," passed in 52 with Pompey's support. This measure exempted Caesar from having to appear in Rome to profess his candidacy for the consulship. As a provincial governor, he could not cross the *pōmerium* ("boundary") of the city of Rome without relinquishing his *imperium.*

7. **aliter . . . nisi:** = *nisi.* —**trādiderit:** this pf. subjn., within an

81

implied indirect statement (AG 592.2), represents a fut. pf. indic. after the primary tense of *cōnstituit* (AG 484c). —**Caesarī . . . persuāsum est:** "Caesar is convinced." Intransitive verbs governing the dat. are used impersonally in the pass., and the dat. is retained (AG 372).

8. **salvum:** without an army under his command, Caesar would be unable to deter attempts by his enemies to prosecute him for illegalities committed during his consulship in 59 (see Historical Introduction, p. 14f.). He would also be powerless against Pompey's armies in Spain. —**posse:** the pres. inf. of *possum* has the meaning of a fut. inf. (AG 584b).

9. **recesserit:** this pf. subjn. in a subordinate clause in indirect statement represents a fut. pf. indic. (AG 484c); see n. 7 on *trādiderit*. —**Fert:** "He (i.e., Caesar) offers." —**condiciōnem:** cf. sections 2.25–27 and 12.18–25. —**ut . . . trādant:** indirect command which depends on a verb of proposing implied in the expression *Fert condiciōnem* (GL 546 n. 2, p. 347).

11. **amōrēs:** "mutual affection." Pompey was married to Julia, Caesar's daughter, from 59 until her death in 54. —**coniūnctiō:** "alliance" (a reference to the so-called "first triumvirate"). —**occultam . . . obtrectātiōnem:** "private bickering."

12. **recidit:** "has degenerated" (pf. of *recidō*, as is clear from *ērūpit*; the pres. of *recidō* has the same spelling). *recidit*, like *ērūpit*, agrees with the nearer subject (*coniunctiō*), and its plural form is understood with *amōrēs* (AG 317c).

13. **meārum rērum quid cōnsilī capiam:** "what decision about my future I am to adopt." The objective gen. *meārum rērum* (AG 347–48) depends on *cōnsilī*, a partitive gen. (AG 346.3). *capiam* is a deliberative subjn. in an indirect question (AG 575b). —**quod:** "in regard to this matter" (i.e., the right course of action for Cicero). *quod* is a connecting relative (AG 308f) and adverbial acc. (AG 397a).

14. **quīn . . . sit perturbātūra:** *quīn*, "that," (lit., "how not"), is derived from *quī*, an old abl., + *-nē*. *quīn* is used with the subjn. after negated verbs of doubting (AG 558a).

15. **hominibus hīs:** Caesar's friends and supporters, such as Curio, Antonius, Quintus Cassius, and Dolabella, Cicero's son-in-law (see list of personal names). —**grātiae et necessitūdinēs:** "ties of obligation and friendship" (SB). —**causam:** i.e., the cause of the *rēs pūblica*, now represented by Pompey, the consuls, and their supporters.

16. **unde:** = *ā quā parte,* "on which side." —**hominēs:** i.e., men such as Domitius Ahenobarbus, the Marcelli, Pompey's father-in-law Scipio, and Appius Claudius (see list of personal names).
17. **Illud tē nōn arbitror fugere quīn:** "I don't think that the following (*illud*) escapes your notice, that . . ." For *illud,* see AG 297e.
18. **dēbeant:** for the subjn., see n. 14 above. —**cīvīliter:** "in the sphere of politics" (as opposed to the battlefield). —**certētur:** impers. pass. of an intrans. verb (AG 208d). It is attracted into the subjn. by *dēbeant* (AG 593).
19. **honestiōrem . . . partem:** "more honorable side." —**bellum et castra:** "open warfare" (an example of hendiadys, in which two coordinate words are combined to express a single idea).
20. **ventum sit:** see n. 18 above on *certētur.* —**firmiōrem:** sc. *partem dēbeant sequī.* —**melius:** predicate adj. modifying *id.* —**statuere:** depends upon *dēbeant* (17). —**quod:** relative pron. of which the antecedent is *id.*
21. **quīque rēs iūdicant:** "and those who decide cases" (*quīque* = *et eōs quī*). These jurors are the *equitēs* and the *tribūnī aerāriī* (see glossary), who since 70 had constituted a two-thirds majority of the jurors, with the senators comprising the remaining third. All these are men of substance, as contrasted with Caesar's followers (lines 22–23), who are characterized as desperate and apprehensive. Although the relative clause is subordinate to an indirect statement, it explains what the writer regards as fact; hence the indic. *iūdicant* (AG 583a).
22. **habitūrum:** sc. *esse* in an indirect statement introduced by *videō* (21); cf. *accessūrōs* (23). —**omnīs:** acc. pl. —**cum timōre aut malā spē:** "in fear (of prosecution) or in desperation." Caelius refers to those ambitious Romans who, under the present circumstances, feel threatened by lawsuits or foresee no hope of political advancement because of the intransigent position of the *optimātēs.* They therefore, like Caesar, would have no qualms about taking extreme measures to satisfy their political and financial ambitions.
23. **vīvant:** generic subjn. (= relative clause of characteristic, AG 535) within an indirect statement (AG 580). —**exercitum:** sc. *Caesaris cum Pompēī exercitū,* "his [Caesar's] army is not to be compared" (i.e., with Pompey's). Clearly Caelius views Caesar's seasoned veterans as the superior fighting force (hence *firmiōrem,* line 20).
24. **Omnīnō:** "to sum up." —**spatī:** "time" (partitive gen., AG 346.4). *spatium* can designate intervals of both time and space.
26. **Ad summam:** "in short." —**putem:** subjn. in an indirect question

83

(AG 574). —**futūrum:** sc. *esse;* fut. inf. in an indirect statement agreeing with *quid.* —**alter uter:** "one or the other," a stock expression sometimes written as one word.

27. **Parthicum bellum:** since 53, when Marcus Crassus had been killed and his army defeated by the Parthians near Carrhae in northern Mesopotamia, there was uneasiness in Rome about the stability of the eastern provinces. As governor of Cilicia since 51, Cicero remained keenly aware of the threat posed by the Parthians, who by midsummer of 50 were besieging Antioch in Syria. Pompey was expected to receive the command to repel the invaders. —**eat:** pres. subjn. in the protasis of a fut. condition within an indirect statement; the meaning of the apodosis (*impendēre*) implies fut. time (AG 589a).

28. **ferrum et vīs:** "force of arms" (for the hendiadys see n. 19). — **animō . . . cōpiīs:** abl. of specification (AG 418). Caelius notes the morale and manpower on both sides despite his confidence in the superiority of Caesar's forces (line 23).

29. **posset:** impers. The subjn. is in the protasis of a condition contrary to fact (AG 517). The apodosis is implied by *magnum et iucūndum* (30).

30. **parābat:** an example of an epistolary tense. In letters, the pf. or the impf. may be used for the pres., and the plupf. for any past tense, as if the letter were being written from the chronological viewpoint of the recipient (AG 479).

2.1. **Fit:** historical pres. In historical narrative the pres. often replaces the pf. for the sake of vividness (AG 469). Either primary or secondary sequence may be used with an historical pres. (AG 485e); cf. *mitterētur* (2). —**ut . . . mitterētur:** the indirect command depends upon a verb of proposing implied in the expression *senātūs cōnsultum,* e.g. *senātus dēcrēvit* (see n. 1.9). This decree was passed in the spring of 50.

3. **neque obscūrē:** an example of litotes, i.e., an understatement which emphasizes by denying the opposite. —**ūnī:** dat. of separation, used especially of persons (AG 381) with verbs of taking away (*dētrahuntur*). The reference is to Caesar.

4. **cōnfectam ex dīlectū prōvinciae Caesaris:** this legion (*legiō prīma*) was mustered (*cōnfectam*) by Pompey as consul in 55 from a recruitment in Caesar's province. Pompey had lent Caesar the legion in the winter of 54–53 at Caesar's request "for the sake of

the state and their friendship" (*Bellum Gallicum* 6.1) to reinforce his troops in Gaul after a revolt.

5. **eam:** refers to *legiōnem* and is best omitted in translation.

7. **suō nōmine:** "on his own behalf" (i.e., "under his name"). The phrase seems to come from the practice of making an entry under the name of a creditor or debtor. Caesar has now repaid the "debt" associated with his name.

8. **Galliā citeriōre:** see glossary s.v. "Prōvincia." —**ex:** "according to" (AG 221.11c).

9. **trādī:** pres. pass. inf.

10. **In eius locum:** "in its place." —**Ītaliam:** i.e., *Gallia citerior.* Since the Rubicon River was the boundary between his province and Italy, Caesar could not cross the Rubicon without relinquishing his command unless he had the approval of the senate. Both Caesar and Hirtius use *Ītalia* loosely to refer either to the country itself or to the province. This same use of *Ītalia* occurs in line 17 below.

11. **tuērētur:** subjn. in a relative clause of purpose.

13. **C. Trebōnium:** Gaius Trebonius, one of Caesar's chief lieutenants in Gaul since early 54 (see list of personal names).

14. **C. Fabium:** another of Caesar's lieutenants in Gaul. —**Aeduōs:** a Gallic tribe living between the rivers *Sēquana* and *Liger* (modern Seine and Loire), which had supported the chieftain Vercingetorix in a revolt against Roman rule in 52.

15. **fore:** = *futūram esse.* —**Belgae:** living north of the Sequana and reputedly the most formidable Gallic tribe.

16. **esset:** subjn. in a subordinate clause in indirect statement (AG 580).

17. **continērentur:** the impf. subjn. represents a fut. indic. in the protasis of a fut. more vivid condition (AG 589a.3). For the mood, see n. 16 above.

18. **Quō:** "there." This relative adv. connects the sentence with the preceding one. —**per:** "through (the agency of)." The phrase *per C. Mārcellum* depends on *trāditās* <*esse*> (20) and *retentās esse* (21). The preposition *per* denotes the mediator through whose voluntary action an effect is produced. Marcellus was one of the two consuls for the year 50 (see list of personal names).

19. **legiōnēs duās:** since a revolt at home had forced the Parthian king to withdraw his army from Syria in July of 50, for the present there was no urgent need to send these legions to the east. The fact

that Pompey still retained the legions under his command tended to strain his relationship with Caesar, who naturally expected at least his own troops (i.e., the fifteenth legion) to be returned to their duty stations in Gaul.

20. **dēbērent:** see n. 16 above.

21. **Italiā:** here the word designates the country itself. —**nūllī:** dat. with adj.

22. **quidnam:** = *quid*, introducing an indirect question.

23. **relinquerētur:** for the mood, see n. 16 above.

24. **disceptandī:** gerund of *disceptāre*, "to settle a dispute." — **belligerandī:** gerund of *belligerāre*. The genitives are objective (AG 347–48) and depend upon *spēs* (23). —**Contendit:** from *contendere*, "to demand" (with *ā/ab* + abl.) —<**per litterās . . . dēfutūrum**> (27): the manuscripts break off with the word *contendit*. Rheinhard's conjectural restoration, quoted in the Loeb edition of H. J. Edwards, *Caesar: The Gallic War* (Cambridge: Harvard University Press, 1970), p. 590, has been adopted to complete the sentence, since it provides a ready transition to the beginning of Caesar's *Bellum Cīvīle*.

25. **litterās:** on January 1, 49 (according to the Roman calendar, which at this time was six weeks ahead of our corrected solar calendar), C. Scribonius Curio, who had served as a *tribūnus plēbis* until December 10, 50 and favored Caesar's cause, probably presented this letter to the senate. Although no contemporary source provides its contents, later authors maintain that in it Caesar summarized his achievements in Gaul and asked the senate not to deprive him of a privilege granted by the "law of the ten tribunes" in 52: the privilege of standing for the consulship *in absentiā*. He further insisted that if he were to hand over his command, the other proconsuls (i.e., Pompey) would have to do the same. According to later sources, Caesar also suggested another possibility whereby he would retain two legions and Cisalpine Gaul with Illyricum or only one legion and Illyricum alone. If the government in Rome rejected his proposals, then he would have to avenge the insults against the Roman people and his *dignitās* (see section 8.8 for Cicero's reference to Caesar's threats). For Curio, see list of personal names. —**imperiō:** abl. of separation (AG 401). —**ut . . . abdicāret:** subjn. in an indirect command (= subst. clause of purpose, AG 563).

26. **sibi . . . patriae:** dat. with *dēfutūrum* <*esse*>. Here Caesar resorts to a veiled threat disguised as a patriotic gesture.

3.1. **cōnsulibus:** since January 1, 49, the two new consuls were Gaius Claudius Marcellus and Lucius Cornelius Lentulus Crus (see list of personal names). The election of these two men was joyfully welcomed by Caesar's political opponents. This Marcellus is the cousin and namesake of the Gaius Marcellus referred to in section 2.18. —**redditīs:** from *reddere*, "to deliver." —**aegrē ab hīs impetrātum est:** "(his) request was obtained from them with difficulty." *impetrātum est* is here impers.

2. **tribūnōrum:** these tribunes were Marcus Antonius and Quintus Cassius Longinus (see list of personal names). —**contentiōne:** "effort" (abl. of manner, AG 412). —**ut . . . recitārentur** (3): the subject is *litterae* understood. The subjn. is in a subst. clause of result which serves as the subject of the impers. pass. *impetrātum est* (AG 569.1).

3. **ex litterīs:** "according to the letter" (AG 221.11c). Caesar's enemies prevented the senate from debating the specific proposals contained in the letter. —**referrētur:** here impers. (*ad senātum referre* is a technical term for raising a matter for debate in the senate. Translate: "(that) a debate be raised before the senate." For the subjn. cf. *recitārentur* in line 2 above.

4. **Referunt cōnsulēs dē rē pūblicā īnfīnītē:** "The consuls raised a discussion about the political situation in general." This was not an unusual procedure at the opening meeting of each new year. But since the presiding consul controlled the daily agenda, such a tactic would also conveniently prevent the discussion of any proposal favorable to Caesar, which his opponents feared might be put to the vote and passed, thereby becoming a decree.

5. **L. Lentulus:** see n. 1 above. —**senātuī:** indirect object of *pollicētur* (6). —**reī pūblicae:** dat. with *dēfutūrum* <*esse*>.

6. **sententiās dīcere:** "to express (their) opinions."

7. **velint . . . respiciant . . . sequantur:** subjn. in a subordinate clause in indirect statement (AG 580). —**respiciant:** "have regard for." —**eius grātiam sequantur:** "curry his favor."

8. **ut . . . fēcerint:** "as they had done" (e.g., in 56 at the conference at Luca and in 50 by supporting, with a vote of 370 to 22, Curio's motion that both Caesar and Pompey lay down their commands). Although *ut*, meaning "as," ordinarily governs the indic., the verb here is subjn. in a subordinate clause within an indirect statement depending on *pollicētur* (6), an historical pres. (see n. 2.1). —**sē sibi cōnsilium captūrum:** "(that) he would look out for his own welfare." *sibi* is a dat. of reference (AG 376–77).

10. **habēre . . . receptum:** "had access" (i.e., "had a way of retreat"). *receptum* is acc. sing. of *receptus, -ūs* and direct object of *habēre*. Lentulus threatens to align himself with Caesar if the senate assumes a position of compromise. A suitable bribe from Caesar would relieve his heavy indebtedness (section 5.3–5).

11. **In eandem sententiam:** "in the same vein." —**Scipiō:** Pompey's father-in-law since 52, when he also shared the consulship with Pompey from August to the end of the year (see list of personal names). —**Pompēiō esse in animō . . . nōn:** "(that) Pompey did not intend" (lit., "[that] it was not in mind to Pompey"). For the case of *Pompēiō*, see n. 8 above on *sibi*.

13. **lēnius:** "too moderately."

16. **Pompēiusque aberat:** Pompey could not cross the sacred inner city boundary, the *pōmerium*, without relinquishing his command (*imperium*). —**mittī:** "to issue" (lit., "to be sent"). The inf. is pres. pass. of *mittere*.

17. **ut:** "as, for example," (cf. lines 21 and 25); sc. *dīxerat. ut*, meaning "as" or "when," governs the indic. mood. —**prīmō:** "at first." Later he changed his mind under duress (lines 28–29). —**M. Mārcellus:** consul in 51 and brother of the present consul, C. Marcellus (see list of personal names).

18. **ingressus in eam ōrātiōnem:** "launching into the following speech." *eam* here anticipates an indirect statement. —**nōn oportēre . . . referrī:** *referrī* is the subject of *oportēre*. Both verbs are impers. (translate: "that a debate ought not to be raised"). —**ante . . . quam** (conj.): "before." The conj. is an example of tmesis, i.e., the "cutting" or separation of a compound word into its original parts with the insertion of one or more words between the parts. —**eā rē:** i.e., the proposal to require Caesar to surrender his command in Gaul. Such a motion would precipitate a civil war.

19. **tōtā Ītaliā:** abl. of place where. When *tōtus* modifies a placename, the prep. *in* is regularly omitted (AG 429.2). —**habitī et . . . cōnscriptī essent:** the plupf. subjn., occurring in indirect statement, represents the fut. pf. indic., which is commonly found with *antequam* to refer to fut. time (AG 551b n. 1 and 551c).

20. **quō praesidiō . . . audēret:** = *ut eō praesidiō . . . audēret* (relative clause of purpose). —**tūtō:** adv.

21. **vellet:** subjn. in an indirect question (AG 574). —**Calidius:** a friend of Cicero and Caesar (see list of personal names).

22. **in suās prōvinciās:** namely, *Hispānia citerior* and *Hispānia ulterior,*

which had been granted to Pompey for five years after his second consulship (in 55) and renewed at the end of his third consulship (in 52) for another five, in direct opposition to one of his own laws. Pompey had been governing these provinces through his *lēgātī* Afranius and Petreius (see list of personal names). —**proficīscerētur:** subjn. in indirect command. —**nē ... esset** (23): negative purpose clause (AG 531.1).

23. **qua:** = *aliqua* after *sī, nisi, nē,* and *num* (AG 310a). —**armōrum:** "armed conflict." —**timēre Caesarem:** the indirect statement marks a change of construction from the preceding indirect command (*ut ... proficīscerētur*). —**ēreptīs ... legiōnibus:** these are the two legions mentioned in section 2.3–9 and 18–21.

24. **nē ... vidērētur** (25): subjn. in a clause of fearing (AG 564). —**ad eius perīculum:** "to endanger him" (i.e., Caesar); *eius* is an objective gen. (AG 347–48).

25. **ad:** "near" (an exaggeration; actually the two legions were stationed at Capua or in Apulia). —**M. Rūfus:** Marcus Caelius Rufus (see section 1 and list of personal names).

26. **paucīs ferē mūtātīs rēbus:** "with only a few items changed" (abl. absol.). —**sequēbātur:** "seconded." —**convīciō L. Lentulī cōnsulis correptī exagitābantur:** "were rebuked (*correptī*) and harassed (*exagitābantur*) by the abuse (*convīciō*) of the consul Lucius Lentulus."

28. **sententiam ... prōnūntiātūrum:** the expression *sententiam prōnūntiāre* means "to put a motion to the vote." —**omnīnō:** "absolutely."

29. **ā suā sententiā discessit:** "withdrew his motion." —**Sīc vōcibus cōnsulis ... sequuntur** (32): construe as though the Latin were written as follows: *Sīc plērīque, invītī et coāctī, compulsī vōcibus* ("outbursts") *cōnsulis, terrōre praesentis exercitūs, minīs amīcōrum Pompēī, sequuntur Scīpiōnis sententiam.* According to the historian Dio Cassius (41.2) only two senators, Curio and Caelius, voted against the motion.

30. **terrōre praesentis exercitūs:** apparently an exaggeration (see n. 25 above).

32. **utī** (= *ut*) **... dīmittat:** indirect command which depends on the idea implied in *sententiam* (31). —**ante certam diem:** the precise day on which Caesar was to disband his army (or even whether a specific day had ever been established by law) has become the subject of extensive scholarly debate. Normally, a magistrate was

authorized to hold *imperium* for a specified period of time or for the duration of a campaign, which could not always be strictly defined.

33. **eum adversus rem pūblicam factūrum vidērī**: "apparently (*vidērī*) he would be acting against the state"; i.e., he would, for all practical purposes, be regarded as a *hostis* or "public enemy." — **faciat**: pres. subjn. in the protasis of a fut. condition within an indirect statement (AG 589a).

34. **Intercēdit**: "exercised the right of veto." The singular verb agrees with the nearer subject (see n. 1.12). A single tribune could veto any senatorial decree deemed contrary to the interests of the people except the *senātūs cōnsultum ultimum*. Antonius and Cassius were attempting to prevent the consuls and their supporters from tampering with Caesar's position. —**Refertur**: see *referrētur* in n. 3 above. Although the veto could not be overridden, Caesar's opponents might argue that motions to arrange successors for provincial governors could not be vetoed by a tribune, according to the provisions of a law of Gaius Gracchus (c. 123). But this position would overlook the argument that Pompey's *lēx dē prōvinciīs,* passed in 52, had superseded Gracchus's law. A motion was nevertheless made to disregard the tribunitial veto, as though Gracchus's law were still in effect.

35. **Dīcuntur**: the third of a series of short clauses, each beginning with a verb, helps to increase the pace of the narrative and create a climax. —**sententiae gravēs**: "strong opinions."

4.1. **ad vesperum**: "towards evening." By a law of the Twelve Tables, no senate meeting or popular assembly could continue after sunset.

2. **ēvocantur**: sc. *ex urbe* (i.e., outside the *pōmerium,* the sacred boundary of the inner city). —**in posterum**: "for the future" or "for the next day" (when the senate may have been reconvened).

4. **ōrdinum**: "promotions."

5. **ēvocantur**: *ēvocāre* in its technical sense means, "to call up (from reserve status)." The same sense applies to *ēvocātīs* in line 7 below. These would include veterans who had served under Pompey in Spain (discharged about twenty years previously) and in the east against Mithridates (discharged about twelve years before). They would now be entitled to higher pay and more privileges.

6. **Complētur . . . ēvocātīs** (7): there are three subjects of *complētur: urbs* (the city itself), *clīvus* (the *Clīvus Capitōlīnus,* a slope of the *Via Sacra* rising from the *Forum* to the Capitoline Hill), and the

comitium (an area of the *Forum* outside the *Curia* or Senate House where assemblies could meet). The sentence provides an example of asyndeton, i.e., the omission of conjunctions between two or more coordinate words, phrases, or clauses. Caesar's point is that armed soldiers do not belong within the center of civil life in Rome.

7. **tribūnīs:** abl. of means (like *centuriōnibus* and *ēvocātīs*), regularly used with verbs of filling (AG 409a). The *tribūnī mīlitum* here must be distinguished from *tribūnī plēbis*. A *tribūnus mīlitum* was one of six senior officers in a legion. —**amīcī:** "political supporters."

8. **necessāriī:** "adherents" (i.e., those connected with a man by ties of friendship, relationship or obligation).

9. **vōcibus et concursū:** take as a single thought (an example of hendiadys; see n. 1.19): "rowdy throngs."

10. **plērīsque:** dat. of separation (see n. 2.3 on *ūnī*).

11. **dēcernendī potestās:** "opportunity to vote." —**L. Pīsō:** Lucius Calpurnius Piso Caesoninus, Caesar's father-in-law since 59. Since 50 Piso had been holding the censorship, an office of eighteen months' duration (see list of personal names).

12. **L. Roscius:** Lucius Roscius Fabatus. Later this man actually carried a message from Pompey to Caesar. He also sponsored a law to grant citizenship to the Transpadanes. In 54, Caesar had placed him in command of the thirteenth legion in Gaul (*Bellum Gallicum* 5.53.6). —**quī . . . doceant** (13): relative clause of purpose. The verb here means "inform."

13. **sex diēs . . . spatī** (14): = *spatium sex diērum,* "an interval of six days." Occasionally a noun that would be in the gen. (of description) is made the leading idea. The six-day interval would enable them to make a round-trip to Ravenna and back.

15. **mittantur:** indirect command which depends on the idea implied in *sententiae* (14): see n. 3.32. These motions may have been voiced because the senate, not fully trusting the volunteers Piso and Roscius, wanted to ensure that its position was properly represented. —**quī . . . prōpōnant** (16): for the subjn., see n. 12 above on *quī . . . doceant.*

5.1. **Omnibus hīs resistitur:** "All these met with resistance." *hīs* is ambiguous; it could be masculine, referring to the proposers, or neuter, referring to their proposals. *resistitur,* a verb governing the dat., is impers. in the pass. (AG 372). Perhaps the *optimātēs* believed that an embassy to Caesar at this time would be tantamount to recognizing his position. As Pompey is alleged to have remarked (*Bellum Cīvīle* 1.32.8), *ad quōs lēgātī mitterentur, hīs auctōritātem attribuī timōremque eōrum, quī mitterent, significārī* ("Recognition is given to those to whom ambassadors are sent, and fear is shown by those who send them.") —**cōnsulis:** i.e., L. Cornelius Lentulus Crus, the presiding consul for the month of January (and of every alternate month in the year: see list of personal names).

2. **Catōnis:** Marcus Porcius Cato, leader of the conservative senators (see list of personal names). —**veterēs inimīcitiae:** the enmity between Cato and Caesar dated from at least 63, when they disagreed over the sentencing of the Catilinarian conspirators. Cato opposed Caesar's candidacy for the consulship in 60 and Caesar's consular legislation in 59. He also opposed in 55 the *lēx Pompēia Licinia*, by which Caesar was given a five-year extension of his command. And later in the year, when the senate wanted to grant Caesar a thanksgiving of twenty days for his many victories in Gaul, Cato made a counter-proposal that Caesar be handed over to the Germans so that the Romans might not be cursed for Caesar's recent breach of faith with the German leaders. Finally, in 52, Cato unsuccessfully attempted to block the "law of the ten tribunes," which extended to Caesar the right to run for consul without the need to canvass in person in Rome (*ratiō absentis*).

3. **Caesaris:** objective gen. (AG 347–48); likewise *repulsae*. —**dolor repulsae:** "resentment over (his) defeat (at the polls)." Cato had suffered two setbacks; first, as a candidate for the praetorship of 55 at an election held in that year because of postponements contrived by Pompey and Crassus (although Cato was elected praetor later in 55 for 54); second, as a candidate for the consulship of 51 because he refused to resort to bribery. —**aeris aliēnī:** from *aes aliēnum*, "debt." As a result of his campaign for the consulship, Lentulus was apparently deep in debt. If Caesar were somehow to be politically neutralized by war or negotiation, Lentulus would expect a proconsulship in a province, where he could enrich himself at the expense of the provincials.

4. **spē exercitūs ac prōvinciārum:** for the case see n. 3 above. The conjunction *ac* connects a closely linked pair. —**rēgum appellandōrum largītiōnbus:** "by bribes for conferring the title of king." Prominent Romans who secured for kings official recognition by Rome would become patrons of those kings and have at

their disposal client kingdoms (and therefore client armies). Such
kings would remain loyal to their Roman sponsors and might be
called upon to provide many forms of support (including military
support). In addition, they would pay handsomely for official
recognition as *rēgēs* and as *amīcī populī Rōmānī*. *rēgum* here is a
subjective gen. (GL 363).

5. **alterum . . . Sullam** (6): Lentulus Crus and Sulla both belonged
to the *gēns Cornēlia,* of which three members were predicted to
rule Rome by a prophecy (said to have been contained in the
Sibylline books). Cornelius Sulla as dictator (82–79) and Cornelius Cinna as consul (87) had already fulfilled this prophecy, which
also encouraged P. Cornelius Lentulus Sura to join the Catilinarian conspiracy (63) in the hope that he would be the third member of the *gēns.* —**fore:** = *futūrum esse.*

6. **summa imperī:** "absolute authority." —**redeat:** generic subjn.
(= relative clause of characteristic; AG 535).

8. **prō necessitūdine:** "in view of his relationship" (for the relationship, see n. 3.11 on *Scipiō*).

9. **iūdiciōrum metus:** his political adversaries had threatened Scipio with prosecution for bribery during the consular elections,
which had been postponed from 53 to 52 because of rioting.
After the senate finally appointed Pompey *cōnsul sine collēgā* (sole
consul) —a political eccentricity and a contradiction in terms —
he chose his new father-in-law as his consular colleague and thus
rendered Scipio immune from prosecution. —**adulātiō atque
ostentātiō suī et potentium:** "(his) boastful display of himself
(*suī*) and of (his friendship with other) powerful men (*potentium*)." The combination of *adulātiō* and *ostentātiō* represents
another example of hendiadys (see n. 1.19). In this difficult expression, both *suī* and *potentium* are construed as objective genitives. But the text is suspect.

10. **rē pūblicā:** "public affairs." —**plūrimum pollēbant:** "were very
influential."

12. **dignitāte:** abl. of specification (AG 418). See n. 1.28 on *animō . . .
cōpiīs.* —**exaequārī:** "to be put on the same level."

13. **in grātiam redierat:** "had become reconciled" (lit., "had come
back into favor").

14. **adfinitātis:** Pompey had been married to Caesar's daughter Julia
from 59 to her death in 54.

15. **iniūnxerat:** "had inflicted upon." Caesar accusingly implies that,
in the relationship which was publicly proclaimed when Pompey

married his daughter Julia, Pompey naturally expected Caesar to regard as enemies those who were opposing his new son-in-law. This tie with Pompey may have adversely affected, since 59, Caesar's relationships with certain *optimātēs* to whom Pompey has now become reconciled. Pompey, Caesar argues, had inflicted upon him a group of enemies which he was forced to share with Pompey after the marriage but with whom Pompey has now mended fences.

16. **Asiae Syriaeque:** "to Asia and Syria" (the words are gen.). See section 2.18–21.

17. **rem ad arma dēdūcī studēbat:** "was eager to have the matter (i.e., the dispute between Caesar and the senate) brought to the issue of war."

6.1. **raptim atque turbātē:** "hastily and in confusion."

  2. **prōpinquīs:** "supporters." —**spatium:** "time." *Caesaris,* modified by the gerundive *docendī,* depends upon *spatium.* —**tribūnīs:** dat. of indirect object with *tribuitur* (5).

  3. **perīculī:** depends upon *facultās* (4), as does *iūris.* —**extrēmī iūris intercessiōne retinendī . . . facultās** (4): "opportunity for keeping their most important right by (exercising their) veto."

  4. **quod L. Sulla relīquerat:** "a right which Lucius Sulla had left intact." Caesar is imprecise here, for in 81, as dictator, Sulla had limited some rights of tribunes, including their right of *intercessiō* (which, under Sulla's reforms, required prior senatorial approval), and he had made tribunes ineligible for other political offices. See section 9.8–10.

  5. **septimō diē:** i.e., of January. Acutally, the tribunes always assumed office on December 10th and so had been holding office since that date in 50.

  6. **quod:** = *id quod* (AG 307d and n.), "a thing which" (direct object of *respicere ac timēre,* lines 7–8). —**turbulentissimī:** "most factious." —**tribūnī:** notable instances are provided by such tribunes as the brothers Tiberius (133) and Gaius (123–22) Gracchus, Lucius Saturninus (100), and Marcus Livius Drusus (91), all of whom had been murdered during periods of extreme social unrest. Caesar's point in mentioning them is that, although they had been able to agitate for months without fear of reprisal, the tribunes of 49 were harassed after only a few days.

  7. **post octō denique mensīs** (acc. pl.): "after a full eight months."

—**variārum actiōnum:** "different official acts." —**respicere ac timēre:** "to regard with fear" (hendiadys).

8. **cōnsuērant:** syncopated form of *cōnsuēverant.* —**Dēcurritur:** "Recourse was had" (another impers. usage).

9. **cōnsultum:** a senatorial decree was not legally binding but had considerable moral impact upon the citizens; the extreme decree (only here described as *ultimum*) established a state of emergency suspending civil rights. Such a decree had been passed seven times before, including the year of the Catilinarian conspiracy (63) and the year of Pompey's sole consulship (52) because of riots during the elections. The historian Sallust (*Bellum Catilīnae* 29) describes the effect of the decree: *ea potestās per senātum mōre Rōmānō magistrātuī maxima permittitur, exercitum parāre, bellum gerere, coercēre omnibus modīs sociōs atque cīvēs, domī mīlitiaeque imperium atque iūdicium summum habēre.* ("This power, granted to a magistrate by the senate in accordance with Roman custom, is the most extensive: to muster an army, to wage war, to keep in order by all means allies and citizens, to hold supreme command and legal jurisdiction at home and abroad.") —**quō . . . lātōrum audāciā numquam ante discessum est** (11): "when never before had the proposers in their boldness put this measure to a vote" (lit., "to which it was never before parted because of the boldness of the proposers"). *quō* is used here because of the motion implied by *discessum est;* the verb expresses the act of voting for or against a specific proposal (*sententia*). A senator voted by moving near the speaker whose position (pro or con) on the specific proposal he supported. —**nisi:** "except." —**paene:** "one might say" (qualifies the expression *in ipsō urbis incendiō*).

10. **incendiō:** arson in Rome often accompanied political riots. Part of Catiline's plan for seizing control of Rome in 63 had called for the burning of sections of the city. During a riot of 52, a fire in the Forum destroyed the Curia and part of the Basilica Porcia next to it.

11. **dent operam:** the expression *operam dare* means "to pay attention," "to see to it." The subjn. is hortatory (jussive): AG 439 and n. 2.

12. **quīque prō cōnsulibus sunt ad urbem:** i.e., Pompey, who as proconsul had been administering the province of Spain from Italy, and Cicero, who had recently returned from Cilicia and was awaiting senatorial approval of a triumph. —**ad:** "near."

95

13. **nē . . . capiat:** subjn. in an indirect command (= subst. clause of purpose, AG 563e) governed by the expression *dent operam*.

14. **a. d. vii Īd. Iān.:** = *ante diem septimum Īdūs Iānuāriās:* = January 7 (see glossary s. v. "Calendar").

16. **biduō exceptō comitiālī:** "with the exception of two assembly days" (abl. absol.). These two assembly days, on which the senate could not meet, were January 3 and 4. Caesar's point is that the senate wasted no time, meeting as often as possible to thwart him.

17. **gravissimē acerbissimēque dēcernitur:** "very severe and harsh decrees were passed" (*dēcernitur* is impers. pass.). These decrees probably stipulated that the senate would not be answerable for the safety of the tribunes, who may even have been declared public enemies (*hostēs*). Clearly, according to Caesar, their inviolability was being threatened.

20. **Ravennae:** loc. case (AG 427.3). Ravenna was located on the Adriatic Sea just north of the provincial boundary marked by the Rubicon River. —**postulātīs:** for the terms see section 2.25–26. —**exspectābatque . . . sī . . . rēs ad ōtium dēdūcī posset** (22): "and he was waiting (to see) . . . if . . . the matter could be brought to a peaceful issue." The subjn. is in an indirect question (AG 576a), which depends upon the idea of "waiting (to see)" contained in *exspectābat*. For the expression *rēs ad ōtium dēdūcī*, see n. 5.17.

21. **quā:** = *aliquā*. Here the adjective modifies *aequitāte*.

7.1. **extrā urbem:** this meeting of the senate was held outside the *pōmerium* in order that Pompey might attend.

2. **ostenderat:** "he had suggested." —**agit:** "discussed."

3. **legiōnēs habēre sēsē parātās x:** sc. *dīxit*, which is also understood with the following indirect statement. It is uncertain how Pompey is alleged to have arrived at this figure of ten legions. Six were stationed in Spain (section 21.33), and two more had been requisitioned from Caesar. There were other troops distributed among such places as Iguvium (section 14.2), Auximum (14.11), Asculum (23.9), Camerinum (23.17), and Corfinium (27.15), although some of these were recent recruits. Caesar, on the other hand, commanded approximately an equal number of legions, but they were stationed at various points in Gaul.

4. **cognitum compertumque:** sc. *esse*, "(that) he knew very well" (lit., "that it was ascertained and known"). These infinitives are used in the impers. pass.

5. **sibi:** dat. of agent (AG 375). —**alienō . . . animō:** abl. of description (AG 415). *alienō* here means "disloyal." The rumor that some of Caesar's troops were disloyal to him was widespread but proved to be false. It may have arisen because of the defection of Titus Labienus, his highest ranking lieutenant (see list of personal names). —**neque eīs posse persuādērī:** "nor could they be persuaded" (lit., "nor could it be persuaded to them"); see n. 1.7 on *Caesarī . . . persuāsum est.*

7. **refertur:** for the meaning see n. 3.3 on *referrētur.* The senate was now able to appoint provincial governors without the interference of Caesar's tribunes. —**tōtā Ītaliā:** abl. of place where (see n. 3.19). —**dīlectus:** according to the historian Appian (fl. 100 A.D.), the senate ordered Pompey to collect an army of 130,000 Italians, including as many veterans as possible, and to enlist from the nearby provinces the strongest force attainable. The senate further authorized Pompey to use all contents of the public treasury to finance the war. Individual senators also pledged their personal fortunes if the expenses of the new army should require them (*Bellum Cīvīle* 2.34).

8. **habeātur . . . mittātur:** subjn. without *ut (utī)* in an indirect command (AG 565a), here governed by *refertur* (7). For the same construction with *ut* cf. lines 9–10 below. —**Faustus Sulla:** son of the dictator and Pompey's son-in-law. Faustus was to be sent into Mauretania (in northwest Africa) because of his father's ties with that country; for the father of one of the present rulers, Bocchus, had assisted the elder Sulla in the war against Jugurtha. This time, however, the prince chose to support Caesar, who later installed him as king. This was precisely the kind of opportunity for which Lentulus had hoped (see n. 5.4 on *rēgum appellandōrum largītiōnibus*). Actually, Faustus remained in Italy, where he raised a legion for Pompey (see sections 31.22 and 32.64 below).

10. **Iubā:** this king of Numidia supported Pompey, who as one of Sulla's lieutenants had restored his father Hiempsal to the throne. Juba later furnished African troops to the Pompeians. He had a personal grudge against Caesar. —**socius . . . atque amīcus:** these formal titles were sometimes granted to a foreign ally as a courtesy. The Romans recognized two broad categories of people outside their state: "allies" (*sociī*) and subjects. In general, *sociī* were pledged by treaty to offer support in war. The title of *amīcus*, on the other hand, implied only diplomatic recognition and did not involve a formal treaty. Such *amīcī* were recorded in an official list.

—**passūrum** <**esse**>: sc. *sē* as subject acc. —**Mārcellus . . . negat**
(11): Marcellus was blocking the proposal concerning the Numidian king Juba. Perhaps he feared that the Numidians, like the
Mauretanians, could not be trusted as firm allies if civil war should
break out. Alternatively, Marcellus may have been unwilling to
provoke Caesar by permitting a formal alliance with Juba, one of
Caesar's long-standing enemies.

11. **in praesentiā:** "for now," "for the present." —**dē Faustō
impedit:** "vetoed the embassy of Faustus" (lit., "stood in the way
concerning Faustus"). —**Philippus:** see n. 15 below.

12. **reliquīs rēbus:** these include the motions to raise troops in all of
Italy and the disbursement of public funds for Pompey's use.

13. **prīvātīs:** according to the *lēx Pompēia dē prōvinciīs,* passed in
Pompey's third consulship (52), an outgoing consul or praetor
could not hold a promagistracy for five years. He would, therefore, be a *prīvātus* when his period of eligibility arrived. Caesar's
grievance here is that, whereas two fully eligible candidates (Philippus and Cotta) were passed over, the two men selected were
both ineligible. This could be done because the tribunes willing to
cast a veto had fled. Scipio had been Pompey's colleague in 52,
and Domitius had held the consulship in 54.

14. **L. Domitiō:** Lucius Domitius Ahenobarbus, a bitter enemy of
Caesar, has now been appointed to succeed him as governor of
Transalpine Gaul, where his grandfather had won military victo-
ries as proconsul in 121–120 or 117 (see list of personal names).

15. **Philippus:** Lucius Marcius Philippus was father of the tribune
mentioned above (line 11). He had been consul in 56. He was the
second husband of Caesar's niece, and his daughter Marcia was
married to Cato. —**Cotta:** Lucius Aurelius Cotta was a relative of
Caesar on his mother's side. He had been consul in 65, when
Caesar assumed office as aedile, and had supported Cicero's suppression of Catiline in 63 by proposing a vote of thanks. —
prīvātō cōnsiliō: "by private arrangement."

16. **dēiciuntur:** sc. *in urnam* (i.e., the *urna* into which the candidates'
lots were thrown).

17. **Neque exspectant . . . ut . . . ferātur** (18): "and they did not
wait . . . for . . . the measure to be brought." The subjn. is in a
subst. clause of result (= explanatory *ut*) in apposition to *id* understood (AG 570; GL 557). Pompey's law required the renewal of
the *imperium,* which should have been conferred by a *plēbīscītum*
(*vote of the people*) as well as by a decree of the senate. —**quod:** = *id*

quod, "as" (lit., "that which"; AG 307d and n.). The same use appears below in line 19.

18. **palūdātī:** from *palūdātus, -a, -um,* "wearing the cloak (*palūdāmentum*) of command."

19. **nuncupātīs:** from *nuncupō, -āre,* "pronounce." Before taking up their commands, generals formally swore vows of allegiance to the state on the Capitoline hill in the presence of priests. —**quod ante id tempus accidit numquam:** since the time of Sulla, consuls had normally spent their terms of office in Rome. Before that time, however, many a consul had taken the field against enemies of the state. Caesar exaggerates here for rhetorical effect; his point is that extraordinary measures were now being taken against him.

20. **lictōrēsque habent . . . prīvātī** (21): Caesar pointedly refers to the promagistrates just mentioned as *prīvātī* because they have not had the *imperium* conferred upon them by the people (see n. 17 above) and because neither private citizens nor promagistrates were entitled to the symbols of authority in the city. Cicero, on the other hand, anticipating a triumph after returning to Italy from his province, followed the standard procedure by remaining outside the city instead of giving up his lictors.

21. **vetustātis exempla:** "precedents of former times."

22. **Tōtā Ītaliā:** abl. of place where (see n. 3.19). With this sentence begins a series of short clauses without conjunctions. This example of asyndeton creates an effect of excitement and haste as Caesar's catalogue of the sudden hostile and illegal acts contrived against him reaches its climax. With this list of grievances, Caesar attempts to justify his own illegal act of crossing the Rubicon.

23. **fānīs:** the word *fānum* designates the sacred precinct within which a temple stood. As a result of the accumulation of votive offerings for many years, a number of temples had become repositories of vast treasures. By merely mentioning that his antagonists have plundered holy places, Caesar charges them with sacrilege and impiety.

8.1. **Tullius et Cicerō, Terentia, Tullia, QQ. Tīrōnī s. p. d.:** = *Tullius et Cicerō, Terentia, Tullia, Quintīque Tīrōnī salūtem plūrimam dīcunt. Tullius* is Marcus Tullius Cicero; *Cicerō* is his son; *Terentia* is his wife; *Tullia* is his daughter. The two *Quintī* are Cicero's brother and nephew, both named Quintus Tullius Cicero. The recipient, Tiro, had been Cicero's personal slave until 53, when he was granted his freedom and remained in the household as Cicero's private secretary. According to custom, he adopted his former master's *praenōmem* and *nōmen* and was now known as Marcus Tullius Tiro.

2. **ad urbem accessī:** Cicero did not actually enter Rome; he could not legally cross the *pōmerium* (sacred boundary) of the city without relinquishing the *imperium* which he still held as proconsul of Cilicia (51–50), from where he had returned in November of 50. He remained outside Rome in the hope that the senate would approve for him a triumph for the limited military exploits of his legions in Cilicia. —**pr. Nōn. Iān.:** = *prīdiē Nōnās Iānuāriās,* January 4 (see glossary s.v. "Calendar"). —**Obviam mihi sīc est prōditum:** "there has been such a turnout to meet me" (*est prōditum* is impers. and pres. pf. in sense, as the primary tense *possit* indicates).

3. **ōrnātius:** "more impressively."

4. **Cui:** a connecting relative (AG 308f) in the f. sing. to refer to *flammam* in the previous sentence; the dat. is governed by *medērī*. —**cum:** introduces a concessive clause.

5. **medērī:** "find a remedy for" (Cicero has mixed his metaphors). Because he enjoyed friendly relations with both Pompey and Caesar and because his absence from the political scene at Rome for the past eighteen months justified, to some extent, a claim of neutrality, Cicero saw himself as a mediator between the opposing sides. Elsewhere he often professes his desire for peace, which would be impossible for him to negotiate if he openly chose one side at the outbreak of hostilities. The medical metaphor in *medērī* suggests Cicero's perception of his role as a doctor who might heal the ills besetting the republic. —**certōrum:** "particular." The adjective suggests that Cicero knows the names of these men but is unwilling to identify them. Among the Pompeians may be included Scipio, Lentulus, Domitius, and the Marcelli; Caesar's partisans include Cassius, Antonius, and Curio.

6. **ex utrāque parte:** "on both sides." —**quī . . . cupiant:** generic subjn. (AG 535).

7. **omnīnō:** "to sum up." —**et:** correlative with *et* in line 10 ("both . . . and"). —**amīcus noster:** Cicero stresses his collegiality with Caesar and his partisans; cf. *Curiō meus* (10) and *Antōnius . . . noster* (10–11).

8. **minācīs . . . et acerbās litterās:** this "threatening and distressing" letter is probably the one delivered to the senate by Curio (see n. 2.25). —**mīserat et erat:** epistolary tenses (see n. 1.30); so also

tenēret (10), *incitābat* (10), *profectī erant* (12), *dederat* (14), *cūrārē-mus* (14), and *caperet* (15).

9. **impudēns quī:** = *tam impudēns ut,* introducing a relative clause of result (AG 537.2 and n. 1).

10. **Curiō:** according to the historian Appian (*Bellum Cīvīle* 2.32), Curio (see list of personal names) advised Caesar to march on Rome at once.

11. **quidem:** "in fact." —**nūllā vī expulsī:** Caesar seems to disagree (section 6.18–19). Although Cicero may be technically right in implying that the tribunes were not physically harmed, neverthe-less they were clearly threatened and intimidated. Cicero himself does not deny that they were driven out of Rome. To this extent, at least, Caesar could maintain that the sovereignty of the *populus Rōmānus,* whom they represented, had been violated (see also n. 6.17). —**ad Caesarem:** Caesar was now in Ravenna (see n. 6.20).

12. **posteāquam:** = *postquam.*

13. **nōbīs, quī prō cōnsulibus sumus:** i.e., Pompey, Cicero himself, and the newly appointed proconsuls Scipio and Domitius.

14. **negōtium dederat:** "had assigned the task." The subject is *senātus* (12). —**nē quid . . . caperet:** this is the language of the *senātūs cōnsultum ultimum* (see n. 6.9).

17. **omnīnō:** "on the whole." —**ex hāc . . . parte:** for meaning see n. 6 above. —**comparātur:** "preparations are being made" (here the verb is impers.).

18. **auctōritāte et studiō:** abl. of cause (AG 404).

20. **Nōbīs:** used here for the sing. *mihi* (AG 143a) and known as the "editorial 'we' " (so also *nōs* in lines 23 and 26 below). — **senātus . . . frequēns:** "a full senate."

21. **quō māius . . . faceret** (22): a purpose clause containing a com-parative is introduced by the conj. *quō* (AG 531.2a). Taken to-gether, *māius facere* means "to enhance." —**suum beneficium:** "his own service." The use of *suum* emphasizes Lentulus's inten-tion to enhance the value of the service performed for Cicero by doing it on his own initiative. *beneficium* has extensive political implications in Roman society. Cicero would then be expected to discharge an *officium* ("obligation") in return.

22. **expedisset:** *expedīre* means "to dispose of." The plupf. subjn., occurring in indirect statement, represents the fut. pf. indic. (cf. n. 3.19). After dealing with Caesar's threats, Lentulus could initiate proceedings for a triumph more suited to Cicero. —**quae essent:** generic subjn. (AG 535).

101

23. **necessāria:** "critical" (i.e., concerned with an effective response to Caesar). —**relātūrum:** sc. *esse.* For the meaning see n. 3.3 on *referrētur.* —**Nōs ... auctōritās** (24): for Cicero's professed neutrality, see n. 5 above.

24. **cupidē:** "to serve myself"; "selfishly." —**eōque:** "and for this reason" (abl. of cause). —**plūris:** gen. of value (AG 417).

25. **quam quisque partem tuērētur:** "for each man to guard a sector" (relative clause of purpose).

26. **Capuam:** a densely populated *mūnicipium* in the heart of the district of Campania and about one hundred miles south of Rome on the *Via Appia.* This assignment would have been very convenient for Cicero, who owned several lodgings nearby. But he may never have officially accepted it.

27. **etiam atque etiam:** "over and over again." —**cūrā ut valeās:** instead of the imperative, *cūrā ut* + subjn. is often used in colloquial language (AG 449c).

28. **habēbis cui dēs:** "you will have someone to whom to give it." The subjn. is generic (AG 535).

29. **D. pr. Īdūs Iān.:** = *Data* (sc. *epistula*) *prīdiē Īdūs Iānuāriās:* i.e., January 12 (see glossary s.v. "Calendar").

9.1. **Quibus rēbus:** i.e., the events around Rome. Here the narrative resumes from section 7, but the scene has now shifted to Ravenna, where Caesar was awaiting a reply to his proposals. It is impossible to ascertain exactly how much Caesar knew before he crossed the Rubicon. Since it would take about three days for news from Rome to reach Ravenna, he may have assembled his men without specific knowledge of any senatorial proceedings which occurred after January 7, when the *senātūs cōnsultum ultimum* was passed.

3. **quibus:** a connecting relative of which the antecedent is *inimīcōrum* (2). —**dēductum ac dēprāvātum:** sc. *esse.* —**invidiā atque obtrectātiōne laudis suae:** "as a result of jealousy and disparagement of his [Caesar's] reputation." *invidiā* and *obtrectātiōne* are abl. of cause, and *laudis* (4) is obj. gen.

4. **cuius:** introduces a relative clause of concession (AG 535e) and is equivalent to *cum eius* (= *Pompēī*). —**honōrī et dignitātī:** "dignity and status."

5. **adiūtorque fuerit:** = *adiūveritque.* Caesar had supported extraordinary commands for Pompey in 67 (to clear the Mediterranean of pirates) and in 66 (against Mithridates, king of Pontus). Upon Pompey's return from the east in 62, Caesar supported measures

for land grants to Pompey's veterans and ratification of his settlement of the east, which were later implemented in Caesar's consulship (59). It was principally the resistance of the conservative aristocrats (such as Cato) to these measures that led to the formation of the so-called "first triumvirate" (with Crassus as the third member) in late 60. Caesar also backed Pompey's candidacy for the consulship of 55. —**Novum . . . exemplum** (6): "an unusual precedent."

6. **intrōductum:** sc. *esse.* —**ut . . . opprimerētur** (7): subst. clause of result (see n. 7.17).

7. **armīs:** contrary to Caesar's assertion, force had often been used against tribunes, e.g. Saturninus, who was killed in office in 100. —**notārētur atque opprimerētur:** "was being censured and suppressed." —**quae . . . restitūta** (8): this clause is contradicted by Caesar's statement in lines 9–10 that Sulla had *not* abolished the tribunes' right to veto. Also, the sources do not mention any use of force (*armīs*) to reestablish the privileges of the tribunes. Furthermore, if Caesar had himself originally written this clause, he would have weakened his own argument by gratuitously acknowledging that a precedent had been set for ignoring a tribune's veto. For these reasons, it seems best to regard the relative clause as spurious.

8. **Sullam . . . relīquisse** (10): sc. *queritur* as the controlling verb of the indirect statement. —**nūdātā . . . tribūniciā potestāte** (9): abl. absol., concessive in sense (AG 420.3). —**omnibus rēbus:** "in every way" (abl. of specification; AG 418 and n. 1.28 on *animō*).

9. **līberam:** "unrestricted." Caesar is exaggerating here, since as dictator Sulla had curtailed the tribunes' right of *intercessiō* (veto) without abolishing it (see n. 6.4).

10. **videātur:** subjn. in a subordinate clause in indirect statement (see n. 2.16). Likewise *habuerint* (11), *sit dēcrētum* (11), and *sit vocātus* (14). —**bona:** in his first consulship (70), Pompey had brought about the restoration of tribunitial powers which had been eliminated or restricted by Sulla. Now, however (Caesar argues), Pompey has in effect removed the tribunitial veto by allowing threats of bodily harm against Antonius and Cassius (thus violating their personal sacrosanctity). Present conditions, in other words, are actually worse than they were under Sulla, whose senate had never driven the tribunes out of Rome.

11. **sit dēcrētum:** here used without *ut* to introduce the hortatory subjn. *darent* (AG 565a), of which the impf. tense results from the

indirect statement (AG 588) governed by the historical pres. *queritur* (6). For the expression *operam dare,* see n. 6.11. For *nē . . . caperet* (13), subjn. in an indirect statement, see n. 6.13.

13. **quā vōce:** "by which declaration" (abl. of means).

14. **factum:** sc. *esse;* the inf. is governed by *queritur* (6). The subject of the inf. is to be supplied from the preceding clause. Translate: "he protested that this had occurred" (*factum <esse>*). —**in:** "in the case of." —**perniciōsīs lēgibus . . . occupātīs** (16): legislation resulting in bloodshed, violence involving tribunes, refusal of the *plēbs* to cooperate in the daily management of the state, and seizure of high ground for defensive purposes in city rioting characterized the years of Tiberius and Gaius Gracchus and Saturninus (last third of the second century).

15. **vī tribūniciā:** "violence involving tribunes" (the adj. here replaces a possessive gen., AG 343 n. 1 and 343a). —**sēcessiōne:** "withdrawal." —**templīs . . . occupātīs** (16): abl. absol., temporal in sense (AG 420.1).

17. **expiāta:** "had been atoned for" (sc. *esse*), a religious metaphor.

18. **quārum rērum:** depends upon *nihil.* —**illō tempore:** i.e., January 49. —**factum . . . cōgitātum:** sc. *esse.*

19. **Hortātur . . . dēfendant** (22): construe as though the Latin were originally written as follows: *Hortātur ut dēfendant ab inimīcīs existimātiōnem dignitātemque eius, cuius imperātōris ductū viiii annīs rem pūblicam fēlicissimē gesserint plūrimaque proelia secunda fēcerint, omnen Galliam Germāniamque pācāverint.* —**cuius imperātōris ductū:** "under whose leadership as a commander" (*imperātōris* is in apposition with *cuius,* and *ductū* is abl. of means). Here the relative pron. precedes its antecedent *eius* (21). —**viiii annīs:** abl. of time refers to the period of Caesar's campaigns in Gaul from 58 to 50 (Romans always counted inclusively). —**rem pūblicam fēlicissimē gesserint:** "they had served the state very successfully." *gesserint* (20), *fēcerint* and *pācāverint* (21) are subjn. in a clause depending upon the indirect command *ut . . . dēfendant* (AG 592.1).

20. **secunda:** "victorious."

21. **eius existimātiōnem dignitātemque:** by using *eius,* ("of that man") instead of the reflexive *suam,* Caesar cleverly makes his point in the form of a dispassionate generalization.

23. **xiii** = *tertiae decimae.* This is the legion mentioned by Hirtius (section 2.10–11). Caesar had moved the thirteenth legion into Cisalpine Gaul in 50 to replace the fifteenth, which he had fur-

nished for the Parthian war in accordance with a decree of the senate (section 2.18–21).

24. **initiō tumultūs:** with this vague expression Caesar may be referring to the events of December 50, when the consul Marcellus (a cousin of the Marcellus who was consul in 49) crossed the *pōmerium* and, without a senatorial decree, entrusted the defense of Rome to Pompey. Marcellus, also on his own initiative, directed Pompey to use the two legions destined for the Parthian campaign as he deemed necessary and to recruit others. — **reliquae:** sc. *legiōnēs.*

25. **imperātōris . . . tribūnōrumque:** objective gen. (AG 347–48). The fusion of Caesar's personal interests (*imperātōris*) with those of the people, whose rights were to be safeguarded by the tribunes (*tribūnōrumque*), makes sense here because Caesar's provincial command in Cisalpine Gaul had been granted through tribunitial legislation in 59, but it also provides a ready justification for his march into Italy.

26. **dēfendere:** Caesar has chosen his words carefully. The verb represents him as the aggrieved party, who must fight in his own defense. The *optimātēs* are portrayed as the aggressors.

10.1. **sublātam . . . intercessiōnem:** see sections 3.34–35; 6.16–19; 9.5–10.

2. **praemissīs . . . cohortibus** (3): these are probably cohorts of the thirteenth legion, which Caesar had recently deployed in Cisalpine Gaul (see n. 9.23).

3. **qua:** = *aliqua* (see n. 3.23).

4. **per dissimulātiōnem:** "for the purpose of concealment." — **fōrmam:** "plan."

5. **erat aedificātūrus:** Caesar's architectural interests are well attested. Like many other prominent Romans (including Pompey), he sought to display his munificence and to prolong the memory of his name by constructing great buildings to serve the needs of his fellow citizens. For example, since 51, he had been lavishing money upon the construction of Rome's first individually financed forum, the *Forum Iūlium,* with its temple to Venus Genetrix, from whom he claimed descent. (Cicero himself had served as the agent who purchased land for the site in 54). By such *beneficia,* Caesar might endear himself to the Roman people and keep his name on their lips during his long absence in Gaul. —**ex:** "according to" (AG 221.11c).

6. **convīviō sē frequentī dedit:** "he attended a large banquet" (lit., "he gave himself to a crowded banquet").

8. **modicō comitātū:** sc. *cum* as the governing prep.

9. **viā:** sc. *ā* as the governing prep.

10. **ad lūcem:** "toward daybreak."

16. **Cūnctantī:** sc. *Caesarī*. —**eximiā magnitūdine et fōrmā:** abl. of description (= abl. of quality, AG 415).

17. **in proximō:** "nearby."

18. **harundine canēns:** "playing on a reed pipe." *harundine* is abl. of means. —**praeter:** "in addition to."

20. **et:** "also." —**ab ūnō:** abl. of separation (AG 401).

21. **ingentī spiritū classicum exōrsus:** "starting with a loud blast on the trumpet" (lit., "having begun a trumpet call with a large blast"). *exōrsus* is the pf. partic. of *exōrdior,* "begin," "embark upon."

22. **Eātur:** "let us go" (lit., "let it be gone." The verb is impers. pass.).

23. **vocat:** sing. in form because it agrees with the nearer subject, *inīquitās,* in spite of the neut. pl. subject *ostenta* (22). —**ālea:** "die" (i.e., sing. of "dice").

11.1. **Cognitā mīlitum voluntāte:** at this point Caesar's narrative is resumed from section 9. Only after determining the intentions of his troops does Caesar begin to march. Contrast Sulla's march on Rome in 88, when all his officers deserted him but one. — **Arīminum:** the mention of this coastal town, about ten miles below the Rubicon, means that Caesar has now crossed the southern boundary of his province and invaded Italy with an armed force. He omits the name of the river, as if to draw attention away from the fact that he has left his province without official authorization. By the morning of January 11, Ariminum had fallen into his hands. The town was strategically important because it provided a command of every direction: Cisalpine Gaul to the north, Etruria to the west, the eastern seaboard and Picenum to the south and east, and a direct route to Rome (by way of the *Via Flāminia*) to the south and west.

3. **convenit:** "he met" (probably on January 11). —**reliquās legiōnēs:** the eighth and twelfth legions, which later joined Caesar in Italy, were now in winter quarters in Gaul (section 2.12–14). *ēvocat* is misleading; Caesar would have had to mobilize the two legions *before* crossing the Rubicon (see n. 23.7 below).

4. **L. Caesar adulescēns:** so mentioned to distinguish him from his

father, consul in 64 and, later, Caesar's *lēgātus* (*Bellum Gallicum* 7.64). The young Caesar was chosen as an emissary because he was both a distant relative of Julius Caesar and a partisan of Pompey.

5. **Is . . . dēmōnstrat** (7): this man, because of his father's connections with Caesar, afforded Pompey a pretext for sending him, without the knowledge of the senate, on a personal mission. The date of the meeting remains uncertain. The expression *reliquō sermōne cōnfectō* may refer merely to an exchange of formalities. Whatever the nature of the *sermō*, Pompey's actual reason for sending an oral communication (*mandāta*) to Caesar now may have been either to buy time for raising troops or to strike an agreement with Caesar at the expense of the senate. The nature of *pauca* (13) remains a matter of pure speculation. Upon his return, L. Caesar, accompanying Roscius, did not meet with Pompey and Cicero until January 23 and probably attended a meeting of the senate in Capua on January 25. See sections 20.6–10, 22.4, and D. R. Shackleton Bailey, *JRS* 50 (1960): 80–83. —**cuius reī causā vēnerat:** sc. *dē rē* as the antecedent of *cuius,* and construe with *habēre . . . mandāta* (6). —**causā:** prep. following its object in the gen. case (AG 404c), as also in line 8 below.

6. **prīvātī officī mandāta:** "instructions involving a personal obligation." *officī* is gen. of description (= gen. of quality, AG 345).

7. **velle Pompēium sē Caesarī pūrgātum:** sc. *esse;* "(that) Pompey wanted himself cleared in Caesar's eyes." *Caesarī* is dat. of reference (AG 378.1). —**nē ea . . . in suam contumēliam vertat** (8): "that he (i.e., Caesar) may not interpret as a personal insult" (lit., "that he may not transfer those things to abuse of himself"). The adjective *suam* here replaces the objective gen. *suī* (AG 348a). The subjn. *ēgerit* (8) is generic (AG 535).

9. **commoda:** "interests." —**necessitūdinibus:** "obligations" (abl. of comparison).

10. **prō:** "in view of."

11. **reī pūblicae:** "for the sake of the state" (dat. of advantage, AG 376).

12. **cum . . . spēret:** temporal clause denoting an action simultaneous with *noceat* (AG 545a). This clause is attracted from the indic. into the subjn. because it is part of the result clause, *ut . . . noceat* (AG 593). —**nocēre:** the pres. inf. (instead of the fut. inf.) after a verb of hoping denotes immediate fulfillment of the hope (GL 531 n. 4).

13. **Pompēī:** the meaning here is ambiguous; as subjective gen., it

means Pompey's justification (i.e., of himself); as objective gen., it means L. Caesar's excuses for Pompey (see AG 348 and n.).

15. **commemorāsse:** syncopated form of *commemorāvisse;* sc. *ea* as object. The meaning of the verb indicates that Roscius's message, like L. Caesar's, was oral.

12.1. **quae:** connecting relative referring to the Pompeians' arguments summarized in section 11.

2. **nactus:** pf. partic. of *nancīscor.* Caesar often uses this verb when describing some unexpectedly favorable opportunity. He excelled at capitalizing upon advantages offered by chance. —**per quōs ea . . . perferrentur** (3): "through whom to communicate these concerns" (lit., "through whom these things might be reported": a relative clause of purpose). Caesar is employing a delaying tactic until his legions arrive. He is also trying to influence public opinion and create disunity in the ranks of his opponents. —**quae vellet:** generic subjn. (see n. 5.6).

3. **eum:** = *Pompēium.* —**quoniam . . . dētulerint** (4): subjn. in a clause depending upon the indirect command *petit . . . nē graventur* (AG 592.1).

4. **sē:** = *Caesarem.* Caesar is also the subject of the main verb *petit* (3).

5. **sī . . . possint** (6): *sī* introduces an indirect question in the sense of "to see if" (see n. 6.20 on *exspectābatque*).

6. **Sibi:** "in his eyes" (dat. of reference, AG 378).

7. **fuisse:** sc. *dīcit* as the controlling verb of this indirect statement. Noteworthy throughout the narrative is the frequency of the word *dignitās,* a concept of crucial significance to Caesar in his assessment of the situation. Like many other Roman aristocrats, Caesar and Pompey were constantly preoccupied with their honorable status in the public eye. Caesar's words represent a rejoinder to Pompey's argument that the interests of the state should outweigh public standing (cf. section 11.9–10). As Cicero himself attests (*Dē Partitiōne Ōrātōriā* 90): *hominum duo esse genera, alterum indoctum et agreste, quod anteferat semper ūtilitātem honestātī, alterum hūmānum atque expolītum, quod rēbus omnibus dignitātem antepōnat.* ("There are two kinds of people: the one, unlearned and boorish, which always prefers expediency to honor; the other, cultured and refined, which prefers genuine worth to everything else"). —**vītā:** abl. of comparison. —**Doluisse:** "(he) had been upset" (for the grammar, see n. on *fuisse* above).

8. **populī Rōmānī beneficium:** a reference to the "law of the ten tribunes" (see n. 1.6 on *Cn. Pompēius . . . trādiderit*). —**sibi:** "from him" (dat. of separation; see n. 2.3 on *ūnī*).

9. **sēmestrī:** "which had six months to run" (agrees with *imperiō* in abl. absol.). Caesar means that, without the "law of the ten tribunes," he would have to canvass in Rome for the consular elections in midsummer 49, instead of remaining in Gaul until he could step directly from his proconsulship into the consulship of 48 on January 1. His personal appearance for the elections would thus cost him approximately six months of *imperium* and force him to give up his troops. The *optimātēs,* of course, seeking to terminate Caesar's command as soon as possible, would find this line of reasoning unacceptable; see n. 3.32 on *ante certam diem.*

10. **cuius absentis ratiōnem habērī proximīs comitiīs populus iussisset:** "although the people had ordered his candidacy (*ratiōnem*) to be considered at the next election in his absence (*absentis*)." *cuius,* modified by *absentis,* introduces a relative clause of concession (i.e., = *cum suī*); AG 535e.

12. **aequō animō:** "patiently" (lit., "with calm mind," an abl. of manner). —**litterās:** this may have been the letter delivered to the senate by Curio on January 1 (see n. 2.25). —**cum . . . mīserit** (13): concessive in sense; for the pf. subjn. cf. *dētulerint* (4) above, where the primary tense is determined by the historical pres. *petit* (3).

13. **discēderent:** subjn. in an indirect command depending upon the idea implied by *litterās* (12). See n. 1.19 on *ut . . . trādant.*

14. **impetrāvisse:** sc. *sē* (i.e., Caesar) as subject. —**Tōtā Ītaliā:** abl. of place where (see n. 3.19).

16. **Quōnam haec onmia nisi ad suam perniciem pertinēre:** "Where did all these actions tend if not to his [Caesar's] destruction?" *quōnam = quō,* interrogative adv. The inf. *pertinēre* is in an indirect statement with *haec omnia* as subject acc.

17. **ad omnia . . . dēscendere:** "to make every concession" (lit., "to stoop to all things").

18. **parātum:** sc. *esse;* the inf. governs *dēscendere* (17) and *patī* (18). —**proficīscātur, dīmittant** (19), **discēdant** (19), **tollātur** (20), **permittātur** (22), **accēdat** (24), **patiātur** (24): subjn. representing imperative forms of direct speech (AG 588).

19. **exercitūs:** direct object of *dīmittant.* Caesar seems to mean only the troops stationed in Italy.

21. **lībera comitia:** sc. *sint.* The implication is that Pompey's forces

near Rome would intimidate the voters. But does Caesar also imply that he is willing to relinquish the privilege of standing for the consulship *in absentiā*? So Cicero, at least, reports (section 21.20–21). —**omnis rēs pūblica . . . permittātur** (22): this proposal would seem to entail the repeal of the *senātūs cōnsultum ultimum.*

22. **permittātur:** from *permittere,* "to entrust." —**quō facilius . . . fiant** (23): purpose clause containing a comparative (AG 531.2a).

23. **iūre iūrandō:** abl. of *iūs iūrandum.* —**sanciantur:** from *sancīre,* "to ratify." —**ipse:** = *Pompēius; sē* (24) = *Caesarem.*

24. **fore utī:** = *futūrum esse ut:* "the result would be that." The expression *fore ut* + subjn. is often used instead of a fut. pass. inf. (AG 569a).

13.1. **Capuam:** see n. 8.26. Actually Lucius Caesar and Roscius met Pompey and the consuls at Teanum Sidicinum, about fifteen miles to the northwest, on January 23 (*Ad Att.* 7.14.1).

3. **dēlīberātā rē:** abl. absol. The meeting was held on January 23. —**scrīptaque . . . mandāta** (4): Pompey's proposals had reached Caesar on January 29 or February 1 (the next day, according to the Roman calendar at that time; see n. 19.21). On February 2, Cicero wrote to Atticus that Pompey had published the proposals. Cicero went on to remark (*Ad Att.* 7.17.2) that Caesar had made his demands "most brazenly."

4. **summa:** from *summa, -ae,* f.

5. **reverterētur . . . excēderet . . . dīmitteret** (6): hortatory subjn. (secondary sequence) within an indirect statement implied by *summa* (AG 588). —**Arīminō:** abl. of place from which (AG 427.1). In summarizing the terms of the *optimātēs,* Caesar mentions only Ariminum. He misleadingly implies that this is the only town he has occupied by the time these terms were drawn up (i.e., no later than January 23). See lines 20–21 and n. 21 below. Cicero, however, states specifically that Caesar had been asked "to withdraw his forces from those towns which he had occupied outside his province" (*Ad Att.* 7.14.1, dated January 25; see section 21.21–22). —**exercitūs dīmitteret:** i.e., in Italy only. Caesar's vagueness may be intended to make the terms seem unfair.

6. **sī fēcisset:** ordinarily, the subjn. would be a fut. pf. indic. in a fut. more vivid condition; but in an indirect statement after a secondary tense, the fut. pf. is replaced by a plupf. subjn. (AG 484c).

7. **quoad . . . esset data:** for the subjn. see n. 6 above. —**fidēs:** "pledge" (i.e., that Caesar would withdraw his troops from Italy).

10. **Erat:** predicate of a series of subjective infinitives: *postulāre* (10), *tenēre* (12), *velle, habēre, pollicērī* (13), *dēfinīre* (14); see AG 452.1 —**condiciō:** predicate nom.

11. **ipsum:** (= *Pompēium*) to be construed as modifying the understood subject (i.e., *eum*) of each inf. above.

12. **legiōnēs aliēnās:** see section 2.3–9. —**tenēre:** by retaining the two legions near Rome, Pompey might be able to influence the immediate political situation and perhaps even the next consular election. —**exercitum . . . dīmittī** (13): a misleading statement, for evidently the senate had insisted only that Caesar withdraw from those areas in Italy south of the Rubicon (see n. 5 above and section 21.21–22).

13. **sē:** = *Pompēium*, also referred to by *ipsum* (11).

14. **itūrum:** sc. *esse.* —**diem:** antecedent of *quem.* The noun has been incorporated into the relative clause (AG 307b). —**itūrus sit:** the primary tense is used for the sake of vividness (AG 585b). —**ut . . . vidērētur** (16): purpose clause (i.e., Pompey's reason). —**sī:** "even if"; concessive because of *tamen* (15).

15. **perāctō cōnsulātū:** abl. absol., temporal in sense (AG 420.1). Caesar hoped to be elected to the consulship in July of 49. —**profectus esset:** for the subjn. see n. 6 above.

16. **mendācī religiōne:** "scruple against lying." *mendācī* (from *mendācium, -ī,* n.) is an objective gen. By declining to set a date for departure to Spain, Pompey could not be accused of breaking his word no matter how long he stayed in Italy. —**obstrictus:** sc. *esse* (the inf. depends upon *vidērētur*). —**tempus:** direct object of *dare* (17). —**colloquiō:** Caesar takes full advantage of Pompey's difficult position. By acceding to a private conference, Pompey would arouse the suspicions of the *optimātēs* that he might strike another agreement with Caesar. Such a move would cost him his position in the state and make him dependent upon Caesar's magnanimity.

17. **dare . . . pollicērī:** inf. subjects of *adferēbat* (18); see n. 10 above. —**accessūrum:** sc. *sē* as subject acc. with the fut. inf. *accessūrum* <*esse*> in an indirect statement governed by *pollicērī.* —**dēspērātiōnem:** direct object of *adferēbat* (18).

18. **Itaque:** here Caesar misrepresents the facts. He did not actually await a reply from the government in Rome since Pompey and the consuls did not receive Caesar's terms, delivered by Lucius Caesar

and Roscius, until January 23. On the other hand, one of Cicero's letters, written about January 21 (cf. section 17), contains the news that Ancona has been taken. Pompey's reply to Caesar's terms was actually issued after the consuls had fled from the advancing thirteenth legion. —**ab Arīminō:** "from the vicinity of Ariminum" (see n. 11.1 on *Arīminum*). The prep. is used with the name of a town because the vicinity is meant, as opposed to simply the town itself (AG 428a).

19. **Arretium:** this town, some fifty miles southwest of Ariminum, is one hundred fifty miles north of Rome and situated on a road joining the *Via Cassia,* which leads directly to the capital. — **Arīminī:** loc. case (see n. 6.20). —**duābus:** sc. *cohortibus.*

20. **Pisaurum, Fānum:** seacoast towns southeast of Ariminum and about eight miles apart. Fanum (Fortunae) is located on the *Via Flāminia,* which connects Rome to the northeast. —**Ancōnam:** a major seaport in the district of Picenum (see n. 14.11) and sixty-six miles from Ariminum, Ancona commands the principal roads to the south. In securing all these towns, Caesar controls access to Rome and can meet any military force approaching from the south. His strategy here required him to split his only legion (ten cohorts) into a two-pronged advance (coastal and inland), a bold tactic but typical of the commander's great daring, adaptability, and ingenuity in the field. —**singulīs cohortibus:** the omission of *cum* is common with certain military phrases (AG 413a).

21. **occupat:** on January 13–14.

14.1. **Īguvium:** object of *tenēre* (2). This was a large, strong town in Umbria near the *Via Flāminia* and about fifty miles inland from Fanum Fortunae. Here Caesar repeats his tactic of a two-pronged advance—inland and coastal (see n. 13.20 on *Ancōnam*). He had conducted the same type of deployment in a combined advance on Arretium and, simultaneously, on the coastal towns of Pisaurum, Fanum, and Ancona. —**Thermum:** acc. subject of *tenēre* and *mūnīre* (2). Quintus Minucius Thermus had been governor of Asia while Cicero was serving in Cilicia. As a former provincial governor, Thermus was probably still holding *imperium* and was summoned to duty under the provisions of the *senātūs cōnsultum ultimum.* Caesar refers to him as a praetor, when in fact he was a propraetor.

2. **cohortibus:** for the omission of *cum* see n. 13.20 on *singulīs cohortibus.*

3. **optimam:** "very friendly." —**voluntātem:** "attitude"; this is acc. subject of *esse* (2) in an indirect statement.

4. **Cuius:** the antecedent of this connecting relative is *Curiōnem* (3).

5. **mūnicipī:** see glossary.

6. **Mīlitēs . . . discēdunt** (7): an exaggeration, for Cicero (*Ad Att.* 7.23.1) reports on February 9 that Thermus arrived at Corfinium accompanied by some troops.

7. **summā omnium voluntāte:** "with the utmost approval of all" (*omnium* is a subjective gen.).

8. **Quibus rēbus cognitīs:** i.e., by January 21 or 22. Iguvium had fallen no earlier than January 20. —**cōnfīsus:** Caesar's confident air is here contrasted with the insecurity of Thermus (*diffīsus,* line 5).

9. **voluntātibus:** "sentiments." —**praesidiīs:** in the towns of Arretium (five cohorts), Fanum Fortunae (one cohort), Ancona (one cohort), and Iguvium (three cohorts). —**cohortīs:** acc. pl.

10. **Auximum:** this town commands another road leading directly to Rome and is just southwest of Ancona (slightly more than ten miles). Auximum stands on the northern fringe of the district of Picenum. Caesar began his advance to Auximum from Ancona on January 28. —**quod:** connecting relative modifying *oppidum.* — **Attius:** Publius Attius Varus, an ex-praetor who had governed Africa, was a long-standing adversary of Caesar.

11. **Pīcēnō:** this district on the northeast Italian coast, where Pompey's family had strong ties, had been the site of a military campaign by his father, Pompeius Strabo. Among the young men who had served under Pompey's father was Cicero himself, then aged seventeen. During this campaign, Cicero had probably made the acquaintance of young Pompey.

13. **Adventū . . . cognitō:** on January 28 or 29. —**decuriōnēs:** "senators." This name was given to members of the senate in *mūnicipia.*

14. **suī iūdicī rem nōn esse:** "(that) the matter was not for their decision" (i.e., the decision to side with either Caesar or Pompey). The local senators were unwilling to close their gates against the armies of either commander. *iūdicī* is a predicate gen. (AG 343c).

15. **C. Caesarem imperātōrem:** an honorific title conferred upon the victorious general by his troops and now included as part of the local senators' diplomatic statement.

16. **bene dē rē pūblicā meritum:** the participle is from *mereor, -ērī, -itus sum.* The expression *bene merērī dē* + abl. means "to deserve well of." —**tantīs rēbus gestīs:** abl. absol., causal in sense (AG 420.2).

17. **prohibērī**: depends upon *patī* (15). —**habeat ratiōnem**: the expression *habēre ratiōnem* (+ gen.) means "to take account (of)." The subjn. *habeat* represents an imperative form of direct speech (see n. 12.18 on *proficīscātur*).
18. **posteritātis**: "the future" (in contrast with *perīculī*, the risk which Varus runs now).
20. **Hunc [= Varum] ex prīmō ōrdine . . . mīlitēs** (21): construe as follows: *paucī mīlitēs Caesaris ex prīmō ōrdine cōnsecūtī hunc*. The *ōrdō prīmus* was the "first century" (of the first cohort). For the terms, see glossary s.v. "Cohort."
22. **nōnnūlla pars**: "a considerable part."
24. **prīmī pīlī centuriō**: "centurion of the first rank." This was the ranking centurion of the first cohort (and therefore the senior centurion of the legion), a position often held by an officer of exemplary courage and considerable combat and administrative experience.
25. **ōrdinem**: for the meaning see n. 20 above.
26. **Attiānōs**: "of Attius (Varus)."

15.1. **Quibus rēbus Rōmam nūntiātīs: Rōmam** is acc. of place to which (AG 427.2) because *nūntiātīs* implies motion (i.e., the physical act of bringing the news to Rome). Rome was abandoned by the government on January 17 and 18 in reaction to the news that Caesar had seized Ariminum and probably Pisaurum, Fanum Fortunae, and Ancona as well.
2. **invāsit**: "gripped" (sc. *urbem* as direct object). —**ad aperiendum aerārium**: located in the Forum, in the temple of Saturn at the foot of the Capitoline hill, the *aerārium* was supervised by the quaestors. It contained public funds and served as the state treasury.
3. **pecūniamque**: the enclitic *-que* is appended to the object of the prep. *ad* instead of to the prep. itself. —**ex**: "according to" (see section 7.9 for the resolution of the senate).
4. **sanctiōre aerāriō**: this "special inner treasury" housed a fund designated as a war reserve for emergencies. Whether Lentulus actually did open the treasury remains doubtful. At any rate, he left Rome without emptying it. Pompey, at least, thought that some money remained in it (section 24.17–19).
5. **Caesar**: sc. *falsō nūntiābātur*. —**iam iamque**: "at any moment."
6. **Hunc**: i.e., Lentulus, the colleague of C. Marcellus.
7. **prīdiē eius diēī**: "on the day before" (AG 359b and n. 2). This must mean that Pompey left Rome for Capua on January 17, i.e.,

about six days *after* the invasion of Italy. Yet only a few paragraphs earlier (section 13.1–2), Caesar's narrative had placed Pompey in Capua *before* his departure from Ariminum (see n. 13.21). Caesar's attempt to distort the truth appears to have caught him in an inconsistency: in reality, he continued his invasion of Italy *before* receiving a reply from the government (see n. 13.18).

8. **iter . . . habēbat:** the expression *iter habēre* means "to make one's way."

9. **Āpūliā:** the district encompassing most of southeastern Italy. — **hībernōrum causā:** = *ut ibi hībernārent. causā* is a prep. following its object in the gen. case (cf. n. 11.5 on *causā*).

10. **citrā Capuam:** i.e., on the northern side, from Caesar's viewpoint.

11. **prīmum:** "for the first time" (AG 322d). —**sēsē cōnfirmant et colligunt:** "they rallied and regrouped" (lit., "they encouraged and gathered themselves").

12. **dīlectum:** Cicero, whose area of responsibility was originally to be Capua (see section 8.26), was expected to assist in this unsuccessful recruitment (*Ad Att.* 7.14.2). —**lēge Iūliā:** abl. of accordance (AG 418a and n.). This famous land law, passed during Caesar's consulship, had provided public land in Campania for thousands of Roman citizens. The measure had come into existence as a result of senatorial opposition to Pompey's attempt to obtain grants of land for his veterans upon his return from Asia in 62. The law, sponsored by Caesar (hence the adj. *Iūliā,* which names Caesar's *gēns*), had enabled him to repay Pompey for his support of Caesar's candidacy for the consulship. —**Capuam:** for the acc. cf. *Rōmam* in n. 1 above. —**dēductī erant:** from *dēdūcere,* "to settle (as colonists)."

13. **gladiātōrēs:** these trained fighters belonged to a school endowed by Caesar earlier in his political career, when he saw to the entertainment of the people as an aedile (in 65). In a letter to Atticus written on January 25, Cicero remarked that the heavily armed fighters in the school were said to be planning a breakout (*Ad Att.* 7.14.2).

15. **iussit:** sc. *hōs* (i.e., *gladiātōrēs*) as subject acc. of *sequī.* —**quōs:** direct object of *distribuit* (18).

16. **iūdiciō:** for the case see n. 12 above on *lēge Iūliā.* —**reprehendēbātur:** the employment of gladiators would inevitably evoke the painful memories of the revolt of Spartacus, a Thracian prisoner-of-war who in 73 had escaped from the very same school in Capua and terrorized the entire country, defeating seven Ro-

man armies and ravaging Lucania. He soon became a legend because of his courage, daring, and leadership. The incident is here recounted by Caesar for its value as propaganda, for it suggests the desperate measures which Lentulus was ready to take.

17. **familiārīs conventūs:** "friendly communities" (i.e., of Roman citizens forming enclaves in non-Roman towns).

18. **causā:** see n. 9 above for use.

16.1. **Atticō:** for Atticus see list of personal names s.v. "Pompōnius." —**sal.:** = *salūtem* (sc. *dīcit*).

2. **cōnsilium cēpī:** the expression *cōnsilium capere* means "to form a plan" or "to make up one's mind." —**ut . . . exīrem:** indirect command depending on the idea implied by *cōnsilium* (see n. 1.9 on *ut . . . trādant*). Cicero uses here the common word for leaving Rome although he had not entered the city. He was still holding *imperium* and awaiting senatorial approval of a triumph. — **antequam lūcēret:** = *ante prīmam lūcem*. The subjn. is in a clause subordinate to an indirect command (AG 592.1).

3. **nē quī cōnspectus fieret aut sermō:** "that no one might see me or talk about me" (lit., "lest any glimpse or talk might happen"). The subjn. is used with an implied verb of fearing (AG 564). *quī* = *aliquī* (adj.) after *nē* (AG 310a). Cicero is here concerned for his reputation (*existimātiō*). —**lictōribus . . . laureātīs** (4): abl. absol., causal in sense. As a proconsul Cicero was entitled to twelve lictors. They carried *fascēs* and, since his troops in Cilicia had hailed him as *imperātor* after a minor military engagement, his lictors bore laurel wreaths in anticipation of a triumph (see n. 7.20). As a victorious commander, Cicero was embarrassed to be fleeing from Rome when the state was endangered.

6. **cōnsilī:** "judgment" (i.e., probably Pompey's decision to abandon Rome on January 17; cf. section 15.1–9). —**Tibi vērō quid suādeam:** "But what advice can I give you?" *quid* is a cognate acc. (AG 390c); the subjn. is deliberative (AG 444).

8. **capiatve:** = *vel capiat;* for the enclitic -*ve* cf. AG 324e. — **coartātus et stupēns:** "tied up and paralyzed."

9. **Omnēs:** Cicero means the *optimātēs* and their supporters. —**ūnā:** i.e., with Pompey. —**cōnsilī rēs est:** "it is a matter for deliberation." For the gen. of description (quality), see AG 345. The frequency of *cōnsilium* in this letter indicates the dilemma which Caesar's actions have thrust upon Cicero. In the coming months he will have to make one of his most difficult decisions: whether

to remain in Italy or leave with Pompey, should Pompey see fit to evacuate the country.

10. **omnia:** sc. *ācta sunt.*

11. **quaesō:** "I implore (you)." The verb is parenthetical. —**vel quod in buccam vēnerit:** "even if (you write) only whatever comes to mind" (lit., "even if only whatever will have come into the jaw").

17.2. **Quaesō:** "I implore (you)." The verb is parenthetical. —**quid agitur:** "what is going on?" (lit., "what is being done?") —**Mihi enim tenebrae sunt:** "For I am in the dark" (lit., "darkness is to me").

3. **Cingulum:** this may be the hometown of Titus Labienus, who rebuilt it at his own expense (see section 23.4–6). It is situated in Picenum about twenty miles from Ancona (less than a full day's march). For Labienus see n. 4 below. —**inquit:** Cicero does not name the subject, but Atticus must have known who Cicero's informant was. —**Ancōnem:** an alternate (third decl.) form of *Ancōnam;* see section 13.20 and n.

4. **Labiēnus:** Caesar never mentions the desertion of this man, one of his ablest and most trusted officers in the Gallic campaign (see list of personal names s.v. "Titus Labienus"). Labienus met Pompey for the first time on January 22. —**Utrum ... an** (5): introduces a double question (AG 335).

5. **Hannibale:** Cicero suggests that Caesar is behaving like a foreign invader—in this case, the most notorious enemy in the history of Rome. —**hominem:** acc. of exclamation (AG 397d).

6. **quī ... vīderit** (7): relative clause of cause, in which *quī = cum is* (AG 535e and n. 1). —**τοῦ καλοῦ:** "of the Right" (pronounced "tou kalou"). The Greek is in the gen. case depending on *umbram.* Cicero here makes a literary reference to the writings of Plato, who frequently uses this term for the concept of absolute Goodness. Cicero often employed Greek to express an idea for which he could not find a suitable Latin word. Since his own treatise on the ideal state had recently been published (in 51), Cicero may be suggesting his literary kinship with the great Greek philosopher whose *Republic* had served as a model for his own work.

7. **dignitātis:** cf. Caesar's remarks (section 12.7 and n.).

8. **honestum:** sc. *est. habēre* and *occupāre* (9) are subjective inf. (see n. 13.10).

9. **nūllō pūblicō cōnsiliō:** "with no authorization by the state" (abl. absol., concessive in sense; AG 420.3). —**urbīs:** acc. pl.

117

10. **quō facilior . . . sit:** purpose clause containing a comparative (AG 531.2a). —**patriam:** i.e., Rome. Cicero occasionally speaks of his two *patriae:* his hometown Arpinum and Rome itself. In general, when Roman citizens spoke of their *patria,* they meant the city-state of Rome, not the country Italy; for it was only at Rome that they could exercise their right to vote and seek their final court of appeals in all legal business.

11. **Mālim:** potential subjn. (AG 447.1).

18.2. **ἥρωα:** acc. of Greek **ἥρως,** "hero" (pronounced "hērōa"). For Labienus, see n. 17.4. By using a Greek word here Cicero may be alluding to the Homeric hero Achilles, who also withdrew his support of a military campaign to uphold his own honor and principles. See also section 19.17. —**iam diū:** sc. *est.* With *iam diū, est* denotes an action begun in the past but continuing into the present (AG 466 and n. 1). In this idiom, the pres. tense is translated by the English pres. pf. ("has been").

3. **quī:** refers to *Labiēnum* (2). —**ut:** "granted that," "suppose that" (AG 527f). sc. *prōfēcit.* —**tamen:** "at least."

4. **illī:** = *Caesarī*. —**ad summam prōfectum <esse>:** the expression *ad summam prōficere* means "to do (something) of general benefit."

5. **Amō etiam Pīsōnem:** for Piso see n. 4.11. Cicero professes affection for Piso because he fled southward from Rome with Pompey in response to the advance of his son-in-law, Caesar—a remarkable change of attitude in view of Cicero's bitter attack (in 55) upon Piso, who had supported Clodius's legislation for Cicero's exile. See also section 19.17. —**vīsum īrī:** fut. pass. inf. from *videor*, "seem."

6. **Quamquam:** Cicero tempers his approval because, even though Piso and Labienus have sided with the legitimate government, *this* civil war has not erupted from violent political differences among Roman citizens. The recklessness of one man, he maintains, has brought it about. —**ita:** "of such a kind." —**cīvīle:** sc. *bellum*.

10. **quod . . . metuās** (11): generic subjn. (AG 535); so also *quī . . . putet* (11–12).

13. **sine magistrātibus:** Cicero acutely identifies a major problem for Caesar throughout the civil war: the fact that few experienced magistrates who were serving or had served the republic were willing to support his attempts to establish a government under

his personal leadership. —**Nē simulāre quidem poterit quic-quam πολιτικῶς** (pronounced "politikos"): "He will not be able to maintain even the pretense of constitutional procedures" (lit., "he will not be able even to pretend constitutionally").

15. **Quōrum:** connecting relative; the antecedent is *nōs* (14). — **quam:** "how" (also in line 16 below). —**ἀστρατήγητος:** "incapable of command" (pronounced "astratēgētos"; sc. *sit* as the verb in the indirect question). —**animadvertis:** Cicero must be referring to a previous letter of Atticus.

16. **cui . . . fuerint:** relative clause of cause (AG 535e and n. 1). — **Pīcēna:** "the business of Picenum" (nom. neut. pl. of *Pīcēnus, -a, -um*). Cicero may be referring to the occupation of Ancona, which Caesar had been able to achieve by surprise. —**sine cōnsiliō:** sc. *sit* for the indirect question, of which the subject is Pompey. For *cōnsilium* ("judgment") cf. n. 16.6. Here Cicero criticizes Pompey's indecisiveness.

17. **rēs:** "situation" (sc. *est*). —**peccāta:** for example, the so-called "First Triumvirate," Pompey's marriage to Julia, the conference at Luca, and Pompey's support of Caesar's *ratiō absentis*.

20. **perturbātius:** "more disorganized."

22. **Spēs omnis:** sc. *est* as the main verb.

23. **aliēnīs:** Cicero may be taking advantage of the ambivalent force of this adj., which means "disloyal" (cf. n. 7.5 on *aliēnō*) and "another's." From his viewpoint, the two legions fit both descriptions.

25. **condiciōnum:** although Caesar has not yet even received the terms of the government, Cicero is convinced, now that Caesar has invaded Italy, that the situation no longer permits any negotiations.

26. **commissum quidem ā nōbīs certē est sīve ā nostrō duce:** "we—or our leader—have without a doubt created such a predicament" (lit., "it has indeed without a doubt been brought about by us or by our leader").

27. **ut . . . trāderēmus** (28): the subjn. is in a subst. clause of result which serves as the subject of the impers. pass. *commissum . . . est* (26). —**ē portū:** the traditional metaphor of the "ship of state."

19.1. **Tullius . . . s. p. d.** (2): for the salutation see n. 8.1. —**animīs:** dat. in apposition to *Terentiae* and *Tulliae*.

4. **ille:** = *Caesar*. Cicero naturally assumes that Caesar will proceed directly to Rome.

5. **in praesentiā:** "for now," "for the present." —**domī:** i.e., Cicero's

house on the Palatine hill, a fashionable and expensive district overlooking the Roman forum. —**esse:** = *manēre*. The same use of *esse* appears below in lines 11 and 13.

6. **homō āmēns:** "as a madman" (to be taken as part of the predicate). —**dīripiendam:** gerundive used as fut. pass. partic. in agreement with *urbem* (AG 500.1). —**ut . . . possit** (7): subjn. in a clause of fearing (AG 564). The same construction occurs in lines 8 (*nē . . . interclūdāmur*) and 14 (*nē . . . sit*) below.

7. **Dolabella:** Publius Cornelius Dolabella, a staunch supporter of Caesar and an officer in his army. As Cicero's son-in-law since his marriage to Tullia in 50, he might be expected to look after his wife and her mother in the event of a civil war around Rome (see list of personal names s.v. "Cornelius"). —**prōdesse:** from *prōsum.*

8. **ut . . . nōn liceat** (9): sc. *vōbīs.* The subjn. is in a result clause (AG 537). —**cum velītis:** concessive clause (AG 549).

9. **Reliquum est, quod:** "There remains the question, which . . ." *quod* = *id quod* (AG 307d and n.), "a thing which" (direct object of *cōnsīderābitis*).

10. **vestrī:** gen. with *similēs*, since with a personal pron. *similis* takes the gen. instead of the dat. (AG 385.2). —**sintne:** *-ne*, "whether," introduces an indirect question.

11. **videndum est:** sc. *vōbīs.* —**ut . . . possītis:** subjn. in a subst. clause of result serving as the subject of the impers. pass. *videndum est* (AG 569.1). —**quidem:** "in fact."

12. **sē rēs habet:** "matters stand." —**modo ut:** "provided that." —**liceat:** subjn. in a clause of proviso introduced by *modo ut* (AG 528 and 528b).

13. **bellissimē:** "very comfortably." —**praediīs:** i.e., at Formiae, Puteoli, Cumae, and Pompeii.

15. **velim . . . cōnsīderētis** (16): "I should like you to think." *velim* is a potential subjn. (AG 447.1) followed by the subjn. *cōnsīderētis* without the introductory *ut* (AG 449c and 565). In colloquial language, this construction often replaces the imperative. —**Pompōniō:** Titus Pomponius Atticus (see list of personal names). —**Camillō:** C. Furius Camillus, a lawyer and friend with whom Cicero was in close contact at this time. The asyndeton here (see n. 4.6) adds emphasis.

16. **vidēbitur:** *vidētur* (impers.) means "it seems best." —**ad summam:** "in short." —**animō fortī:** abl. of description (AG 415). —**sītis:** for the construction see n. 15 above on *cōnsīderētis.*

17. **Labiēnus:** see section 17.4 (with n.) and 18.1. —**rem meliōrem**

fēcit: "has made the situation better" (cf. *māius . . . facere,* n. 8.21). —**Pīsō:** see n. 4.11 and section 18.5 with n.

20. **quid agātis:** "how you are doing." —**quid . . . agātur:** "what is going on."

21. **Rūfus:** this is either Lucius Mescinius Rufus, who had served under Cicero as a quaestor in Cilicia, or Marcus Caelius Rufus (see list of personal names). —**viii K.:** = *octāvō <diē ante> Kalendās <Februāriās>,* January 22. This date (like all others in the text) is based on the calendar *before* Caesar revised it, when all months had twenty-nine days except for February (twenty-eight days) and March, May, July, and October (thirty-one days each). For dates in general, see glossary s.v. "Calendar." —**Menturnīs:** locative. Menturnae was a seacoast town northwest of Capua on the *Via Appia.*

20.2. **quīn . . . darem** (3): *quīn* is used with the subjn. after negative expressions (*nūllum . . . diem*) implying delay (AG 558).

3. **nōn quō:** = *nōn quod* and takes the subjn. in a causal clause when the clause is to be denied (AG 540 n. 3). —**magnō opere:** "particularly."

4. **quod scrīberem:** generic subjn. (AG 535). —**quō:** abl. of comparison (AG 406).

6. **a. d. vi. Kal.:** = *ante diem sextum Kalendās <Februāriās>,* January 25. —**prīdiē quam:** "on the day before" (AG 434). *quam* is a conj. introducing *dedī* (7).

8. **abductīs praesidiīs:** Caesar's opponents made this a prerequisite for further negotiation (cf. n. 13.5 on *Arīminō* and section 21.21–22).

9. **iīs:** = *eīs.* —**quās tulisset:** "because he had offered them" (relative clause of cause; AG 535e). —**Favōniō:** Marcus Favonius, a praetor in 49 and a zealous admirer and imitator of the reactionary Cato. His name, like Cato's, eventually became synonymous with uncompromising republicanism. He had prosecuted Scipio, Pompey's future father-in-law, in 60 and had for years been an enemy of Pompey himself. The reaction of Favonius to Caesar's terms in the meeting on January 25 was stronger than that of Cato, whom Cicero describes as less than belligerent. —**nōbīs:** dat. governed by the compound *impōnī* (pres. pass. inf.).

10. **cōnsiliō:** "meeting."

12. **agātur:** used impersonally.

13. **adductus sit:** the pf. subj. in a subordinate clause in primary

sequence in indirect statement represents a fut. pf. indic. (AG 484c). —**ut . . . dēdūcat:** indirect command introduced by *adductus sit.*

15. **interposita esse:** *interpōnere* means "to introduce" (for purposes of hindering or preventing); sc. *dīcunt.*

16. **quōminus:** the conj. is used with the subjn. after verbs of hindering, especially after a controlling verb which is not negative (AG 558b); see n. 20.2 on *quīn.* —**quod (= id quod) opus esset:** "what was essential." The subjn. is generic (AG 535) used in a noun clause as the subject of *parārētur.*

17. **ut . . . dēdūcat:** subst. clause of result after *factūrum <esse>* (AG 568). Here the expression *facere ut* means "to decide to" (lit., "to bring it about that").

18. **minōre scelere vīcerit quam quō ingressus est:** "he will have prevailed with less scandal than with his present course of action" (lit., "than that on which he has embarked").

20. **cum . . . tum:** "not only . . . but also" (correlatives, usually used with the indic.; AG 323g and 549b). —*ā:* "from the viewpoint of."

22. **relīquimus:** see section 15.1–5.

23. **legiōnēs Appiānās:** these troops (also mentioned in section 2.1–9) are so described here because an officer named Appius had marched them from Gaul into Italy. This Appius may have been a nephew of the Appius Claudius Pulcher whom Cicero succeeded as governor of Cilicia.

24. **Fōrmiās:** one of Cicero's villas was located at Formiae, a coastal town about forty miles northwest of Capua. Cicero probably used this residence as his headquarters at the time.

25. **cōgitābam:** epistolary impf. (see n. 1.30).

21.2. **versētur:** = *sit.* —**salūs:** sc. *salūs* also with *bonōrum* and *reī pūblicae* (3). For the significance of *bonōrum,* see n. 10 below.

3. **ex eō . . . quod:** "from the fact that."

4. **patriam:** cf. n. 17.10 on *patriam.* —**dīripiendam . . . īnflammandam:** gerundives used as fut. pass. partic. modifying *patriam* (AG 500.1).

5. **eum:** the demonstrative meaning "such" often anticipates a result clause (here *ut . . . nequeāmus*). —**rēs dēducta est:** for the idiom, see n. 5.17. —**quī:** = *aliquī* (adj.).

6. **cāsus:** "lucky break." —**subvēnerit:** pf. subjn. by attraction representing a fut. pf. indic. (AG 484c).

7. **Equidem:** "I, for my part" (used *only* with the first person sing.).
   —**ad urbem:** see n. 8.2.
8. **quae . . . pertinērent:** generic subjn. (AG 535).
9. **improbīs . . . iīs** (= *eīs*): dat. governed by *invāserat,* which usually governs the acc. in Cicero. As a political term, *improbī* is used as the antonym of *bonī* (see below).
10. **bonī:** Cicero often uses this term to refer to the conservative oligarchy committed to maintaining the political prestige of the senate in accordance with long-standing Roman traditions. Many of these men, as landowners, sought to uphold the rights of private property and supported the political, social, and economic status quo. Their opponents (*populārēs*), whom Cicero here refers to as *improbī,* usually sought to establish their own personal advancement by using *tribūnī plēbis* to obtain from the assembly of the people such prerogatives as special military commands and exemptions from normal constitutional requirements (e.g., Caesar's *ratiō absentis*). Often the *bonī,* who also called themselves *optimātēs,* differed from the *populārēs* only in the methods by which they sought to achieve their political objectives. And sometimes, if they had the *tribūnī plēbis* in their employment, even their methods were identical to those of the *populārēs* (see Historical Introduction, p. 14f.). —**ut . . . cuperent:** result clause.
14. **quam:** "how." —**nihil attinet disputārī:** "it is pointless to argue" (lit., "it is not at all relevant to be argued").
15. **Feruntur:** "are being offered."
16. **illō:** = *Caesare.* —**ut . . . eat . . . dīmittantur** (17): indirect command depending on the idea implied by *condiciōnēs* (GL 546 n. 2, p. 347).
17. **sē . . . trāditūrum** (19): sc. *Caesar dīcit* as the controlling verb of the indirect statement and *esse* with *trāditūrum.*
18. **Cōnsidiō Noniānō:** M. Considius Nonianus, whom Caesar has overlooked in his remarks about the reassignment of Gaul (section 7.14). In mid-February, Considius helped Cicero to supervise the recruitment of troops in Capua. —**obtigērunt:** sc. *Galliae* as subject. Cicero refers to the normal practice of awarding provincial commands by drawing lots (see section 7.15–16).
19. **cōnsulātūs:** objective gen. (AG 347–48). —**neque . . . iam** (20): "and no longer."
20. **absente sē:** abl. absol. —**ratiōnem habērī:** "(his) candidacy to be considered."
21. **trīnum nūndinum:** "for the interval of three eight-day periods"

(i.e., twenty-four days). A *nūndinum* was the period of time from one market day to the next (i.e., eight days). This was the interval, required by law, between a candidate's formal announcement (*prō-fessiō*) of his candidacy and the day of the elections. During this time, the candidate was expected to remain in Rome as a *prīvātus*. The same interval was required by law between the proposal of a bill and the vote on it. —**petitūrum:** for meaning cf. *petitiōnem* (19). —**condiciōnēs:** compare these terms with those summarized by Caesar (section 12.18–25 and 13.4–9). A careful comparison reveals the vagueness of Caesar's language, which constitutes a clever use of propaganda. Obviously neither Caesar nor Pompey wished to be the first to dismiss his troops. Nowhere does Cicero mention Caesar's proposal that Caesar and Pompey meet; in fact, Caesar reports that Pompey refused (section 13.16–18)—a situation providing Caesar with a pretext for pursuing him through Italy and using the breakdown of negotiations as propaganda. If Caesar's terms seemed too reasonable to be sincere, it may be that, in his shrewed assessment of the attitudes of the *optimātēs* in power, he expected his terms to be rejected. Any time he might gain by preoccupying his opponents (and causing dissension among them) with his proposals would enable him to exploit his tactical advantage in northern Italy while pointing to the reluctance of the legitimate government to honor a compromise with him. Some, as Cicero himself states (section 20.14–16), suspected that Caesar's aim was to thwart the military preparations of the *optimātēs* by diverting their attention from the war effort with his apparent willingness to compromise. —**ita ut:** "on condition that" (lit., "in such a way that"), introducing a clause of proviso (AG 528b and n.).

24. **honestae:** agrees with *pācis.* —**lēgēs:** "terms."
25. **impōnuntur:** i.e., upon the Pompeians.
26. **condiciōnibus:** abl. of specification (AG 418a).
27. **eius modī:** gen. of description depending on *bellum* (26). —**quod . . . possit:** generic subjn. (AG 535).
28. **ā . . . fūgerit:** "has rejected" (lit., "has retreated from"). Cicero's reaction suggests that he doubted the sincerity of Caesar's terms. —**tantum modo ut:** "provided only that" (introducing a subjn. in a clause of proviso; AG 528 and 528b).
29. **nē . . . possit:** like *quōminus, nē* is used with the subjn. after verbs of hindering (AG 558b). —**quod:** connecting relative.
30. **spērābāmus . . . habēbāmus putābāmusque:** epistolary impf.

(see n. 1.30). The change of tone here contrasts markedly with the desperation of the opening paragraph. Perhaps Cicero was trying to spare the convalescing Tiro any further stress (see lines 46–47). —**Dīlectūs . . . magnōs:** there is no evidence to corroborate this statement. By early February, in fact, Cicero realized that the recruiting in the vicinity of Capua had not been very successful, and, as later events would prove, the government was able to enlist few troops anywhere in Italy (see section 24. 8–9).

31. **coepisset:** plupf. subjn. replacing a fut. pf. indic. (see n. 13.6). —**nē . . . āmitteret** (32): subjn. in a clause of fearing.

32. **ambās:** i.e., Cisalpine Gaul and Transalpine Gaul. —**inimīcissimās:** although the Transalpine Gauls may still have been hostile, their spirit had been broken with the defeat of Vercingetorix in 52. They would therefore pose little threat to Caesar at this time.

33. **Trānspadānōs:** these people would favor Caesar because he had recently supported their enfranchisement as Roman citizens. —**ex Hispānia:** "in Spain." The prep. *ex* is used to indicate the direction of movement.

34. **Āfrāniō et Petreiō:** see list of personal names. —**ā tergō:** "in his rear" (AG 429b).

35. **modo ut:** sc. *opprimātur.* Translate: "provided only that he is checked," a clause of proviso with the connotations of a wish (cf. n. 19.12 on *liceat*). —**urbe salvā:** abl. absol.

36. **quod:** "the fact that." —**illīus:** = *Caesaris.*

37. **T. Labiēnus:** *T.* = *Titus* (see n. 17.4 and sections 18.1 and 19.17).

38. **multīque idem . . . dīcuntur** (39): see n. 7.5 on *aliēnō.*

40. **Fōrmiīs:** see n. 20.24.

41. **quō plūs . . . valērent** (42): purpose clause containing a comparative (AG 531.2a).

43. **certīs:** i.e., specific legions to be assigned to Cicero.

44. **quod:** "the fact that." —**Dolabella:** see list of personal names.

46. **quae:** connecting relative, subject of *perturbent et impediant.* —**cavē nē . . . perturbent et impediant:** *cavē* (*nē*) is used with the pres. subjn. to express a prohibition (AG 450 and n. 2).

47. **dā operam:** "see to it." —**ut valeās . . . navigēs** (48): subjn. in an indirect command (AG 563e).

48. **cum rectē navigārī poterit:** "when you can make a safe voyage" (lit., "when it will be possible to be sailed safely"). For the future tense in temporal clauses with *cum,* see AG 547. Sailing in winter was dangerous because of storms.

49. **Cicerō . . . Terentia et Tullia:** see n. 8.1. —**Fōrmiānō:** "the villa

at Formiae" (situated on the *Via Appia* about eighty-eight miles south of Rome; see n. 20.24). —**erat:** epistolary impf. —**Rōmae:** Cicero left his wife and daughter in Rome for their own personal safety or perhaps because their presence would suggest that Cicero, anxious to appear neutral, had not made a full commitment to Pompey.

50. **Cūrā ut valeās:** see n. 8.27 for the construction. —**iiii K. Febr.:** = *quartō <diē ante> Kalendās Februāriās,* January 27 (see glossary s.v. "Calendar"). —**Capuā:** abl. of place.

22.2. **scrībam:** generic subjn. (AG 535). —**quī . . . dederim** (3): relative clause of cause (AG 535e). As Cicero goes on to explain, he did not send his previous letter because subsequent events proved that it had been too optimistic.

3. **eram ēlūcubrātus:** *ēlūcubrārī* means "to burn the midnight oil over (a literary work)."

4. **spеī bonae:** "optimism." —**contiōnis:** here Cicero probably refers to the meeting of the senate at Capua on January 25 (see section 20) to consider Caesar's terms, which had been brought by Roscius and L. Caesar (section 12.18–13.3). For the terms as reported by Cicero, see section 21.15–21. —**voluntātem:** "attitude." —**audieram:** the alternate third principal part of *audīre* is *audiī*. —**illum:** = *Caesarem*.

5. **Ecce tibi:** "Observe this!" —**tibi:** ethical dat., used to indicate the person to whom the thought expressed is of particular importance (AG 380).

6. **iii Nōnās Febr.:** = *tertiō <diē ante> Nōnās Februāriās.* To calculate this date see glossary s.v. "Calendar." —**Philotimī:** sc. *et litterās.* Philotimus, Terentia's steward and a freedman, was an exceedingly conservative supporter of Pompey. —**Furnī:** C. Furnius, a former pupil of Cicero, had been tribune in 50 and was acting as an intermediary between Cicero and Caesar, whose cause he favored. He had supported a thanksgiving for Cicero's achievements in Cilicia.

7. **Curiōnis:** see list of personal names and n. 8.10. —**inrīdet:** sc. *Curiō* as subject. Apparently Curio considered the unofficial "embassy" of L. Caesar to be so doomed to failure that he could make fun of it before the negotiations actually broke down.

8. **oppressī:** sc. *esse.* —**capiam:** deliberative subjn. in an indirect question (AG 575b). The same construction appears in line 9 below (*quid agam*).

9. **labōrō:** "I worry." —**puerīs:** i.e., Cicero's son and nephew. — **habeō:** "I have (knowledge)" or "I know."
10. **proficīscēbar:** epistolary impf.

23.1. **Auximō . . . prōgressus:** i.e., no later than February 1 and possibly as early as January 29. After his description of the capture of Auximum (section 14) and the consequent abandoning of Rome (section 15), Caesar's narrative resumes with the occupation of Picenum. —**Pīcēnum:** modifying *agrum* ("district"). —**percurrit:** i.e., during the first week of February.
2. **praefectūrae:** "towns." Unlike the *mūnicipium*, which elected its own senate and magistrates, the *praefectūra* was governed by magistrates (*praefectī*) appointed directly by Rome.
3. **omnibus rēbus:** "in every way" (abl. of specification).
4. **Cingulō:** see n. 17.3. —**quod oppidum:** the antecedent (*oppidum*), when in apposition to a word in the main clause (*Cingulō*), is often in the same case as the relative pron. (*quod*). See AG 307e. —**cōnstituerat:** from *cōnstituere*, here used in the technical meaning of "to settle" (i.e., with some of Pompey's veterans).
5. **quaeque:** = *et ea quae.*
6. **imperāverit:** *imperāre* + acc. means "to demand." The pf. subjn. in a subordinate clause in indirect statement represents a fut. pf. indic. (AG 484c).
7. **imperat: mittunt:** the asyndeton expresses the promptness of the response to Caesar's demands. —**legiō xii:** = *legiō duodecima.* This was most likely one of the four legions which had been wintering among the Aedui under the command of Fabius (section 2.14 and n.). —**cōnsequitur:** to reach Caesar at this time, the twelfth legion must have been summoned from Gaul no later than December 21. Obviously Caesar had already considered the possibility of invading Italy at that time.
8. **hīs duābus:** sc. *legiōnibus,* i.e., the twelfth and thirteenth, for by this time the five cohorts commanded by Antonius (section 13.18–19) and the three commanded by Curio (section 14.3–4) would probably have rejoined Caesar. —**Āsculum Pīcēnum:** Asculum was a stongly fortified town in the Apennine mountains and about sixty miles south of Auximum. Asculum was occupied on February 4. For *Pīcēnum,* see n. 1 above.
9. **Lentulus Spinther:** Publius Cornelius Lentulus Spinther, a political ally and close friend of Cicero since at least 63 (see list of per-

sonal names). —**x cohortibus:** the omission of *cum* is common with certain military phrases (AG 413a). Since ten cohorts normally comprise a full legion, the expression here (instead of *ūna legiō*) may mean that these cohorts had belonged to different legions or had been recruited at different times and places. They therefore had not yet been incorporated into a uniform fighting force.

10. **cohortīs:** acc. pl.

12. **Vibullium Rūfum:** Lucius Vibullius Rufus, a messenger and informant for Pompey, praised by Cicero for his courage and energy (*Ad Att.* 8.11B.1).

13. **quō:** connecting relative referring to Lentulus Spinther.

15. **ipsum:** "the commander" (lit., "him himself"). —**dīmittit:** the verb suggests that Lentulus, an ex-consul, was curtly sent away by a man of inferior rank. At this point, Lentulus proceeded to Corfinium. —**quās potest:** sc. *contrahere.*

16. **cohortīs:** acc. pl. —**in hīs:** sc. *cohortibus.*

17. **Camerīnō:** an old town about thirty miles northwest of Asculum. —**Lucilium Hirrum:** C. Lucilius Hirrus, a cousin of Pompey and a partisan of Domitius Ahenobarbus.

18. **quibus:** sc. *cohortibus.* —**xiii:** sc. *cohortīs* (acc. pl.).

19. **Domitium Ahēnobarbum:** see list of personal names and n. 7.14. —**Corfīnium:** located about eighty miles east of Rome on the *Via Valeria*, which led directly to the capital, this *mūnicipium* was a natural stronghold. Corfinium was the chief city of the Paeligni (22). —**magnīs itineribus:** the expression *magnum iter* means "forced march" (i.e., 25–30 miles per day).

21. **per sē:** "by his own efforts." —**Albā:** abl. Alba Fucens was a town of the Aequi on the *Via Valeria* about twenty miles west of Corfinium and about a two days' march from the capital. Rome had planted a colony there in 303. The Marsi, allies of the Paeligni both ethnically and politically, had been friendly to Rome as early as the fourth century.

24.2. **prius . . . quam:** = *priusquam,* "before." The divided word is an example of tmesis (see n. 3.18 on *ante . . . quam*). —**Istim:** "from your direction" (i.e., north, from Cicero's standpoint).

3. **ēmānant:** sc. *mala* as subject. —**bonī:** gen. of the whole with *nihil.*

4. **ad Nōnās Febr.:** "by February 5th." Cicero had actually arrived the day before.

5. **omnīnō nōn:** "not at all." —**vii Īdūs:** = *septimō <diē ante> Īdūs <Febr.>*, i.e. February 7.

6. **Calibus:** loc. case of *Calēs, -ium,* f., "Cales" (a town in the district of Campania a few miles north of Capua, where Cicero had a *dēversōrium* or "lodging").

8. **nihil in cōnsulibus:** sc. *esse.* Translate: "that the consuls are worthless" (lit., "that nothing is in the consuls").

9. **φαινοπροσωπεῖν:** "to show their faces" (pronounced "phaino-prosopein").

10. **ille:** = *Caesar.* —**contrā:** adv.

11. **nōmina dant:** the expression *nōmina dare* means "to enlist."

12. **ō rem:** acc. of exclamation (AG 397d). —**ut tōtus iacet:** "how completely he's lying down on the job!"

14. **Mittam:** "I shall omit." By mentioning the points which he says he will omit, Cicero uses a rhetorical device known as *praeteritiō.*

15. **adversārī:** possessive gen. depending upon *cōpiārum* (16).

16. **hoc cuius modī est?:** "What sort of performance is this?" (lit., "of what sort is this?") —**vii Īdūs Febr.:** see n. 5 above.

17. **C. Cassius:** Gaius Cassius Longinus, a relative of Quintus Cassius Longinus and, like him, a tribune of 49. Gaius is best known as one of Caesar's assassins in 44 (see list of personal names).

18. **sanctiōre aerāriō:** see section 15.2–5 and n. 15.4.

19. **redeant . . . exeant** (20): hortatory subjn. Cicero ridicules the idea that the consuls could safely return to the city which they have already abandoned and then leave it again with state money but without interference.

20. **sinat:** potential subjn. (AG 447.1).

21. **ut:** sc. *venīret* in an indirect command. Lentulus answers Pompey's "instructions" with a suggestion of his own. Unlike Pompey, Lentulus did not know that Picenum had been overrun. Moreover, the fact that no commander for the troops of the legitimate government held supreme command (*imperium māius*) presented a serious obstacle for Pompey—a situation which Caesar exploited without having to deal with similar complications in his own army. —**ipse:** = *Pompēius.* —**illud:** sc. *Pīcēnum.* While Cicero may here be exaggerating, it is probable that, since Asculum lies in the southern sector of Picenum, most of the district had been overrun by February 4. —**erat āmissum . . . sciēbat** (22) **. . . erat** (23): epistolary tenses.

23. **iam iamque:** "at any moment." —**quīn . . . foret** (= *esset*): *quīn* is

used with the subjn. after negated expressions of doubting (AG 558a). See also n. 1.14. —Āpūliā: see n. 15.9.

24. **in nāvī:** Cicero already suspected that Pompey would leave Italy—a tactic with which Cicero would have little sympathy after regarding the abandonment of Rome as *fugam turpissimam* (14).

25. **quid agam:** deliberative subjn. in an indirect question (AG 575b). — **σκέμμα:** "dilemma" (pronounced "skemma"); sc. *est.*

26. **ūllum:** sc. **σκέμμα** *esset* in the apodosis of a mixed contrary-to-fact condition. —**ego:** sc. *sum.*

27. **quid mē deceat:** sc. **σκέμμα** *magnum est* to resume *quid agam* (25) and introduce the indirect question *quid . . . deceat* (SB).

28. **antīquiōrēs . . . quam:** = *antequam* in sense. —**litterae:** sc. *scrīptae sunt.*

29. **ruere:** "to run wild." Cicero uses the verb to describe actions performed with complete disregard for constitutional procedures. —**Dolabella, Caelius:** sc. *dīcunt.*

30. **Mīra mē ἀπορία torquet:** "I am at my wits' end" (lit., "an extraordinary helplessness torments me"). **ἀπορία** is pronounced "aporia."

31. **ista:** "your own affairs." —**quantum:** with *possum* = "to what degree" (i.e., "as much as"). Cicero's request for advice, combined with a sensitivity to his friend's own concerns, appears also in a letter written just three days previously (*Ad Att.* 7.20.2, February 5) in similar language: *Haec velim explicēs et mē iuvēs cōnsiliō, etsī tē ipsum istīc iam calēre putō; sed tamen quantum poteris.* ("I would like you to sort out these things and help me with your advice, although I suppose that you yourself now have your hands full (*calēre*) in Rome (*istīc*). But nevertheless do as much as you can.")

32. **perturbātiōne:** abl. of cause. —**scrībam:** generic subjn. (AG 535).

25.1. **Cn. Magnus:** = *Gnaeus Pompēius Magnus.* —**prōcōs.:** = *prōcōnsul.* —**imp.:** = *imperātōrī.* Here Pompey recognizes Cicero's title *imperātor*, which had been conferred upon him by some troops in Cilicia during his tenure as governor in 51–50. Pompey's use of the title may be intended to show his support of a triumph for Cicero.

2. **Q. Fabius:** this may be Quintus Fabius Vergilianus, who served as *lēgātus* under Appius Claudius Pulcher, Cicero's predecessor in Cilicia. —**a. d. iiii Īdūs Febr.:** for the form (as well as that in line 5 below) see glossary s.v. "Calendar" and n. 6.14.

3. **cohortibus xii:** there is a discrepancy with Caesar's account (sec-

130

tion 23.21), where "about twenty" cohorts are ascribed to Domitius. —**cohortibus xiiii quās Vibullius addūxerit:** on the other hand, Caesar implies (section 23.17–19) that Vibullius had seven cohorts and combined them with six which had been under the command of Hirrus (for a total of thirteen, not fourteen). For Vibullius, see n. 23.12.

5. **v cohortibus:** Caesar thought he had six (see n. 3 above).

6. **Cēnseō:** governs *veniās* without *ut* in an indirect command (AG 565a). Pompey does not *order* Cicero, since both are proconsuls and, without specific authorization from the senate, neither can act as ranking officer. For this lack of a clearly defined chain of command, see n. 24.21. —**Lūceriam:** this large old town on the northern border of Apulia was situated nearly one hundred miles southeast of Corfinium. A road directly east from Capua made Luceria accessible to Pompey. It was now his headquarters.

26.3. **dē rē pūblicā:** i.e., with reference to the military situation, not the political one (SB). —**disiectā manū:** abl. absol.

4. **contractīs nostrīs cōpiīs:** the exact opposite of *disiectā manū* (3) in meaning.

5. **prōdesse:** behind the vagueness of Pompey's language lies a strategy not shared with Domitius: the evacuation of Italy. Perhaps Pompey feared that the *optimātēs* might withdraw their support if such a plan were to be widely circulated.

6. **posse:** the pres. inf. of *possum* often has a fut. meaning (AG 584b). —**cum:** here causal or concessive in sense.

7. **a. d. v Īd. Febr.:** for the form of the date see glossary s.v. "Calendar."

8. **fuerit . . . mūtārīs (9):** subjn. in an indirect question. —**quā rē:** this expression is much more common than *cur* for introducing indirect questions.

9. **mūtārīs:** syncopated form of *mūtāverīs*.

10. **propterea . . . quod:** = *quod.* —**audierīs:** pf. subjn. in a subordinate clause in an indirect statement (AG 580). *audierīs* is an alternate form for *audīverīs*.

11. **Firmō:** Firmum was situated near the coast about twenty-five miles southeast of Auximum and about one hundred miles north of Corfinium. —**Castrum Truentīnum:** a coastal town about twenty-five miles south of Firmum. From here Caesar had an almost direct route to Rome from the northeast along the *Via Salāria* and access to points south along the coast. Since Domitius

could not determine which direction Caesar would take, he held his position at Corfinium, as Pompey acknowledges to Domitius in a letter (*Ad Att.* 8.12C.1) of February 16: *scrībis tibi in animō esse observāre Caesarem, et, sī secundum mare ad mē īre coepisset, cōnfestim in Samnium ad mē ventūrum, sīn autem ille circum istaec loca commorārētur, tē eī, sī propius accessisset, resistere velle.* ("You write that you intend to keep an eye on Caesar, and, if he should begin to advance toward me along the seacoast, that you will at once join me in Samnium. But if he should linger in your vicinity, you say that you want to oppose him if he should draw nearer").

12. **Quantō ... māgis ... eō ... celerius** (13): "the more ... the more quickly." The abl. *quantō* and *eō* express degree of difference (AG 414a).

13. **ut ... coniungerēs:** purpose. —**priusquam ... posset** (15): here the subjn. in a temporal clause implies purpose (AG 551b).

16. **etiam atque etiam:** "over and over again." —**rogō et hortor:** Pompey addresses Domitius as an equal (cf. the salutation of the letter).

18. **prīmō quōque diē:** "on the earliest possible day" (AG 313b). —**advenīrēs:** although the subjn. is governed by *rogō et hortor* (16), the secondary sequence is the result of the parenthetical *dēstitī* (17). —**antequam ... distrahant** (20): rarely is the pres. subjn. found in temporal clauses with *antequam* and *priusquam* (AG 551c). —**cōpiae:** in addition to his own legions from Gaul and the deserting Pompeian forces, Caesar has been recruiting additional troops on the way down through northern Italy.

19. **coāctae:** translate as though this participle were parallel to *distrahant* (20).

20. **impediant:** generic subjn. (AG 535).

21. **servent:** mindful of the dictatorship of Sulla, these local landowners might well fear not only the depradations of Caesar's soldiers but also the confiscation of their property, for by such means a victorious commander could reward his veterans or enrich himself, as Crassus once did while serving under Sulla. —**ut ... faciās** (23): subst. clause of result (AG 568). —**cohortīs:** acc. direct object of *faciās* (23).

22. **Camerīnō:** see n. 23.17. —**fortūnās:** "property."

23. **missum faciās:** the expression *missum facere* means "to release," "to let go." Instead of *missum*, Pompey might have written *missās* to agree with *cohortīs* (21) or perhaps *missōs* (i.e., the soldiers in the

cohorts). Consequently, some scholars have criticized Pompey's Latinity, but others construe *missum* here as indeclinable.

27.1. **Receptō Firmō:** Caesar's narrative resumes from section 23, where he described the occupation of Picenum, and, in particular, of Asculum, which had been held by Lentulus Spinther. For Firmum, see n. 26.11. —**expulsōque Lentulō:** see section 23.8–11.

2. **ūnum diem:** February 4.

3. **ibi:** Asculum, from which Lentulus had been routed. —**Corfinium contendit:** Caesar does not describe his line of march from the area of Asculum through rugged, mountainous terrain for a distance of about eighty-five miles.

4. **Eō cum vēnisset:** i.e., a point just north of the town, on about February 14.

5. **flūminis:** i.e., the Aternus. —**interrumpēbant:** "were trying to tear down," a conative impf. (AG 471c).

7. **Domitiānī:** "the men of Domitius" (cf. *mīlitēs Attiānōs,* section 14.25–26).

9. **castra posuit:** i.e., on the east side of Corfinium.

10. **perītōs regiōnum:** such volunteers were needed to evade Caesar's scouts and outposts. Their destination was Luceria.

12. **sibi:** = *Domitiō.* —**duōbus exercitibus:** i.e., his own at Corfinium, Alba, and Sulmo as well as Pompey's at Luceria.

13. **locōrum angustiīs:** "narrow pass" (lit., "the narrowness of the places"). Between Amiternum and Corfinium stretches a road flanked by high ground as it approaches the river. Perhaps Domitius envisioned a pincer movement on this site.

14. **fēcerit:** this pf. subjn. in an indirect statement represents a fut. pf. indic. (AG 484c).

15. **amplius xxx:** sc. *cohortīs.* The total was probably thirty-one. For *amplius* without *quam* see AG 407c and n.

17. **partīs:** "function" (with this meaning *pars* is usually plural). —**ad custōdiam urbis:** = *ad custōdiendam urbem.*

19. **possessiōnibus:** Domitius had profited from Sulla's confiscations of land; as Caesar mentions elsewhere (*Bellum Cīvīle* 1.34.2), he was wealthy enough to furnish manpower for seven transport ships. The extent of Domitius's land holdings suggests why he, and others of similar status, would vehemently oppose any agrarian law. —**xl:** = *quadrāgēna,* a distributive numeral (AG 136–7a) here amounting to about twenty-five acres, but since that number

seems excessively large for individual grants of land, some scholars prefer the reading *quaterna*. —**in singulōs:** "to each man" (another distributive). —**prō ratā parte:** "in due proportion" (AG 221.19a). Since most centurions received one-and-one-half times the pay of the ordinary soldier (some senior officers received double pay), and *ēvocātī* (see n. 4.5) were also paid at a somewhat higher rate, these men might expect to receive a correspondingly greater share of acres as a bonus.

28.1. **Sulmōnensēs:** Caesar uses the name of the people to refer to the town itself. Sulmo was situated on the *Via Minucia*, which offered a way of retreat southward to the district of Apulia, where Luceria lies. The poet Ovid was born in Sulmo in 43. —**quod oppidum:** for the construction see n. 23.4. —**ā Corfīniō:** see n. 13.18 on *ab Arīminō*.

2. **mīlium:** sc. *passuum*. The gen. is one of measurement after *intervallō*, an abl. of degree of difference (AG 414). —**vellet:** generic subjn. (AG 535).

3. **Q. Lucrētiō:** Quintus Lucretius Vespillo later served as Pompey's naval commander and became consul under Augustus in 19. —**Attiō Paelignō:** "Attius the Pelignian." Caesar distinguishes him from Attius Varus, who had held Auximum (section 14.10–12).

4. **tenēbant:** indicative here, even though subordinate to an indirect statement, because the relative clause is furnished as an explanation by the writer (AG 583).

5. **xiii:** = *tertiae decimae*.

8. **sē dēiēcērunt:** i.e., to escape, not to commit suicide.

12. **incolumem:** this is one of the first instances of Caesar's clemency toward the republicans, a policy which Caesar later publicizes to develop more propaganda for his cause, and which Cicero would describe as *insidiōsa clēmentia* (*Ad Att.* 8.16.2).

13. **prīmīs diēbus:** i.e., beginning with February 14.

15. **Eō trīduō:** abl. of time within which (AG 423.1); i.e., February 15–17. —**viii:** = *octāva*. It is uncertain whether this was another of Fabius's legions or one of those under the command of Trebonius, originally stationed among the Belgians (see section 2.12–14).

16. **cohortēsque . . . xxii** (= *vīgintī duae*): sc. *vēnērunt* here as well as with *equitēs*. With the addition of these twenty-two cohorts and the seven cohorts collected at Sulmo, plus the soldiers who joined him at Auximum and Asculum, Caesar now has a total force of

about six legions. —**Galliae:** i.e., Cisalpine Gaul, where Caesar was popular.

17. **Nōricō:** "of Noricum." Located north of Cisalpine Gaul between the Alps and the Danube, Noricum was not conquered until 13. It had been a Roman custom to use foreign cavalry as support for the legions. Caesar deployed Gallic squadrons throughout his campaigns in their native land. —**ccc:** = *trēcentī*, agreeing with *equitēs* (16).

19. **vallō castellīsque:** in 1879 a trapezoidal ditch over 427 feet long, 8.5 feet wide, and 4 feet deep was found outside the town walls. It has been identifed as part of Caesar's siege lines.

21. **ad Pompēium:** to be taken with *missī* (sc. ā Domitiō), which refers to the volunteers sent by Domitius to Pompey (section 27. 10–12).

29.2. **Litterae:** for Caesar's reference to the contents of this letter, see section 27.10–16. —**redditae sunt:** from *reddere*, "to deliver." — **a. d. xiii Kal. Mārtiās:** see glossary s.v. "Calendar."

4. **Quod:** = *id quod* (AG 397d and n.), "a thing which" (direct object of *putāvī* and *praemonuī*). —**ut . . . velit et . . . implicet** (5): the subst. clause of result serves as the subject of *fit* (AG 569.1). The subject of both verbs is Caesar. —**in praesentiā:** "for now"; "for the present."

7. **hīs legiōnibus:** these two legions Caesar had sent in compliance with a decree of the senate (section 2.1–9). In addition, Pompey requested from Domitius the cohorts recruited from Picenum and Camerinum (section 26.21–23) to reinforce them. Evidently Pompey had more confidence in the recruits than in the veteran legions supplied by Caesar.

8. **voluntāte:** "attitude." The same meaning is found in line 9 below. —**Quō:** connecting relative (abl. of cause).

9. **voluntāte:** abl. with *cōnfīdō*, "trust in" (AG 431).

10. **ut . . . dīmicem** (11): result clause.

11. **etiam:** = *adhūc* (SB). —**cōnsulibus:** "for the consuls" (dat. of advantage, AG 376).

13. **dā operam:** "see to it."

14. **ut . . . explicēs:** subst. clause of result (AG 568). —**hōc:** = *hūc* (here and in line 16 below). —**veniās:** depends upon *dā operam* (13), which here governs the subjn. without *ut* (AG 563 and 565a). —**antequam . . . conveniant** (15): rarely is the pres. subjn. found in temporal clauses with *antequam* and *priusquam* (AG 551c). Here Pompey is expressing his fears that additional legions from Gaul

may catch up to Caesar before Domitius can escape and join Pompey in Luceria. —**adversārium:** gen. pl. (AG 49d).

16. **sī convenīrent:** impf. subjn. in the protasis of a mixed contrary to fact condition.

17. **quantum . . . praeterit** (18): construe as though the Latin read: *nōn tē praeterit quantum contrā veterānās legiōnēs committendum sit iīs quī inter sē nē nōtī quidem sunt. quantum* refers to how little the recruits could be trusted (cf. the facetious reproach, "That shows how much you know!") *nōn tē praeterit* may be translated, "you cannot fail to see" (lit., "it does not go past you").

30.1. **Litterīs:** this dispatch may be the letter of section 29. — **dissimulāns:** i.e., concealing the actual contents of the letter. — **cōnsiliō:** "meeting."

2. **subsidiō:** dat. of purpose (AG 382), like *ūsuī* (3).

3. **quaeque:** = *et ea quae* (cf. n. 23.5).

4. **sint:** generic subjn. (AG 535). —**parent:** sc. introductory *ut*, suggested by the preceding *nē* (3). —**arcānō:** a rare adv., found only here in Caesar's writings.

5. **cōnsiliumque fugae:** i.e., for himself and a few chosen comrades. Caesar's pejorative *fugae* may be a distortion of Domitius's actual intent to appeal in person to Pompey for help. Domitius had been a political adversary of both Caesar and Pompey for so long that neither could be impartial in dealing with him. —**cum:** causal conj. governing four verbs. *cōnsentīret* (6), *ageret* (7), *colloquerētur* (9), and *fugeret* (10).

8. **cōnsuēsset:** syncopated form of *cōnsuēvisset* and subjn. in a comparative clause (GL 298, n. 2).

10. **rēs:** i.e., Pompey's actual reply.

11. **rem:** i.e., Pompey's tactical position, for he did not want to narrow the distance between himself and Caesar.

12. **neque:** negates *cōnsiliō* and *voluntāte*, not *contulisse* (13). — **cōnsiliō aut voluntāte:** abl. of accordance (AG 418 and n.). By publishing his correspondence with Domitius and the consuls, Pompey may have sought to absolve himself of all responsibility for the situation at Corfinium.

13. **qua:** = *aliqua* after *sī, nisi, nē,* and *num* (AG 310a). —**fuisset:** for the subjn. see n. 13.6.

14. **venīret:** hortatory subjn. (secondary sequence) in an indirect statement (AG 588). —**nē:** used instead of *ut nōn* to introduce a subst. clause of result (AG 569) because of the prevention implied by the

abl. of cause *obsidiōne* (15) and *circummunitiōne* (AG 558b). This final sentence of the paragraph represents an editorial comment by Caesar, not a part of Pompey's reply to Domitius.

17. **prīmō vesperī:** "early in the evening." —**sēcessiōnem:** i.e., a mutiny. —**ita:** modifies *colloquuntur* (19). —**inter sē:** regularly used to express a reciprocal relationship (AG 145c and 301f). —**per:** "through (the agency of)."

18. **honestissimōs suī generis:** i.e., common soldiers, not officers.

20. **cuius:** objective gen. after the causal abl. *spē atque fīduciā,* an example of hendiadys. Translate: "because of their hopeful confidence in whom."

21. **omnibus:** masculine.

22. **ratiōnem habēre:** "to take account of."

23. **Marsī:** these troops had been recruited primarily from Alba (see n. 23.21 on *Albā*).

24. **vidērētur:** subjn. because it reflects the thinking of the Marsi, not Caesar (AG 592.3).

25. **manum cōnserere:** "to join in close combat."

27. **dē . . . fugā:** explains *quae ignōrābant.*

28. **ūnō cōnsiliō:** i.e., with a single purpose.

30. **sēsē parātōs esse:** sc. *dīcunt.* Compare this entire episode, in which Domitius is said to have deceived his troops and fallen victim to a mutiny, with Caesar's description of his own soldiers' behavior at Ravenna (section 9.22–26).

31.1. **cōss.:** = *cōnsulibus.*

3. **ūtilīs:** acc. pl.

4. **litterās:** for the reference see section 26. —**utī . . . venīret** (5): sc. *hortātus* to govern the indirect command here and also with *ut . . . mitteret* (5–6). See n. 1.9 on *ut . . . trādant.*

5. **dubitāret:** subjn. in a clause within an indirect command (AG 592.1).

6. **iter habēbant:** Pompey implies here that these cohorts were detained by Domitius while marching to Apulia. As if to emphasize that he expected to have them, he describes them as *meās* below (8). —**quod:** = *id quod,* "what" (lit., "that which"; AG 307d and n.).

7. **ut:** introduces a subst. result clause (AG 569.1) containing three parallel verbs: *implicārētur* (7), *esset* (8), *posset* (11).

9. **habēret:** subjn. to represent the excuse of Domitius rather than the justification of Pompey himself (AG 540.2).

10. **Sulmōne:** loc. case with the alternative ending *-e* (AG 80). — **conlocāvit:** sc. *cohortīs* as direct object.
11. **vellet:** subjn. by attraction (AG 593).
12. **scītōte:** fut. imperative second person pl., regularly used with *sciō* (AG 449a).
13. **subsidiō:** dat. of purpose (AG 382).
14. **quod hīs duābus legiōnibus nōn putō esse committendum ut illūc dūcantur:** "because I don't think that these two legions should be trusted to march there" (lit., "because I don't think that it should be entrusted to these two legions that they be led there"). *esse committendum* is impers. The subst. clause of result *ut . . . dūcantur* (15) serves as its subject (see n. 7 above). These are the legions referred to in n. 29.7.
15. **illūc:** i.e., Corfinium. —**nōn amplius . . . potuī** (16): Pompey seems unaware of the irony of situation here. After pointing out to the consuls that Domitius could not resist Caesar at Corfinium because he had deployed his forces in three different locations, Pompey explained his own failure to help Domitius because he also had divided his troops.
16. **Brundisium:** the major port of embarkation from Italy to Greece and the best harbor on the eastern seaboard. —**praesidium:** i.e., two cohorts (see section 32.63).
17. **Canusium:** a *mūnicipium* strategically located on the road from Luceria to Brundisium. Pompey was protecting his line of retreat with a garrison there.
19. **D. Laeliō:** Decimus Laelius, a long-standing friend of Pompey's family. —**mandāram:** syncopated plupf. = *mandāveram*. These instructions were sent no later than February 15. By this time, Domitius was already under siege. —**quod . . . habitūrōs** (20): an implied criticism of Domitius.
20. **ut:** introduces an indirect command after *mandāram* (19), containing five parallel verbs: *venīret* (21), *proficīscerētur* (23), *adiungerētur* (23), *cōgerentur* (24), and *trānsportārentur* (25). —**sī vōbīs vidērētur:** with this expression Pompey addresses the consuls as equals but refrains from asking for their advice. For the subjn. see n. 5 above on *dubitāret*. —**alter uter:** "one or the other."
21. **circum Capuam:** i.e., the district of Campania, within which Cicero and the consuls had been mustering troops. Despite Cicero's complaints about the recruiting (section 24.7–11), the volunteers from Campania substantially reinforced Pompey at Brundisium.

138

22. **comparāstis:** syncopated pf. = *comparāvistis.* —**Faustus:** see n. 7.8.

23. **Domitius ... eōdem adiungerētur:** here Pompey writes as though Domitius were expected to proceed to Sicily instead of joining him in Brundisium.

25. **Dyrrachium:** this major Adriatic port for embarkation to Italy had for more than a century functioned as a Roman army base. This first official notice by Pompey that Italy was to be abandoned had for some time been anticipated by Cicero (see section 24.24). Domitius, on the other hand, was not informed of Pompey's plans even when he was being urged to abandon Corfinium. —**cum:** causal in sense.

27. **nōn est nōbīs committendum ut:** "we must not run the risk that" (lit., "it must not be brought about by us that"). Cf. the idiom in n. 14 above.

28. **animō:** abl. of description.

29. **hostis:** the singular refers to Caesar, who is elsewhere referred to as an *adversārius* (see, e.g., section 29.15). The word *hostis* was normally reserved for individuals designated by the state as national enemies.

30. **placitum est mihi:** "I decided" (literally, "it was pleasing to me"). The verb is here used in a depon. sense.

31. **M. Mārcellō ... cēterīs:** dat. of agent. For Marcellus, see n. 3.17. —**nostrī ōrdinis:** i.e., members of the senate. —**hīc:** i.e., in Luceria.

32. **Vōs hortor ut ... eōdem Brundisium veniātis** (34): Pompey seems to have changed his plans. In view of Domitius's predicament, he now proposed that *both* consuls consolidate their forces at Brundisium. Sicily is evidently no longer a factor.

33. **quodcumque mīlitum:** "whatever soldiers" (*mīlitum* is gen. of the whole).

34. **Arma:** this form, attracted into the case of the relative *quae,* would normally have been abl. of means, as is the pron. *īs* (= *eīs*) which resumes it.

35. **armētis:** subjn. without *ut* in an indirect command introduced by *cēnseō* (AG 565a).

36. **Quae arma ... ea:** construe as though the Latin read: *ea arma quae.* —**superābunt:** from *superāre,* "to be left over."

37. **dēportāritis:** syncopated form (= *dēportāveritis*) in the protasis of a fut. more vivid condition. The fut. pf. *prōfueritis* is in the apodosis (AG 516c n.).

38. **velim . . . faciātis:** *velim* is a potential subjn. (AG 447.1) followed by the subjn. *faciātis* without the introductory *ut* (AG 449c and 565). —**P. Lupum:** Publius Rutilius Lupus, one of the praetors, was stationed at Tarracina with three cohorts who soon deserted him.

39. **C. Copōnium:** Gaius Coponius, another of the praetors and a supporter of Pompey. —**mīsī:** sc. *litterās* as direct object. The expression introduces an indirect command (*ut . . . coniungerent et . . . dēdūcerent*).

40. **mīlitum quod:** = *quodcumque mīlitum* (for the gen. see. n. 33 above). —**habērent:** subjn. in a clause within an indirect command (AG 592.1).

32.5. **quod:** = *id quod* (AG 307d and n.), "a thing which" (direct object of *factūrum esse*). —**suspicor:** cf. section 24.24 and n.

6. **agendum:** sc. *esse*. —**putēs:** subjn. in an indirect question implied by *dēlīberātiō* (4).

7. **in utramque partem:** "on both sides." —**mihi:** dat. of reference used instead of *meam* (AG 377). This dat. often replaces a possessive gen. or, as here, a pronominal adj.

9. **Cum . . . tum** (10): "Not only . . . but also" (correlatives, usually used with the indic., AG 323g and 549b). —**merita:** for an explanation of these, see below, n. 17 and 32.

11. **addūcit:** has three subjects—*merita* (9), *familiāritās* (9), and *causa* (10). The verb agrees with the nearest subject. When it means "convince" (as here), it introduces an indirect command (*ut . . . videātur*). —**mihi . . . coniungenda esse videātur** (12): "apparently ought to be coordinated" (lit., "seems to me to have to be coordinated").

13. **Accēdit illud:** "The following (*illud*) is an additional factor." For this use of *illud*, see AG 297e. —**optimōrum et clārissimōrum cīvium:** i.e., the *optimātēs* or, as Cicero often designates them, the *bonī* (see n. 21.10). Elsewhere, in periods of disillusionment, Cicero often defines the *optimātēs* or *bonī* in less complimentary fashion. Cf. *Ad Att.* 8.1.3: *videō bonōrum, id est lautōrum et locuplētum, urbem refertam fore . . .* ("I see that the city will be packed with 'good' men, that is, the stylish and the rich.")

14. **cadendum est:** sc. *mihi* as dat. of agent. —**ūnīus:** = *Caesaris*.

15. **multīs rēbus:** "in many ways" (abl. of specification, AG 418).

16. **ut esset:** sc. *amīcus* as predicate nom. The subjn. is in a subst. clause of result which serves as the subject of *est . . . prōvīsum* (AG

140

569.1). —**ā mē est . . . prōvīsum** (17): the pass. equivalent of *ego prōvīdī*. —**tūte:** *-te* is enclitic (like *-que*) and emphasizes the pronoun. Since it does not depend upon anything in the sentence, the expression *tūte scīs* is parenthetical.

17. **multō ante prōvīsum:** shortly after Cicero was recalled from exile back to Rome (September 57), largely because of Pompey's influence, he resumed his efforts to revive a political harmony of moderate senators, businessmen (*equitēs*), and others who were loyal to either group. To achieve this union (*concordia ōrdinum*) Cicero hoped to conciliate Pompey while dissolving the "triumvirate" and rallying under Pompey's leadership all supporters of constitutional government. When, however, Pompey accepted the invitation of Caesar and Crassus to renew their pact in April 56 at Luca, Cicero's hopes were crushed. As an important public figure, moreover, he was forced to cooperate with the triumvirs by defending in the courts some of their protégés (among them Balbus, Vatinius, and Gabinius), by supporting the extension of Caesar's command in Gaul with a speech (*Dē Prōvinciīs Cōnsulāribus*) before the senate in which he lavished praises upon Caesar's achievements, and in general by serving as a spokesman for the political maneuvers of the "triumvirs." This period of personal compromise was the unhappiest of Cicero's political career; his disillusionment, frustration, and embarrassment made him a reluctant participant in public life for several years. Hardly more comforting was the fact that, in 49, Cicero was still indebted to Caesar, who had lent him money to restore a house in Rome and two villas which had been destroyed by political enemies during his exile.

18. **utrumque:** "each of two points." —**fidēs eī sit habenda:** *fidem habēre* (+ dat.) means "to trust." The dat. is retained in the pass. The subjn. is in an indirect question.

19. **explōrātum sit:** impers. The verb, attracted into the subjn. (AG 593) by *sit habenda* (18), introduces an indirect statement. —**amīcum:** here an adj. —**sitne virī fortis et bonī cīvis:** "whether it is the mark of a brave man and a loyal citizen." The enclitic *-ne*, "whether," introduces an indirect question. *virī* and *cīvis* are predicate gen. (AG 343c).

20. **cum:** concessive in sense.

21. **honōribus imperiīsque:** among these would be included all the magistracies (*honōrēs*) held by Cicero within the *cursus honōrum*, especially the consulship, and his proconsulship in Cilicia. —**rēs:** here Cicero refers especially to his suppression of the Catilinarian

conspiracy in 63, when he was consul, and possibly to the recognition (*salūtātiō imperātōria*) afforded him by his troops while he
governed Cilicia. —**sacerdōtiō:** in 53 Cicero had been elected to
the college of augurs to replace Crassus, who as proconsul in
Syria, had been killed in a battle with the Parthians. As one of
sixteen *augurēs,* Cicero was responsible for determining, by observation of natural phenomena, whether the gods approved or disapproved of a proposed course of action by the state.

22. **nōn futūrus <sit quī fuerit>:** "he is not going to be the sort of
man he was." *futūrus sit* is subjn. by attraction and the predicate of
the relative clause introduced by *in quā* (20). The subjn. *fuerit* is
generic (AG 535).

23. **forte:** = *fortāsse,* but the reading is highly suspect.

24. **reciperārit:** syncopated pf. subjn. (= *reciperāverit*) representing a
pres. subjn. in the protasis of a fut. less vivid condition (AG 516c).
—**In hāc parte haec sunt:** "On this side are these arguments."
haec (n. pl.) refers to what precedes (AG 297e). With these words,
Cicero concludes the arguments for joining Pompey.

26. **in alterā:** sc. *parte.* Cicero now prepares to list the arguments for
remaining in Italy with Caesar.

27. **addō etiam nihil:** sc. *āctum esse.*

28. **illa vetera:** Cicero actually refers to Pompey's errors of judgment
as *peccāta* in section 18.17.

29. **quod:** "the fact that" (AG 572 and n.). This word introduces a
series of arguments that were to be passed over without comment:
omittō illa vetera (28). The whole sentence represents another example of *praeteritiō* (see n. 24.14). —**istum:** = *Caesarem.* The
pronoun expresses contempt. —**ille:** = *Pompēius.* —**aluit, auxit,
armāvit:** asyndeton (i.e., omission of conj.) is combined with
alliteration and homoioteleuton (end-rhyme). —**ille lēgibus . . .
ferendīs auctor** (30): "that man supported the passing of laws"
(lit., "that man was a supporter for passing laws"). The dat. of the
gerund and gerundive is used in certain technical phrases (AG
505b) to indicate the function of a noun (sc. *fuit* here and in all
subsequent clauses which begin with *ille*). The *lēgēs* mentioned
here include the agrarian measure which provided land grants for
Pompey's veterans (see n. 9.5). That measure was accompanied by
violence against the opposing tribunes (*per vim*) and enacted despite the unfavorable omens (*contrā auspicia*) announced by Bibulus, who had been Caesar's consular colleague in 59. As an augur

since 53, Cicero could well profess horror at this flagrant disregard of the state religion. See also n. 15.12 on *lēge Iūliā*.

31. **Galliae ulteriōris adiūnctor:** "the one who added Transalpine Gaul" (lit., "the joiner of further Gaul"). Cicero means that Pompey persuaded the senate to add Transalpine Gaul to Caesar's provincial command in Cisalpine Gaul, which had been secured by the legislation of Vatinius (*lēx Vatīnia*), a tribune in Caesar's service in 59. The latter procedure circumvented the senate, which oversaw the distribution of provinces (see n. 9.25). —**ille gener:** sc. *Caesaris* (see n. 5.14). —**ille in adoptandō P. Clōdiō augur:** as an augur Pompey had officiated at the ceremony in which Publius Clodius Pulcher, a bitter enemy of Cicero, formally abandoned his patrician status and became a plebeian in order to stand for the tribunate. Upon election to that office, Clodius passed legislation which forced Cicero into exile in March 58.

32. **ille restituendī meī quam retinendī studiōsior:** "he was more eager to restore me than to hold me back (from exile)." Here the gerundives modify the pron. *meī*, which is an objective gen. after *studiōsior*. Although Cicero acknowledges that Pompey was instrumental in his recall (see n. 17 above), Cicero cannot forget that Pompey had first betrayed him by doing nothing to prevent his exile.

33. **ille prōvinciae propāgātor:** "he was the one who extended (Caesar's) provincial command" (lit., "he was the extender of the province"). See note 5.2 (on the *lēx Pompēia Licinia* sponsored jointly by Pompey and Crassus in 55) and n. 17 above (on Cicero's support of that legislation). —**absentis:** sc. *Caesaris.* —**in omnibus:** sc. *rēbus.*

34. **īdem etiam:** with these words Cicero criticizes the inconsistency of Pompey, who, after Julia's death in 54, began to align himself with the *optimātēs* (e.g., by marrying the daughter of Scipio during his third consulship) despite his continued efforts to protect the interests of Caesar with such actions as his support of the law of the ten tribunes. —**tertiō cōnsulātū:** in 52, as *cōnsul sine collēgā* until August, when he shared the office with Scipio, his new father-in-law. Pompey's two previous consulships had been served with Crassus in 70 and 55 (see n. 5.9).

35. **contendit:** from *contendere*, "to demand." —**decem tribūnī plēbis:** see n. 5.2.

36. **ferrent:** from *ferre*, here meaning "to propose (a bill)," with the

implication that the bill became a law. —**absentis ratiō**: "(his) candidacy in (his) absence." —**quod**: = *id quod* (AG 307d and n.), "a thing which." —**sanxit**: from *sancīre*, "to ratify."

37. **lēge**: Cicero means that, by this provision, Caesar was exempted from compliance with the *lēx Pompēia dē iūre magistrātuum* of 52, which reiterated the general policy that politicians announce their candidacy for office in person in Rome (see n. 7.13). —**quādam**: suggests Cicero's doubt about the validity of the *lēx* (SB 153.3) — **Mārcōque Mārcellō cōnsulī**: dat. with *restitit* (38). Marcus Marcellus, brother of Gaius, was consul in 51 (see list of personal names). —**fīnientī prōvinciās Galliās**: "when he was trying to terminate Caesar's command in Gaul" (lit., "ending the Gallic provinces"). In the winter of 51, the consul Marcellus was making every effort to relieve Caesar of his proconsulship.

38. **Kalendārum Mārtiārum diē restitit**: in a meeting of the senate on March 1, 51, Pompey opposed Marcellus so effectively that the question of Caesar's tenure was deferred until June 1. Subsequently, at the suggestion of Pompey's father-in-law Scipio, March 1, 50 was reserved for that question only. At that time, Pompey no longer objected to the replacement of Caesar, who would then have to surrender his army and depend upon Pompey for further political advancement, particularly support in the consular elections. This arrangement would allow Pompey to retain his army in Spain and thus establish an advantage which Caesar wanted to prevent at all costs. —**ut haec omittam**: resumes *Omittō illa vetera* (28) and marks the conclusion of Cicero's list of grievances.

39. **quid foedius, quid perturbātius**: sc. *est* with each of these clauses. —**perturbātius**: "more disorganized."

41. **relinquenda patria**: "having to abandon Rome" (lit., "the fatherland to be abandoned"). See n. 17.10.

42. **sed num quid**: sc. *est*. —**hōc**: abl. of comparison. The word refers to the act of abandoning the *patria*.

43. **quid ad eam spem est parātī**: "what preparations have been made to justify this hope?" (lit., "what preparation is for this hope?") *parātī* is a partitive gen. depending on *quid*.

44. **āmissus . . . patēfactum . . . trādita** (46): sc. *est* with each partic. —**ager Pīcēnus**: see n. 14.11. Cicero implies that this district, with which Pompey's family had strong ties, should not have been abandoned.

45. **pecūnia . . . pūblica**: see sections 15.2–5 and 24.18–19.

47. **quō concurrant quī rem pūblicam dēfensam velint:** "where the kind of people who want the state defended may gather." *concurrant* is subjn. in a relative clause of purpose. *velint* is a generic subjn. (AG 535).

48. **inānissima:** reserved largely for pasture land maintained by slaves and therefore very sparsely populated by free-born Italians, Apulia would make a poor recruiting ground.

49. **fuga et maritīma opportūnitās:** "flight afforded by easy access to the sea" (lit., "flight and the convenience of the sea"). The expression is an example of hendiadys (see n. 1.19).

51. **rem:** acc. of exclamation (AG 397d).

52. **nē . . . existimārīs:** prohibitions (negative commands) are often expressed by *nē* with the pf. subjn. (AG 450), here syncopated.

53. **partem:** for the meaning, see n. 24 above.

54. **quod:** = *id quod* (AG 307d and n.), "a thing which."

55. **rēs . . . haec:** "the latter argument" (*illa*, therefore, means "the former argument").

56. **ut . . . dēlīberantī, ita mihi:** "as to one pondering, so to me." Both indirect objects are governed by *dēs*. —**aequō animō:** "patiently" (lit., "with calm mind," an abl. of manner).

57. **velim:** potential subjn. (AG 447.1) governing the subjn. *dēs* (56) without the introductory *ut* (AG 449c and 565). —**Cāiētā:** i.e., the harbor of Caieta, located a few miles south of Formiae.

59. **ecce nūntiī . . . ecce litterae** (60): sc. *adsunt.* —**Calēnō:** "the lodging at Cales" (see n. 24.6).

60. **Caesarem:** sc. *adesse* with this subject acc. as well as with *Domitium.*

61. **etiam hoc . . . commissūrum** <esse> **ut** (62): "will go so far as to" (lit., "will bring even this about, that"). *hoc* is direct object of the inf.

62. **ut . . . relinquat:** subst. clause of result (AG 568). —**etsī:** construe with both *praemīserat* (63) and *scrīpserat* (65). For the strategy see section 31.19–25.

63. **Scipiōnem:** see list of personal names.

64. **Faustō:** see n. 7.8. —**sibi placēre:** "(that) he had decided" (lit., "[that] it was pleasing to him"). —**ā cōnsule:** "by *a* consul" (i.e., either Marcellus or Lentulus).

65. **Domitium:** object of *dēserere* (66); sc. *Pompēium* as subject acc.

67. **mihi:** "in my opinion" (dat. of reference, AG 378). —**Āfrānium:** see n. 3.22.

68. **Trebōniō:** see section 2.13 and n.—**Fabium:** see section 2.14 and n.

69. **summa:** sc. *spēs est.* All the hopes mentioned by Cicero turned out to be fruitless.

70. **Id sī est:** sc. *ita.* —**manēbitur:** impers.; sc. *ā nōbīs.*

71. **esset . . . putābātur (72) . . . mīsī (72) . . . revertī (73):** epistolary tenses (see n. 1.30). —**ad Capuam . . . ad Lūceriam (72):** for the meaning with prep., see n. 13.18 on *ab Arīminō.* Since both Capua and Luceria were republican strongholds, Caesar could not expect cooperation from the townspeople, as at Iguvium, Auximum, and Sulmo.

72. **itūrus:** sc. *esse.* This fut. inf. depends upon *putābātur.* —**Leptam:** Quintus Lepta had been a staff officer (*praefectus fabrum*) for Cicero during his proconsulship in Cilicia and remained a friend thereafter. See n. 38.12 on *praefectus fabrum.*

73. **nē quō inciderem:** "in order not to meet up with some obstacle" (i.e., Caesar). As usual, *quō* replaces *aliquō* after *nē.*

75. **proximē:** "recently" (i.e., in Cicero's previous letter to Atticus).

33.1. **Quibus rēbus cognitīs:** refers to the offer (mentioned in section 30.27–32) of the garrison at Corfinium to surrender the town and their commander Domitius to Caesar. —**magnī:** genitive of value (AG 355 n. 2) with *interesse.*

3. **qua:** = *aliqua,* agreeing with *commūtātiō* (4).

5. **quod parvīs mōmentīs magnī cāsūs intercēderent:** "because from insignificant disturbances great events developed." The subjn. may be attracted (AG 593) to *fieret* (4), or it may indicate that Caesar, as writer, is attributing this generalization—a rarity in his works—to himself in his role as commander (AG 540).

6. **veritus nē . . . oppidum dīriperētur (7):** Caesar's concern that his soldiers do nothing to antagonize the townspeople can be compared with an incident of the American Civil War. Preparing to invade Maryland, General Lee issued, on September 9, 1862, Special Order No. 191, which stipulated that "all officers and men of this army are strictly prohibited from visiting Fredericktown except on business, in which case they will bear evidence of this in writing from division commanders." —**nocturnī temporis:** "provided by the night time." *temporis,* like *mīlitum* (6), is a subjective gen. (AG 343 n. 1).

10. **nōn certīs spatiīs intermissīs:** "not leaving fixed intervals" (lit., "fixed intervals not having been placed between").

12. **ut contingant . . . atque . . . expleant (13):** result clause.

13. **praefectōs:** i.e., cavalry officers (unlike *tribūnī*, who commanded infantry).

14. **hortātur:** governs *caveant* and *asservent* (15) in an indirect command without *ut* (AG 565a). —**singulōrum hominum:** by ensuring that no one escaped from Corfinium during the night, Caesar afforded himself an opportunity to demonstrate his clemency on a large scale and win the indebtedness of several prominent Romans for his *beneficium*. Furthermore, the news that Caesar was not vindictive would spread rapidly to other forces of the legitimate government and encourage them to abandon the cause, since they would have nothing to fear in doing so but risked their lives if they offered resistance.

16. **animō:** abl. of description (AG 415).

17. **conquiēverit:** subjn. in a relative clause of result (AG 537.2 and n. 1). —**summae rērum:** i.e., the outcome of events. —**alius in aliam partem mente atque animō trāherētur, quid . . . accideret** (20): "everyone's thoughts and feelings raced in different directions, as they wondered what would happen. . . ." (lit., "one was dragged by his mind and heart in one direction, another in another, [pondering] what would happen. . . ."). *quid . . . accideret* is an indirect question with an introductory verb such as *reputāns* understood; likewise *quī . . . exciperent* (20). This psychological analysis, unusual in Caesar's narrative, marks the climax of an operation which succeeded far beyond his expectations.

20. **quōsque:** the plural is used to refer to the three groups (citizens, troops under siege, and besiegers) waiting to see what fate would overtake them.

34.1. **Quartā vigiliā:** the Romans divided their night watches into four approximately equal periods from sunset to sunrise. At this time of the year, the *quarta vigilia* extended from about 4 A.M. to about 7:30 A.M. —**Lentulus Spinther:** see list of personal names and section 23.9.

2. **velle:** sc. *sē* (i.e., Lentulus Spinther) as subject acc. —**sī . . . fiat:** subjn. in a subordinate clause in indirect statement (AG 580).

3. **convenīre:** "to meet."

4. **mittitur:** i.e., he was escorted by a detachment of Domitius' men. —**prius . . . quam . . . dēdūcātur** (5): the subjn. with *priusquam* denotes purpose (AG 551b and n. 2). *prius . . . quam* is another example of tmesis (see n. 3.18 on *ante . . . quam*).

7. **sē:** acc.
8. **quod:** "the fact that." —**per:** "through (the agency of)." —**eum:** = *Caesarem.* Caesar had been elected chief priest (*pontifex maximus*) in 63. —**collēgium pontificum:** this "board of priests" consisted, in Cicero's time, of fifteen members, whose original responsibility was to assist the chief magistrate as he discharged his religious functions. The *pontificēs* ascertained that all state ceremonies were performed at the proper time and place according to the proper ritual. They also controlled the state calendar, which restricted the days on which magistrates could convoke the people. Since this calendar occasionally required the insertion of extra days to bring the Roman lunar year (355 days) into harmony with the sun, the *pontificēs* could lengthen or shorten the magisterial year to suit their own political interests. Of Caesar's support for Lentulus's candidacy nothing is known, but his use of the indic. *vēnerat* (9), *habuerat* (9), and *erat sublevātus* (10) subtly implies that Caesar is himself attesting to the list of *beneficia* extended to Lentulus.
9. **ex praetūrā:** "immediately after his praetorship" (AG 221.11c). Lentulus, who was praetor in 60, took over from Caesar as governor of *Hispānia citerior* in the following year. This appointment he might have owed to Caesar's influence.
10. **in petitiōne cōnsulātūs:** Lentulus had campaigned successfully in 58 for the consulship of 57, when he was instrumental in the recall of Cicero from exile. *cōnsulātūs* is an objective gen. (AG 347–8).
11. **nōn maleficī causā . . . sed utī . . . dēfenderet** (12): the two different expressions of purpose balance each other.
12. **ēgressum:** sc. *esse.* —**utī . . . ut . . . ut** (14): the omission of connectives between these purpose clauses provides an example of asyndeton.
13. **in eā rē:** i.e., their attempts to protect Caesar's interests in Rome by using their power of veto. —**suam:** here used to refer to *tribūnōs*, not to the subject. Similarly, in line 17 *suam* refers to *reliquīs*.
14. **factiōne:** the expression *factiō paucōrum* was a term of opprobrium usually employed by the political enemies of the self-styled *optimātēs* to describe them.
15. **in lībertātem vindicāret:** a legal phrase referring to an action by which one restores to freedom an enslaved individual or country. In the American Civil War, General Lee issued a proclamation to the people of Maryland on September 8, 1862, which included the following remarks: "the people of the South have long

wished . . . to enable you again to enjoy the inalienable rights of freedom, and restore independence and sovereignty to your State. In obedience to this wish, our army has come among you, and is prepared to assist with the power of its arms in regaining the rights of which you have been despoiled."

16. **liceat:** sc. *sibi.*

17. **quod:** "the fact that." The clause *quod . . . impetrāverit* is the subject of *fore* (= *futūrum esse*). *impetrāverit* is pf. subjn. in a subordinate clause in indirect statement and represents a fut. pf. indic. (AG 484c). With *fore,* as with *esse perterritōs* (18), sc. *dīcit* to control these indirect statements. —**reliquīs . . . sōlāciō** (18): double dat. —**ad:** "for (the fulfillment of)."

18. **suae vītae dūrius cōnsulere:** "to commit suicide" (lit., "to look out for their own lives too harshly").

35.1. **Cn. Magnus . . . imp.:** for the salutation see n. 25.1.

2. **s. v. b. e.:** = *sī valēs, bene est.* So common was this type of greeting in Roman correspondence that it could routinely be abbreviated. —**Tuās litterās:** Cicero had written a reply to Pompey's initial request (section 25) that Cicero join him in Luceria. In that reply (*Ad Att.* 8.11B.3), Cicero had expressed uncertainty about whether Pompey wanted to hold the west coast, which would require a commander, or to concentrate his forces in southern Italy. Hence Cicero had hesitated to leave the vicinity of Capua.

3. **pristinam:** the flattering adj. implies that Cicero's *virtūs* had already existed for a considerable time. Perhaps Pompey is ingratiatingly recalling Cicero's consulship. —**etiam:** "yet again."

4. **exercitum:** see n. 29.7. —**vēnērunt:** as Pompey had finally requested after changing his plans (cf. n. 31.32). —**magnō opere:** = *magnopere.*

5. **prō:** "in view of."

7. **Cēnseō:** governs *faciās* (8) and *veniās* (8) without *ut* in an indirect command (AG 565a). —**viā Appiā:** begun by Appius Claudius Caecus, censor in 312, this famous old road stretched from Rome southward to Capua and, by 244, southeastward from there to Brundisium. By the time of the Gracchi, it had been paved. This route would enable Cicero to escape detection by Caesar's forces.

36.2. **amīcō nostrō:** dat. of reference (AG 377). —**ut . . . subveniat** (3): subst. clause of result (see n. 7.17), explaining *ūnum.* Cicero's bitter disappointment and frustration can be clearly seen here.

3. **quīn . . . ventūrus sit:** *quīn* is used with the subjn. after negated verbs of doubting (AG 558a). —**subsidiō:** dat. of purpose (AG 382.2).

4. **tālem cīvem:** Cicero, who was not particularly fond of Domitius, realized nevertheless his standing among the prominent *optimātēs* in the state.

5. **eōs <quōs> ūnā sci<t e>sse:** for their names, see section 37.3–5. —**cum . . . praesertim:** "and that, too (*praesertim*), although." —**xx . . . cohortīs:** i.e., the two legions requested from Caesar and commanded by Appius (see n. 2.19 and n. 20.23). See also Pompey's assessment of his forces in section 31.12–18. —**ipse:** = *Pompēius.*

7. **Cui:** connecting relative, dat. of reference (AG 377).

8. **vērō:** "certainly" (as also in lines 11 and 12 below). —**fugiam . . . sequar** (9): generic subjn. (AG 535).

9. **Quod:** = *id quod* (AG 307d and n.), "a thing which" (direct object of *laudās* and *dīcis*).

10. **quod:** = *id quod,* "as" (lit., "that which", AG 307d and n.). —**dīxerim:** subjn. in a subordinate clause in indirect statement (AG 580). In a letter to Atticus written in October of 50 (*Ad Att.* 7.1.4), Cicero had remarked: *sī enim castrīs rēs gerētur, videō cum alterō vincī satius esse quam cum alterō vincere* ("For if the matter is to be decided on the battlefield, I see that it is better to be defeated with the one than to be victorious with the other.")

12. **cum hōc:** sc. *vincī* as a complementary inf. to be construed with *māluī* (14).

13. **ante . . . quam:** tmesis (see n. 3.18 on the same word).

14. **patriam:** see n. 17.10.

15. **Quod superest:** "As for the rest" (lit., "as for that which remains"). The antecedent of the nom. *quod* is an understood *id,* which is to be construed as an adverbial acc. (acc. of respect); cf. *quod sī,* "but if" (lit., "as to which if"; AG 397a). —**ista:** "those actions" (i.e., of Caesar). —**vidēre:** "to face."

16. **istum:** = *Caesarem.*

17. **mihi . . . carendum est:** "I must be deprived of." The impers. gerundive, used with a dat. of personal agent (*mihi*), retains the abl. (*meīs, mēmet ipsō*) normally found with the verb *careō* (GL 217 and Remark 1). —**meīs:** n. pl. (= "my status"). —**mēmet ipsō:** "my very identity." The suffix *-met* on the personal pronoun adds intensive force and emphasis. Cicero here bemoans the loss

150

of what he had accomplished and of the standing he held in the republic before the civil war broke out. Cf. the sentiment in section 32.20–23.

37.1. **lūxit:** this daybreak refers to the morning of February 21. Here the narrative resumes Caesar's description of the events at Corfinium.

3. **Erant quinque senātōriī ōrdinis:** Caesar lists them in the order of their seniority.

4. **L. Caecilius Rūfus:** he had supported Cicero in 63 as tribune and in 57 as praetor. He was now siding with Pompey. —**Sex. Quintilius Varus:** one of the quaestors of 49.

5. **L. Rubrius:** mentioned only here in the sources. —**praetereā:** sc. *erant.*

6. **decuriōnum:** "of senators" (see n. 14.13).

9. **quod:** "the fact that." —**relāta nōn sit:** if the text is sound, the subjn. is used to attribute the words to Caesar the *general* (as opposed to Caesar the *author;* but see GL 525.1 n. 7). —**ā parte eōrum:** "on their part" (lit., "from their side.") Here *ab* denotes not an agent, but rather the direction from which the gratitude comes.

10. **dīmittit omnīs incolumīs:** Caesar's pardon is so accommodating that he does not even require an oath of loyalty, which he will demand of the rank and file at once (lines 15–16). According to several of Cicero's letters (e.g., section 41.7–10), this merciful act by Caesar won him many friends throughout Italy. It must also have provided great relief to those who were dreading a repetition of the bloodbath during the dictatorship of Sulla. Every one of these pardoned senators would leave Corfinium only to fight Caesar again.

11. **HS⎡lx⎤:** the symbol *HS* represents a *sestertius,* which is a shortened form of *sēmis tertius* and means lit., "the third (unit is a) half." This expression refers to the fact that a *sestertius* consists of two and one-half *assēs* (AG 633–34). The lines on either side of and above the number indicate "hundred-thousands"; therefore *HS* ⎡*lx*⎤ equals 6,000,000 *sestertiī* (60 × 100,000). This sum would have been enough to furnish a year's base pay for more than 6,600 legionary soldiers. (The annual pay for that number of American soldiers today would require well over 50 million dollars!) The Latin figure should be read as follows: *sestertiōrum sexāgiēs centēna mīlia.* In Caesar's narrative, the amount is the direct object of

reddit (12). In a letter to Atticus (*Ad Att.* 8.14.3) dated March 2, however, Cicero reports hearsay to the effect that the money was *not* returned to Domitius. —**in pūblicō:** sc. *aerāriō*.

12. **iiiivirīs:** these were the chief magistrates of Corfinium. A board of four magistrates (each called a *quattorvir* or *quattervir* in local inscriptions) represented the government of a typical *mūnicipium*.

13. **in:** "in the case of" (AG 221.12.2).

15. **in stipendium:** "for pay" (i.e., for the soldiers).

16. **iūstum . . . iter:** "an ordinary day's march." Caesar must have left Corfinium well after daybreak, and yet his men evidently managed a full day's march (about twenty miles) with a late start, since ordinarily his army would have broken camp at dawn and departed at once. Caesar was obviously hurrying to overtake Pompey. —**vii . . . diēs** (17): the dates were February 15 through 21. In a letter to Atticus (*Ad Att.* 8.14.1), Cicero explicitly mentions Caesar's date of departure.

17. **Marrūcīnōrum, Frentānōrum, Lārīnātium:** the *Marrūcīnī* inhabited a seacoast area south of the river Aternus. The *Frentānī* were located on their southern border. The *Lārīnātēs* occupied the northern boundary of Apulia. All these tribes had by now received Roman citizenship.

18. **Āpūliam:** see n. 15.9.

38.2. **Lūceriā proficīscitur:** since Pompey was in Canusium (see n. 31.17) on February 20 (see section 35), he must have left Luceria no later than early on the 19th, two days before Caesar's departure from Corfinium. Pompey could not, therefore, have left Luceria in reaction to the surrender of Corfinium, as Caesar implies (*hīs rēbus cognitīs,* line 1). To avoid the risk of opposing Caesar with men whose loyalty and capabilities he criticized (see section 31.27–29) seems to have been Pompey's sole concern while marching to Brundisium, the principal Italian port for embarkation to the east. Luceria, a major stronghold in northern Apulia, had been Pompey's headquarters for several weeks. Canusium, about ten miles from the seacoast, was a *mūnicipium* located some fifty miles south of Luceria. Pompey departed from Canusium on February 21 (*Ad Att.* 8.14.1). He arrived in Brundisium, about one hundred miles to the southeast, on February 25 (*Ad Att.* 9.10.8).

3. **Cōpiās . . . iubet:** for Pompey's suggestion that the forces be con-

solidated at Brundisium, see section 31.32–34. At this time, the only regular troops under Pompey's command consisted of two legions taken from Caesar. Of the twenty cohorts in these two legions, fourteen had encamped at Luceria (section 31.16), and the remaining six had either been sent to Brundisium or stationed at Canusium (section 31.16–18).

4. **servōs:** this may have been a standard political slur intended to evoke memories of infamous public enemies and revolutionaries of an earlier day, such as the legendary Spartacus (73) or Catiline (63), whom Cicero labelled a "recruiter of slaves" (*In Catilīnam* 1.27), although we have no evidence to support that accusation. The arming of slaves would represent the last resort of an extremely desperate man (see n. 15.16). —**eīs equōs attribuit:** i.e., Pompey is converting them into cavalrymen.

5. **L. Manlius:** Lucius Manlius Torquatus, a personal friend of Cicero and apparently one of the praetors of 49, although Cicero (*Ad Att.* 8.11B.1) names him without the title. The marriage celebrated in an *epithalamium* ("bridal song") by the lyric poet Catullus (poem 61) may have been his. —**Albā:** see n. 23.21.

6. **Rutilius Lupus:** see n. 31.38. —**Tarracīnā:** an old coastal town on the *Via Appia*, about sixty-five miles south of Rome.

7. **quae:** i.e., *cohortēs.*

8. **Vibius Curius:** mentioned only here in the ancient sources. —**signa . . . trānsferunt** (9): i.e., they transferred their allegiance.

9. **reliquīs itineribus:** "on subsequent marches."

10. **nōnnūllae:** = *aliae.*

11. **ex itinere:** = *in itinere.* —**N. Magius:** Numerius Magius was probably sent out from Brundisium by Pompey to survey the area. At this point, Caesar was approaching the town from the north.

12. **Cremōnā:** abl. of source (AG 403a n. 2). This town, located on the north bank of the Po River, would soon become famous as the place where the epic poet Vergil was educated. —**praefectus fabrum:** "staff officer." The term *praefectus fabrum*, which had originally designated the commander of a separate unit of engineers (*fabrī;* gen. pl. *fabrum*), was retained in later Republican times to designate a staff officer or aide-de-camp.

13. **fuerit . . . sit ventūrus** (14): subjn. in a subordinate clause in indirect statement (AG 580). Caesar mentions his imminent arrival in Brundisium in a casual, almost matter-of-fact way, as if he were arriving there for some other reason than a confrontation

with Pompey. This statement, characteristic of Caesar's "objective" style, creates an impression of distance and impartiality on the part of the narrator. —**ad id tempus:** "up to this time."

15. **interesse:** sc. *dīcit* to control the indirect statement implied by *mandātīs* (13).

16. **idem:** correlative with *ac* (17). Words expressing likeness or similarity are regularly followed by *atque* or *ac,* "as" (AG 384 n. 2). — **longō itineris spatiō:** abl. absol. —**cum:** introduces a causal clause.

18. **disceptētur:** impers. pass. (AG 208d) subjn. in a conditional clause of comparison (AG 524 and n. 2).

39.1. **Balbus:** L. Cornelius Balbus (see list of personal names).

2. **suscipe cūram et cōgitātiōnem:** "give careful consideration" (lit., "take up care and thought"), an example of hendiadys (see n. 1.19 on *bellum et castra*).

3. **virtūtis:** "character" (here the gen. is used instead of the more common abl. with *dignus*). —**ut . . . redūcās** (4): the clause explains *cūram et cōgitātiōnem*. The subjn. is in a subst. clause of result (AG 570; GL 557). —**perfidiā hominum:** here Balbus echoes Caesar's remarks to his soldiers at Ravenna (section 9.2–5), where the *optimātēs,* not Pompey himself, are blamed for the split between Caesar and Pompey. Also, when Caesar assesses the motives of his opponents (section 5.11–18), Pompey is described as being prodded by Caesar's enemies.

5. **in tuā potestāte:** "in your debt."

7. **hōc:** = *hūc.* —**tē rēicis:** the expression *sē rēicere* means "to devote oneself." The colloquial use of the present tense occurs despite a fut. (*iūdicātūram,* line 6) in the protasis of the condition (AG 516a n. and 468). —**velim:** potential subjn. (AG 447.1) followed by the subjn. *faciat* without the introductory *ut* (AG 449c and 565).

8. **māgis optō quam spērō:** *optō,* suggesting a hope for some highly unlikely or practically impossible turn of events, is contrasted with *spērō,* anticipating what remains feasible or what one can expect as being possible.

9. **cōnstiterit . . . dēsierit:** fut. pf. to express a fut. action before another future action where English often uses the pres. tense. *cōnsistere* here means "to be in control" (i.e., of oneself).

12. **Quod:** "as to the fact that" (acc. of specification, AG 572a). — **meum:** "my friend." The adjective here may refer to Balbus's

personal relationship to Lentulus, who had perhaps granted him Roman citizenship and whose *praenōmen* and *nōmen*, Lucius Cornelius, he may therefore have assumed. The family name, at least, probably refers to the patronage of the *gēns Cornēlia*, which had close ties with the Spanish Gades, Balbus's native town, since about the year 200.

13. **Caesarī grātum . . . fēcistī:** the expression *grātum facere alicui* means "to do someone a favor." —**medius fidius:** "so help me God" (= *mē dius Fidius*). The expression *dius Fidius,* possibly a title of Jupiter, was commonly used in oaths.

14. **tantī:** gen. of value (AG 417). —**faciō:** with a gen. of value *facere* means "to value," "to esteem." —**sī passus esset . . . et . . . āvertisset (16) . . . essem** (17): a mixed contrary to fact condition (AG 517).

15. **nōs:** an example of the "editorial 'we' " (AG 143a).

16. **etiam atque etiam:** "over and over again."

17. **cavē putēs:** = *nōlī putāre* (for the construction see n. 21.46). —**mē:** abl. of comparison.

19. **Quod sī:** "but if " (AG 397a).

22. **auctōre tē, illō relātōre:** abl. absol. (*illō* refers to Lentulus).

23. **Quod:** connecting relative.

26. **quō modō in eius modī rē:** "under the present circumstances" (lit., "as [it is] in a situation of this kind"). —**potuit:** impers.

27. **ut . . . cōnfieret:** subst. clause of result with *ut* following *quam* after the comparative *commodius* (AG 571a). Occasionally *fiō* is used in compounds to form the passive voice (AG 204a–c).

28. **Balbī:** this nephew of the writer of the letter was undertaking a diplomatic mission for Caesar. The words *quaeque Caesar scrīpsit* may mean that the younger Balbus had actually delivered to Cicero a letter from Caesar.

30. **rē:** "by his actions." —**probābit:** governs *scrīpsisse* (31); the subject is Caesar. —**quaecumque fortūna eius fuerit:** Balbus probably means that Caesar will pursue a policy of clemency despite any obstacles thrust into his path by the *optimātēs;* that is, he will not be vindictive even if it should become easy (and justifiable) to treat his opposition in such a manner. —**fuerit:** fut. pf. indic.

31. **scrīpsisse:** sc. *sē* as subject acc.

40.2. **vīs:** i.e., force of character.

3. **illīus virī:** the guardian of the state, analogous to the philosopher-king in Plato's *Republic.* —**nostrīs librīs:** i.e., Cicero's work *Dē Rē*

Pūblicā (see n. 17.6). —**ut tibi quidem vidēmur:** "as you think, at least" (lit., "as we seem to you, at least").

4. **Tenēsne:** sc. *memoriā* (abl.). The idiom *memoriā tenēre* means "to remember." Construe as though the Latin read: *Tenēsne igitur quō velimus moderātōrem illum reī pūblicae referre omnia?*

5. **quō:** "to which (standard)"; *quō* is here a relative adv. —**velimus:** subjn. in an indirect question (AG 574).

6. **Scipiō:** P. Cornelius Scipio Aemilianus, the son of L. Aemilius Paullus, who defeated Perseus in the Third Macedonian War (168). He was also the adopted son of the P. Cornelius Scipio whose father had defeated Hannibal. This Scipio Aemilianus, a central figure in three of Cicero's philosophical works (*Dē Rē Pūblicā, Dē Senectūte,* and *Dē Amīcitiā*), had become celebrated as a man of culture, political distinction, and military excellence. As a man of culture, he fostered an interest in Greek literature and philosophy. As a statesman, he was elected consul in 147 by special legislation because at that time he was still under the legal minimum age. As a soldier, he achieved success (149 and 148) in the Third Punic War against the Carthaginians, whose city he destroyed in 146. For all these reasons, Cicero idealized him as a model statesman. —**cursus . . . salūs** (7) **. . . victōria** (7): like *vīta* (8), these are all subjects of *prōposita est* (8), which agrees with the nearest of them.

8. **ut . . . sit** (9): purpose clause (sc. *vīta* as subject). —**opibus . . . cōpiīs** (9) **. . . glōriā . . . virtūte:** abl. of specification.

11. **cum . . . tum** (12): "not only . . . but also" (AG 323g).

13. **āctum:** sc. *est.*

14. **ille:** = *Pompēius.* —**quod . . . posset nec . . . quod . . . pellerētur** (15): the subjn. is used in a causal clause with *quod,* when the reason is attributed to someone other than the writer (AG 540.2).

15. **eā:** abl. of place from which. —**ā prīmō:** Cicero seems to have changed his mind. Having formerly criticized Pompey's failure to plan and to act (section 16. 7–8 and 24.12–16), he now regards Pompey's behavior as evidence of a master plan, formed from the very beginning (*ā prīmō*), to evacuate Italy in order to return, like Sulla, with an invading force.

16. **movēre:** i.e., to throw into turmoil.

18. **rēgnī:** such a regime would be expected to conduct a thorough purge of its enemies, like the dreaded proscriptions of Sulla. —**iam prīdem:** used with the pres. tense to denote an action begun

in the past but continuing into the present. The verb should be translated as a pres. pf. (AG 466).

19. **multīs ... cupientibus:** abl. absol. —**nihil:** subject acc. of *convenīre* (20).

20. **convenīre:** the impers. *convenit* means "it is agreed"; the inf. depends upon *potuisse.*

21. **σκοπός:** "aim" (nom.; modified by *ille* and pronounced "skopos"). —**ut ... sīmus:** subjn. in a subst. clause of result (AG 570; GL 557). —**uterque rēgnāre vult:** Cicero reveals his psychological insight into the motives of contemporary Roman politicians. As he would have each of them say: *Sulla potuit, ego nōn poterō?* (*Ad Att.* 9.10.2), i.e., "Sulla could; why can't I?"

41.2. **Lippitūdinis:** gen. of *lippitūdō,* "inflammation of the eyes." In other letters, Cicero complains of this chronic ailment. —**sit:** hortatory subjn. (AG 439 and n. 2). —**manus:** i.e., handwriting. *manus* is the subject of the clause, and *signum* is a predicate nom.

3. **eadem:** predicate adj. —**causa:** sc. *sit.* —**etsī:** "and yet" (here introducing a main clause).

4. **erat:** both occurrences of this verb are epistolary tenses.

5. **nactus ... esset:** epistolary plupf. Occasionally, the verb in the protasis of a future less vivid condition appears in the pf. subjn. (instead of the pres. subjn.) when the action expressed is regarded as completed before the action of the protasis begins (AG 516c); here, however, the plupf., as an epistolary tense, has replaced the pf. —**spēs:** sc. *erat,* another epistolary tense, here and with *metus* (7).

6. **ante:** adv. —**trāmīsisset:** i.e., to Greece (for the tense see n. 5 above).

7. **quem:** = *quālem.* —**hominem:** = *Caesarem.*

8. **quam:** "how."

9. **cuiquam:** dat. of separation (AG 381). Cicero is thinking especially of Caesar's behavior at Corfinium (section 37.7–10 and n. 37.10).

11. **mūnicipālēs ... rusticānī** (12): "townspeople" ... "country people."

12. **nihil prorsus aliud:** "nothing else at all."

13. **vīllulās ... nummulōs:** "(their) little farmsteads, (their) meager incomes." The diminutives express Cicero's contempt for those who, preoccupied with their own fortunes, have not responded patriotically to the cause of the republic. Cf. Pompey's comment

to Domitius: *erunt quī tē impediant ut vīllās suās servent* (section 26.20–21).

14. **quō:** the abl. with *cōnfīdēbant* replaces the usual dat. (AG 431).

15. **quantīs ... peccātīs vitiīsque:** abl. of cause. —**ēvēnerit:** subjn. in an indirect question (AG 574). Cicero probably refers to Pompey's precipitous flight from Rome. Elsewhere he mentions rumors of proscriptions if the *optimātēs* recover control of Italy (see, e.g., section 40.18 and n.). Moreover, in *Ad Att.* 8.16.2, Cicero describes the townspeople thus: *huius īnsidiōsā clēmentiā dēlectantur, illīus īrācundiam formīdant* ("they are pleased with this man's deceitful mercy, they dread that man's wrath").

16. **Quae ... putārem** (17): indirect question (AG 574). —**impendēre:** for Cicero's dire predictions, see section 40.15–19.

17. **scrīpseram ... exspectābam:** epistolary tenses.

42.1. **Oppiō, Cornēliō:** both these men were agents of Caesar. C. Oppius was a Roman *eques* with whom Cicero was on friendly terms. Some think (Suetonius, *Dīvus Iūlius* 56.1) that he wrote the historical account of Caesar's war in Egypt in 48–47 (*Bellum Alexandrīnum*). For Cornelius Balbus, see section 39 and list of personal names.

3. **probētis:** subjn. in an indirect question (AG 574). —**ea quae ... sunt gesta:** a reference to Caesar's policy of *clēmentia*.

4. **hōc:** abl. of cause.

5. **ut ... praebērem:** subst. clause of result (AG 568).

6. **ut ... reconciliārem:** indirect command (AG 563e). —**sī:** "(to see) if." —**possīmus:** subjn. in an indirect question (AG 576a).

8. **reliquī:** Caesar refers to leaders such as Marius and Sulla, who resorted to proscriptions and confiscations after attaining victory in civil wars.

9. **diutius:** "for any period of time." —**quem imitātūrus nōn sum:** aware of the fact that, like Sulla, he was marching against the legitimate government at the head of an army, Caesar here repudiates any further comparison between himself and the dictator by renouncing Sulla's punitive policies, which the *optimātēs* were alleged to be adopting.

10. **ratiō:** Caesar's policy of clemency gave him several advantages: (1) a moral position and cause superior to that of his opponents; (2) propaganda that would win adherents from the class of *nōbilēs*, for whom the label *ingrātī* would be especially abhorrent; (3) a reversal of public opinion (encouraged, if not initiated, by the

optimātēs), which had represented Caesar as a traitor to his *patria* (see section 18.11–12) and as another Sulla. No wonder that Cicero suspiciously regarded the policy as *insidiōsa clēmentia*! (see n. 41.15). —**ut . . . mūniāmus** (11): an appropriate military metaphor; the subjn. is in a subst. clause of result (AG 570; GL 557) in apposition to *haec . . . ratiō* (10).

11. **nōs:** reflexive pron.
12. **possit:** for the subjn. see n. 3 above. —**mī:** = *mihi* (dat. of reference, AG 376–77).
13. **Dē hīs rēbus:** the phrase is best construed as part of the clause *ut . . . suscipiātis* (the subjn. is in an indirect command, AG 563).
14. **N. Magium:** see section 38.11–12 and n.
15. **missum fēcī:** "I released" (for the idiom see n. 26.23). —**duo praefectī fabrum:** the other one, L. Vibullius Rufus, had been captured at Corfinium, as Caesar himself attests (section 52.1–3).
18. **ut mālit:** the same construction as *ut . . . suscipiātis* in n. 13 above. —**iīs:** = *eīs.* Among these Caesar would include Cato, Scipio, Domitius, the Marcelli, and Lentulus Crus (see Caesar's grievance in section 5.11–15).
20. **ut . . . pervenīret:** for the subjn. see n. 5 above.

43.1. **Caesar imp.:** unlike Pompey, Caesar does not refer to himself as *prōcōs*. Caesar's choice of titles thus puts him on an equal footing with Cicero.
2. **Cum:** concessive in sense, as indicated by *tamen* (4). The conj. governs *vīdissem, potuissem* (3), *properārem* (3), and *essem* (3). — **Furnium:** see n. 22.6.
3. **meō commodō:** abl. of specification (AG 418a).
5. **quīn . . . scrīberem . . . mitterem . . . agerem:** the subjn. is introduced by *quīn* after negated verbs of refusing, hindering, neglecting, etc. (AG 558).
6. **mihi factūrus videor:** "I think I shall do" (lit., "I seem to myself to be about to do"). —**ita dē mē mereris:** Caesar may here be expressing appreciation for Cicero's neutrality now as well as for his previous support of the "triumvirate" after Luca (see n. 32.17).
7. **in prīmīs:** "above all."
8. **ut . . . videam:** indirect command (AG 563). —**ut . . . possim** (9): purpose clause. —**tuō cōnsiliō, grātiā, dignitāte, ope omnium rērum:** so intently did Cicero ponder the meaning of Caesar's words that, on March 19, he showed the letter to his friend Matius. Whereas Cicero suspected (*Ad Att.* 9.9.3) that Caesar was referring

to plans to hold the upcoming consular elections without the supervision of the current consuls, an unlawful and unprecedented procedure, Matius offered (*Ad Att.* 9.11.2) another interpretation: *[Matius] respondit sē nōn dubitāre quīn et opem et grātiam meam ille ad pācificātiōnem quaereret* ("Matius replied that he did not doubt that he [Caesar] was asking for both my cooperation and my influence with regard to a peaceful solution").

44.1. **Hīs datīs mandātīs:** the narrative here resumes from section 38, where Caesar describes his efforts to arrange a conference with the retreating Pompey by means of the instructions given to Numerius Magius (section 38.12–18). —**Brundisium . . . pervēnit** (2): i.e., on March 9, as we know from a letter of Caesar to Oppius (*Ad Att.* 9.13A.1): *a. d. vii Īd. Mārt. Brundisium vēnī; ad mūrum castra posuī. Pompēius est Brundisī.* —**cum legiōnibus vi:** see n. 28.16.

2. **veterānīs iii:** the thirteenth (section 2.10), twelfth (section 23.7), and eighth (section 28.15) legions. Together these represent about thirty cohorts. —**ex novō dīlectū:** see sections 13.19–20, 27.2, and 28.16.

3. **in itinere complēverat:** in addition to an undertermined number of deserters from Attius Varus (section 14.22–23) and from Lentulus (section 27.1–2), Caesar had gained seven cohorts from Lucretius and Attius (section 28.4 and 10–11), about thirty from Domitius (sections 27.15 and 33.2–3), six from Manlius, and three from Rutilius Lupus (section 38.5–9). Even allowing for the dismissal of some of these soldiers, by a conservative estimate Caesar commanded at least nine legions in Italy, of which three would now be sent to Sicily.

4. **ā Corfīniō:** "from the vicinity of Corfinium" (for the expression see n. 13.18 on *ab Arīminō*). —**in Siciliam:** this province was now in the charge of Cato (*Ad Att.* 10.16.3), who was about to embark for Dyrrachium in Greece.

5. **cōnsulēs Dyrrachium profectōs:** they had set out with thirty cohorts about March 4. The Greek seaport of Dyrrachium served as a major port of embarkation for points west. By controlling Dyrrachium as well as Brundisium, Pompey could secure the entire Adriatic and direct the war from these two extreme points.

7. **obtinendīne . . . an** (10): the suffix *-ne,* "whether," introduces a double indirect question (AG 331n. and 335).

8. **quō facilius . . . habēret** (9): purpose clause (see n. 8.21). —**ex**

ultimīs . . . Graeciae (9): by holding the extreme points of Brundisium in southeastern Italy and Dyrrachium directly across the sea (in northwestern Greece), Pompey could control access to the Adriatic Sea and the east coast of Italy.

10. **ex utrāque parte:** "on both sides."

11. **restitisset:** from *restāre*, not *resistere*. —**veritus . . . īnstituit** (13): aware that Pompey might choose to stand and fight rather than abandon Italy, Caesar began operations to deny him efficient use of the harbor. The resulting blockade would force Pompey to retreat as soon as possible without awaiting reinforcements, or seal off Pompey's retreat if he should delay his departure in the hope of making a stand in Italy with additional troops. As Caesar himself wrote on March 14 in a letter quoted by Cicero (*Ad Att.* 9.14.1): *ab utrōque portūs cornū mōlēs iacimus, ut aut illum quam prīmum trāicere quod habet Brundisī cōpiārum cōgāmus aut exitū prohibeāmus* ("We are building piers on either end of the harbor either to force him [Pompey] to take across whatever troops he has as soon as possible or to prevent his escape"). —**nē . . . nōn existimāret** (12): clause of fearing (AG 564). —**dīmittendam:** sc. *esse*, as with *dīmittendās* (15) below.

12. **exitūs administrātiōnēsque . . . impedīre** (13): "to block the way out and hinder the operation."

14. **haec:** i.e., the operations to blockade Brundisium. These included the construction of piers at the narrowest points of the harbor, where the water was shallow. In the deeper water, he lashed together large rafts anchored at each corner. Each raft was screened for protection, and every fourth one fitted with a tower. Against this tactic Pompey commandeered some merchant ships, rigged towers on them, and rammed Caesar's line of rafts.

16. **quem . . . remittī** (17): on or after February 25, Magius had been sent to Pompey in Brundisium (section 38.12–13) and later had returned to Caesar, according to a letter from Cornelius Balbus to Cicero, which quotes Caesar as reporting that he reached Brundisium on March 9 and encamped there (see n. 1 above on *Brundisium . . . pervēnit*). Caesar is further quoted as follows: *[Pompēius] mīsit ad mē N. Magium dē pāce. Quae vīsa sunt respondī* (*Ad Att.* 9.13A.1). This seems to imply that Caesar had sent Numerius back to Pompey with a *second* message, containing "what seemed fitting." The *second* message, whatever its contents, must have offered Pompey no encouragement, since he did not pursue the matter.

17. **rēs:** i.e., the negotiations. —**etsī:** introduces the clause *ea rēs . . . tardābat* (18).
18. **omnibus rēbus:** "in every way" (abl. of specification, AG 418). — **in eō:** "in this course."
19. **perserverandum:** sc. *esse* and *sibi* (dat. of agent). —**Canīnium Rebilum:** he had served as a *lēgātus* under Caesar in Gaul. Later Caesar appointed him to the consulship on December 31, 45 for the rest of that day to fill the gap created by the death of the consul Q. Fabius Maximus. See section 54 for Cicero's reactions to this maneuver.
20. **Scrībōnī Libōnis:** an ardent Pompeian and commander of a division of the Adriatic fleet after the retreat to Brundisium. His sister Scribonia was to become the third wife of Octavian. —**eum:** = *Libōnem.*
21. **mandat ut . . . hortētur:** the primary sequence of this indirect command may be compared with the secondary sequence of *ut . . . colloquerētur postulat* (22); for the sequence, see n. 2.1.
22. **in prīmīs:** "above all." —**ipse:** = *Caesar.*
23. **sit . . . facta** (24): this pf. subjn. in a subordinate clause in indirect statement represents a fut. pf. indic. (AG 484c).
24. **fore ut aequīs condiciōnibus ab armīs discēdātur:** "that they would lay down their arms under fair terms" (lit., "that in accordance with fair terms it might be departed from arms"). For the construction, see n. 12.24. *discēdātur* is impers. Cf. the idiom in section 12.19–20.
25. **cuius reī:** "for this accomplishment" (objective gen. depending upon *laudis atque existimātiōnis*). *cuius* is a connecting relative.
26. **illō auctōre atque agente:** "with his support and initiative" (abl. absol.).
27. **sit discessum:** for the subjn. see n. 23 above.
28. **post:** = *posteā.*
29. **sine illīs nōn posse agī dē compositiōne:** this obstacle had been anticipated by Cicero (section 18.12–13). *agī:* the impers. idiom *agitur dē* (+ abl.) means "it is a question of." See also line 31 below. —**saepius:** "too often." —**rem:** for the meaning here see n. 17 above.
31. **dē bellō agendum:** sc. *esse.* Caesar implies that, until now, he had not been contemplating war. Thus his decision at this point is presented as a last resort after many frustrating and unsuccessful attempts to negotiate.
32. **operis:** i.e., the task of placing and connecting rafts for the blockade

across the harbor channel, which measured about three hundred and fifty yards across. —**diēbusque . . . viiii** (33): i.e., March 9 to March 17, when Caesar finally entered Brundisium. On that same day Pompey made his escape (see below, section 46.2–5).

35. **operibus Caesaris:** see lines 11–13 and n. 11 above.

38. **Hīs parātīs rēbus:** to slow Caesar's advance into Brundisium and the harbor beyond it, Pompey had barricaded the gates and streets, dug trenches across the main thoroughfares and in the trenches planted sharpened stakes, which he had then camouflaged. —**iubet:** i.e., by March 15.

39. **Brundisīnī . . . favēbant** (40): for this typical response, see sections 14.2–3, 14.15–17, and 28.5–8. For an observation by Cicero to the same effect, see sections 40.15–19 and 41.14–15. —**mīlitum . . . atque ipsīus Pompēī:** subjective gen. The Pompeians' reprehensible behavior may be contrasted with the restraint imposed upon Caesar's troops at Corfinium (section 33.1–9). Such conduct by the Pompeians would promote fears of another Sullan proscription.

40. **rēbus:** "cause."

41. **illīs:** i.e., the Pompeian soldiers. —**rē:** i.e., the operations for departing.

42. **vulgō:** modifies *significābant.*

43. **quam:** = *aliquam.*

44. **sub noctem:** here again Caesar suggests the desperation of the Pompeians, since putting out to sea just before nightfall in winter was a particularly risky enterprise.

46. **priusquam . . . cōnfirmāret** (47): temporal clause (AG 551b).

47. **ille:** = *Pompēius.* —**eius reī:** i.e., the collecting of vessels with which to pursue Pompey.

50. **Relinquēbātur ut . . . nāvēs essent exspectandae** (51): "The only course of action left was to wait for ships" (lit., "it was left that ships were to be waited for"). The subst. clause of result (*ut . . . essent exspectandae*) is used as the subject of *relinquēbātur* (AG 569.2). —**regiōnibus Galliae:** i.e, the Adriatic coast of Cisalpine Gaul.

51. **ā frētō:** i.e., the Strait of Messina, between Italy and Sicily. The ships had transported to Sicily the cohorts surrendered by Domitius at Corfinium (lines 3–4 above).

53. **veterem exercitum:** i.e., six legions in Spain under Pompey's command (see section 21.33). —**duās Hispāniās:** i.e., *Hispānia citerior* and *Hispānia ulterior.* These provinces, acquired from Car-

thage in 206 as a result of the conquests of Scipio Africanus, were extremely important to Rome. *Hispānia citerior,* the stronger and wealthier, had been indebted to Pompey for putting an end to Sertorius's war of rebellion in 72 and reorganizing the government. *Hispānia ulterior,* on the other hand, leaned toward Caesar, who as propraetor there in 61 had befriended many inhabitants while discovering that military leadership was his forte. —**cōnfirmārī:** i.e., in their allegiance to Pompey.

54. **altera:** i.e., *Hispānia citerior.*

45.3. **ut . . . essem:** indirect command (AG 563). —**ad urbem:** for the reason see n. 8.2. —**"cōnsiliō et dignitāte meā"** . . . **dē "grātiā" et dē "ope"** (4): see section 43.8–9 and n. In this carefully composed letter, Cicero employs the structure of a speech as follows: *exordium* (introduction), lines 2–9; *praemūnītiō* (preparation for the argument, which is here a *captātiō benevolentiae* as well), lines 10–21; *argūmentātiō* (presentation of the argument), lines 22–30; and *perōrātiō* (conclusion), lines 31–36.

4. **minus:** = *nōn.*

6. **ut . . . arbitrārer** (8): subst. clause of result in apposition to *eam cōgitātiōnem* (AG 570; GL 557). —**prō:** "in view of." —**tē:** subject acc. of *velle* (7). —**admīrābilī . . . sapientiā** (7): this praise of Caesar would later cause Cicero embarrassment (see n. 49.15 on *causam eius probō*).

7. **dē ōtiō, dē pāce, dē concordiā cīvium:** these three expressions are virtually synonymous. They emphasize Cicero's wish to serve as a negotiator of peace rather than as a political supporter of Caesar in his bid for a second consulship. For the importance of *concordia,* see section 21.7–8. —**agī:** impers. (for the idiom, see n. 44.29).

10. **tuendō:** i.e., protecting Pompey's interests.

11. **tibi ac reī pūblicae:** Cicero flatters Caesar by identifying him with the state and by implying that Pompey is the *hostis!* Here begins Cicero's use of a rhetorical tactic (*captātiō benevolentiae*) designed to secure Caesar's good will. If anti-Caesarians did not take offense at Cicero's fulsome praise of Caesar's *sapientia* (7), they certainly would be perturbed at this gratuitous compliment. Cicero's diction here illustrates his difficult position: he was repelled by Caesar's cause but attracted by his methods. On the other hand, the anti-Caesarians, who could claim the cause favored by Cicero, were inclined to vindicate their position with revenge. Caelius

faced a similar dilemma (section 1.15–16). —**reconciliandō:** gerundive agreeing with *Pompēiō* (10), governing the dative, and parallel to *tuendō* (10).

12. **profectō:** "in my opinion" (the adv. expresses the personal view of the speaker).

13. **et illī . . . et senātuī:** dat. of reference (AG 378). —**cum prīmum potuī:** "as soon as I could" (i.e., after Cicero returned to Italy from Cilicia late in 50). —**auctor:** Cicero had always championed the cause of peace (see lines 8–9 above).

14. **nec . . . bellī ūllam partem attigī:** perhaps an accurate claim, in that Cicero may never have discharged his assignment as supervisor of recruiting around Capua (see n. 8.26).

15. **eō bellō tē violārī:** with the substitution of *mē* for *tē* these words could have been written by Caesar himself! They express the very opposite of Cicero's sentiments elsewhere (see, e.g., sections 17.4–5 and 8–10; 18.6–12; and 21.11–13). —**honōrem:** Cicero probably means the consulship itself, to which Caesar's election would have been virtually assured. —**populī Rōmānī beneficiō:** a Caesarian expression (section 12.8 and n.), which very likely was circulating as propaganda. The *beneficium* had been conferred by the law of the ten tribunes.

16. **inimīcī atque invidī:** note again the Caesarian viewpoint (see sections 5.13–14; 9.2–5; 34.12; and 42.17–20). —**eō tempore:** i.e., the year 52.

17. **fautor dignitātis:** an exaggeration containing a grain of truth: namely, that although Cicero disapproved of the *ratiō absentis,* he also opposed the measures to withdraw it once it had been granted (*Ad Att.* 7.7.6). For a more accurate expression of Cicero's opinion of Caesar's *dignitās,* see section 17.7–10.

18. **auctor:** sc. *fuī.* This is a colloquial expression from *auctor esse* (+ dat.), "to advise"; "to be an advisor (to)." —**Pompēī dignitās:** Cicero had carefully prepared for this expression by using the parallel *fautor dignitātis* (17). In Cicero's eyes, not only Caesar but also Pompey and the other magistrates of the state had a justifiable claim to *dignitās.* Caesar blames Pompey for wanting no rival in *dignitās* (section 5.12). Cicero, on the other hand, realized that respect for the *dignitās* of all concerned was the only way to avoid civil war and bring about a *concordia ōrdinum* (see Historical Introduction, p. 14). Given the personalities involved in this conflict of ideologies, however, such a course was also impossible.

19. **aliquot . . . sunt annī:** for the idiom see n. 40.18 on *iam prīdem.*

—**cum**: takes the indicative here because the time of the action is defined in the main clause (*aliquot . . . annī*), and the principal idea is expressed in the subordinate clause. The construction is known as *cum inversum* (AG 546a) because the logical relationship between the two clauses is inverted. —**vōs duo dēlēgī**: see n. 32.17.

20. **quōs . . . colerem et . . . essem**: generic subjn. (AG 535).

22. **Quam ob rem**: here Cicero gets to the point; he wishes to preserve his neutrality in order to maintain his ties with Pompey.

23. **ut . . . impertiās**: indirect command (AG 563).

24. **ut . . . possim** (25): defines *cōgitātiōnī*. The subjn. is in a subst. clause of result (= explanatory *ut*, AG 570; GL 557). —**beneficiō**: abl. of cause.

25. **beneficī**: i.e., Pompey's. The *beneficium*, of course, involved the recall of Cicero from exile (see section 32.9).

27. **fidem**: "credibility."

29. **<et ad vestram> et ad cīvium concordiam**: "to peace both between you (*vestram*) and among our fellow citizens." The whole phrase is dependent upon *quam accommodātissimum*. *vestram* stands for the objective gen. *vestrī*, and *cīvium* is an objective gen. Cicero did not yet know that Pompey had evacuated Brundisium on March 17 (section 46.2) and that therefore Caesar no longer needed him as a mediator. —**per**: "through (the agency of)." —**quam accommodātissimum**: "in a position as favorable as possible." The superlative modifies *mē* (28) and is to be translated in the predicate after *cōnservārī* (30): Cicero means that he wants Caesar to honor his neutral position. This neutrality would be jeopardized if Cicero were to return to Rome, where he would appear to be cooperating with Caesar's political reorganization.

31. **cum . . . ēgissem**: concessive clause. —**dē Lentulō**: i.e., for sparing Lentulus Spinther at Corfinium (sections 34 and 37). —**cum . . . fuissēs** (32): causal clause. —**eī salūtī**: double dat.

32. **mihi**: sc. *salūtī*. Lentulus Spinther had worked for Cicero's recall from exile in 57.

33. **animō**: abl. of manner (AG 412).

34. **<putāvī>**: a disputed reading supplied by some editors because a main verb is lacking in the manuscripts. Others suggest *mihi videor.*

35. **quem**: = *Lentulum*. —**cūrā . . . ut . . . possim** (36): instead of the imperative, *cūrā ut* + subjn. is often used in colloquial language (AG 449c).

46.1. Matius et Trebātius: for Matius, see list of personal names. C. Trebatius Testa was a lawyer and friend of Cicero, whose letter of recommendation (*Ad Fam.* 7.5) induced Caesar to appoint him to his staff in Gaul. Later he was also included among the friends of the poet Horace (*Satires* 2.1) and was the addressee of Cicero's *Topica*.

4. **habuerit:** this pf. subjn., in a clause subordinate to an indirect statement, is used although the controlling verb, *audīvimus* (2), is in a secondary tense (AG 585b). The construction developed from the custom of using the time of the narrator (i.e., the present) as a reference point for events described.

7. **nōn aliēnum:** an example of litotes (see n. 2.3).

8. **prō certō habēbāmus:** the expression *prō certō habēre* means "to consider as a certainty."

9. **Mandāta tua:** these may be instructions relating to Cicero's forthcoming conference with Caesar.

10. **postulārit:** syncopated fut. pf. indic.

11. **ut antecēdat:** i.e., before Caesar does. Trebatius intends to prepare Cicero for his conference with Caesar. The subjn. is in a subst. clause of result (AG 568).

13. **Beneventī . . . Capuae . . . Sinuessae** (14): Caesar left Brundisium for Rome on the *Via Appia,* which extends west to Tarentum and then turns northwest to Rome via Beneventum, Capua, and Sinuessa. A journey of five or six days covered the two hundred miles from Brundisium to Beneventum. Caesar travelled the thirty miles from Beneventum to Capua and the twenty miles from Capua to Sinuessa in one day each. From Sinuessa a journey of about one hundred miles stood between him and Rome. Cicero's villa at Formiae, where the meeting was to take place, was situated only about twenty miles north of Sinuessa and directly on Caesar's route.

14. **prō certō:** see n. 8 above.

47.2. scrīberem . . . habērem . . . intermitterem (3): epistolary impf. The sequence is controlled by the epistolary *dedī* (3).

4. **nūntiābant:** another epistolary tense (sc. *Matius et Trebātius* as subjects).

5. **opēs:** Caesar had used the singular of this noun (section 43.9); hence the plural here puzzles Cicero because of the difference in meaning. Whereas the singular means "help," the plural means "influence" (i.e., "power exercised over others"). Cicero's concern

with this single term suggests once again (see n. 43.8 on *tuō cōnsiliō*) how closely he studied Caesar's every word.

7. **illam:** the position of this demonstrative (i.e., *after* the noun which it modifies) indicates that Caesar's merciful conduct at Corfinium has already become well known. —**per litterās:** probably the letter referred to in section 45.31 (*cum anteā tibi dē Lentulō grātiās ēgissem*).

8. **hōc exemplō:** abl. absol.

10. **augurāris:** Caesar's choice of this verb, coincidence or not, is amusing in view of Cicero's position as augur. —**cognitus:** here an adj.

11. **cum . . . tum** (12): "not only . . . but also" (AG 323g).

13. **triumphō gaudiō** (12): "I am jubilant" (lit., "I exult with joy.") *gaudiō* is an abl. of cause. —**quod:** "the fact that" (AG 572 and n.). —**iī:** = *eī*. These included Attius Varus, who had been set free by Caesar after the capitulation of Sulmo (section 28.12). As a Pompeian, Varus eventually usurped the province of Africa, where he had governed as propraetor in 52. Likewise Vibullius Rufus, who had been pardoned at Corfinium, served in Spain; and Domitius Ahenobarbus assumed command of the Pompeian forces at Massilia.

15. **meī . . . suī** (16): gen. with *similem,* since with a personal pron. *similis* takes the gen. instead of the dat. (AG 385.2).

16. **velim:** potential subjn. (AG 447.1) followed by the subjn. *sīs* without the introductory *ut* (AG 449c and 565). —**praestō:** adv. with dat.

18. **Dolabellā:** abl. of comparison. Cicero's son-in-law might have been expected to desert Caesar's cause even before Titus Labienus. The fact that he did not, however, must have pleased Caesar (who praises him in glowing terms) as much as it discomfited Cicero (see list of personal names). —**scītō:** fut. imperative second person sing. (AG 449a). —**Hanc . . . grātiam** (19): = *grātiam huius reī* (i.e., Dolabella's act of securing Cicero's consent to meet with Caesar in Rome). —**adeō:** "in fact" (emphasizes *hanc*).

19. **neque enim:** = *nōn enim.*

20. **is:** here = *tālis,* as does *ea* also.

48.2. **Utrumque:** sc. *ēgī.* As the following remarks imply, Atticus evidently advised Cicero on two points: first, to say nothing that would cause Caesar to think less of him; and second, to stay away from Rome. —**ex:** "according to" (AG 221.11c). —**et . . . et** (4): "both . . . and." —**ea:** the demonstrative, meaning "such," often anticipates a result clause. —**ōrātiō:** i.e., the tone of Cicero's language.

4. **nē ad urbem:** sc. *īrēmus*. The implied indirect command explains *eō*. —**fefellērunt:** sc. *nōs* as direct object. Cicero now uses the first person plural to mean Atticus and himself instead of simply himself, as previously in this letter. —**facilem:** predicate adj. after *illum fore,* to be supplied (cf. the construction in line 6). In fact, on the evidence of his remarks in an earlier letter (*Ad Att.* 9.15.2), Cicero had anticipated that Caesar would be anything but *facilis*.

5. **quod:** "the fact that" (AG 572 and n.). —**putārāmus:** syncopated plupf. indic.

6. **venīrēmus:** the impf. subjn. represents a fut. indic. in the protasis of a fut. more vivid condition in an indirect statement (AG 589a.3). —**dīcere:** in lively descriptions, the pres. inf., known as an "historical inf." (AG 463), often replaces the impf. or perf. indic. and regularly uses secondary sequence (AG 485f). The understood subject is *Caesar*. The inf. *dīcere* governs both *damnārī* (5) and *fore*. —**Ego:** sc. *respondī*.

7. **illōrum . . . causam:** i.e., the position of those described as *reliquōs* (6). Cicero saw his own situation as unique in view of his exceptional political career, his particular indebtedness to Pompey, and his role as a mediator between Caesar and the *optimātēs*. — **multa:** sc. *dicta essent*. —**Vēnī igitur:** sc. *inquit*.

8. **Meōne . . . arbitrātū:** abl. of manner (AG 412b). Cicero's words imply his doubts about Caesar's tolerance of republican sentiments. The doubts were confirmed by Caesar's peremptory remark below: *Ego vērō ista dīcī nōlō* (12).

10. **placēre:** impers., in implied indirect statement. —**īrī:** impers. (sc. *ā tē*).

13. **eō:** abl. of cause anticipating the following clause. —**quod:** see n. 5 above. —**sīc:** refers to the thoughts in lines 9–11 above. — **multaque:** sc. *dīcenda sunt*.

14. **aut nōn veniendum:** balances *aut . . . mihi dīcendum est* (13).

15. **Summa:** from *summa, -ae* (f.). —**<rogāret>:** subjn. in a subst. clause of result (= explanatory *ut*) in apposition to *summa* (AG 570; GL 557). —**ut dēlīberārem:** depends upon *<rogāret>*.

16. **negandum:** sc. *mihi*. —**Ita discessimus:** their parting marked a turning point for Cicero, who now realized that his function as a

mediator was no longer possible since Caesar would tolerate no pleas for Pompey's position and would readily proceed without Cicero's support if necessary.

17. **quod:** = *id quod* (AG 307d and n.), "a thing which."

18. **ūsū . . . venit:** the expression *ūsū venīre* (+ dat.) means "to happen (in one's experience)." *venit* is pres. with *iam prīdem* (see n. 18.2 on *iam diū*).

49.2. **quod:** "as to the fact that" (acc. of specification, AG 572a). —**ferō moleste:** the idiom *moleste ferre* means "to be upset." Here Cicero's sincerity is highly suspect. The fact that his letter to Caesar had now become a vehicle of Caesarian propaganda must have caused him acute embarrassment at the very least.

3. **quīn etiam:** "and furthermore." —**ea:** see n. 48.2 on *ea*.

5. **eam:** i.e., *pācem*.

6. **quam sī . . . dīcerem** (7): a conditional clause of comparison, which takes the subjn. (usually the impf.) after *quam sī* (AG 524a and n.).

8. **cum . . . hortābar:** note the indic. mood here, since the time expressed by the verb is absolutely identical with that of *dīxī* (AG 545a).

9. **cui:** dat. of reference (AG 376–77) to be construed with *ad pedēs* (10), "at whose feet."

10. **abiēcissem:** plupf. subjn. in the apodosis of a past contrary-to-fact condition with the protasis implied by *tālī in rē* (9); AG 521. —**Quā:** sc. *parte epistulae*.

11. **dē pāce . . . officiō** (12): construe with *ut . . . cōgitet* (12). Cicero here explains what he meant when he wrote *aliquid impertiās temporis* to Caesar. Cicero hoped that Caesar would show some consideration for Cicero's obligation to Pompey (see section 45.23–25).

12. **quod:** for the use see line 2 above.

13. **rē:** "by my actions." —**eō:** for the use see n. 48.13.

14. **quō . . . habērem:** purpose clause (AG 531.2a). —**eōdem pertinet:** "amounts to the same thing."

15. **quod:** "the fact that." The clause *quod . . . probō* is the subject of *pertinet.* —**causam eius probō:** these words of Cicero's rebuttal comprise the only reference to those remarks which would have seemed most offensive to the republicans (see section 45.10–11 and 14–16). Rather than dwell upon this point, however, Cicero

expounds at some length upon two other expressions, *prō tuā admīrābilī ac singulārī sapientiā* and *aliquid impertiās temporis* (45.6–7 and 23–24), which might have caused the *optimātēs* only a minor irritation. Thus he deliberately diverts attention from the flattery which he could not defend: namely, the identification of Caesar's interests with those of the *rēs pūblica* and his reference to Caesar's enemies as *invidī*.

16. **haec**: sc. *dīcam*.

17. **Ne** (affirmative particle): "certainly."

18. **ille**: = *Pompēius*. —**eundem**: = *Caesarem*. —**epistulam illam**: the position of *illam* suggests that Pompey's letter to Caesar (now lost) had been well known to Atticus and, presumably, to many others. Evidently in that letter Pompey extolled Caesar with the words *prō tuīs rēbus gestīs amplissimīs* (19). Cicero is irked by his critics, who carp at his compliments of Caesar but ignore those of Pompey.

19. **prō**: "in view of."

20. **ampliōribus**: Cicero pretends to take Pompey's use of the word *amplisimīs* in an absolute sense: i.e., to mean "most illustrious (of all)" and then proceeds to make a flippant comparison with Pompey's own achievements or those of Scipio Africanus. —**Āfricānī**: Probably P. Cornelius Scipio Aemilianus, recognized by the name *Āfricānus* for his victory over the Carthaginians in the Third Punic War (149–146); he was one of Cicero's most respected models; see n. 40.6 for his achievements. —**Ita tempus ferēbat**: "So the occasion demanded."

21. **Quantō**: abl. of degree of difference (AG 414). —**ille**: = *Caesar*.

22. **vōs**: Atticus and Sextus Peducaeus, a mutual friend under whose father Cicero had served (in 75) as quaestor in Sicily. —**vestrī**: for the use, see n. 47.15.

26. **apertius**: sc. the epistolary *scrībēbam*.

50.2. **omnīs dīligenter scrīptās**: Cicero has carefully read his friend's correspondence.

3. **legendam**: "worth reading" (lit., "to be read").

4. **In quā**: connecting relative of which the antecedent is the letter referred to by *eam* (3).

5. **pergrātum fēcistī**: the expression *pergrātum facere* means "to do a great favor." —**ut . . . faciās** (6): indirect command governed by *rogō* (7).

8. **dēplōrandī:** gen. depending upon *fīnis* (9) and *moderātiō*.

10. **profectō:** "in my opinion" (the adv. expresses the personal view of the speaker).

11. **sed:** sc. *cōgitō* to introduce the subsequent indirect questions.

13. **quid intersit:** "what difference there is." —**istōs:** i.e., Caesar and Pompey. —**propter:** governs *quōs,* which precedes it (a rhetorical figure known as anastrophe).

14. **mē cīvitāte expulissent:** i.e., into exile in 58. For the subjn., see n. 13.6.

15. **posse:** the pres. inf. of *possum* often has the meaning of a fut. inf. (AG 584b).

16. **societātis . . . cōnsēnsiōnis:** the so-called "first triumvirate."

18. **remittit aliquid:** the expression *remittere aliquid* means "to ease off," "to relax," "to abate."

19. **in diēs:** "day by day." —**<generum>:** since a direct object is needed with *expulit,* Kayser's suggestion at least preserves the contrast with *socerī* (25).

20. **ex aliā:** sc. *parte* (cf. *aliā ex parte*). —**prōvinciā:** abl. of separation.

22. **tyrannus:** Cicero here refers to Caesar's aspirations to be named *dictātor,* which could not be legitimately achieved without action by the senate. For the same sentiment cf. *uterque rēgnāre vult* (section 40.21–22). Caesar's greatest political problem was the legalization of his position.

23. **sibi:** "his" (dat. of reference with *pedēs;* cf. the same construction in section 49.9 and n.).

24. **sublevābat:** although this is probably not literally true, Pompey had nevertheless not seen fit to accede to Cicero's appeal to prevent Clodius from forcing him into exile. When a number of Cicero's distinguished friends actually visited Pompey to plead for Cicero, they were told that he could do nothing without authorization from the senate (*In Pīsōnem* 77). Cicero viewed this failure to act as a betrayal (see also n. 32.32). —**huius:** = *Caesaris.*

25. **facere posse:** sc. *aiēbat.*

26. **ille:** = *Pompēius.*

30. **quā:** connecting relative referring to *fortūnam* and modified by both *flōrentissimā* and *dūriōre* (31). —**illī:** sc. *cōnflictātī esse videntur.* The use of *cōnflictātī* with the contradictory ideas, *flōrentissimā* (*fortūnā*) and *dūriōre* (*fortūnā*), represents an example of zeugma, by which two substantives are joined to a verb appropriate for only one of them but suggesting another verb appropri-

ate for the other. Translate: "They seem to have been favored with remarkable prosperity, I to have been beset with harsh adversity."

32. **dēsertā . . . oppressā:** *dēsertā* refers to Pompey's actions, whereas *oppressā* describes Caesar's. —**per sē:** "by his own efforts."

33. **nōs:** used here for *ego* (AG 143a) and known as the "editorial 'we'." —**in illīs librīs:** in a work entitled *Dē Lēgibus,* begun in 51, Cicero (*Dē Lēgibus* 1.55) quotes the Greek Stoic philosopher Ariston of Chios (3rd century B.C.) as follows: *Chius Aristō dīxit sōlum bonum esse quod honestum esset, malumque quod turpe* ("Ariston of Chios said the only good is that which is honorable and the only evil that which is disgraceful"). This dogma is frequently repeated or re-stated in several of Cicero's later philosophical treatises as well.

36. **dominātiōne:** abl. of comparison, as is *commodīs* (37). For the language and the ideas expressed here, see section 40.12–13.

38. **Praeclārā . . . cōnscientiā:** i.e., a clear conscience.

39. **dē rē pūblicā . . . meruisse optimē:** see n. 14.16 for the idiom.

40. **ēversam esse:** sc. *cum cōgitō* as the controlling construction.

41. **quam:** the antecedent is *tempestāte* (40). —**xiiii annīs ante:** i.e., in 63, when the Catilinarian conspiracy was suppressed under Cicero's consulship (see also n. 32.21). Here Cicero suggests that even then Caesar was a threat to the republic.

42. **Hāc . . . comite:** abl. absol.

43. **tam . . . quam** (44): "so much . . . as." —**id:** i.e., the idea contained in *proficīscar magnō . . . cum dolōre.*

44. **puerōs:** i.e., Cicero's son Marcus and his brother's son Quintus.

45. **etiam:** "also" (i.e., in addition to their inheritance).

51.3. **iūdicāram:** syncopated form of *iūdicāveram.* —**scrībendum:** sc. *esse mihi,* as with *petendum* (4).

4. **quō:** = *aliquō.*

5. **prōclīnātā iam rē:** "now that matters have veered my way" (abl. absol.). —**integrā etiam:** "when matters were still undecided" (sc. *rē* in another abl. absol.). —**prōgrediendum:** sc. *esse.*

6. **existimāssēs:** syncopated plupf. subjn. form of *existimāvissēs* in a subordinate clause dependent upon an indirect command (AG 592.1). —**amīcitiae:** objective gen.

8. **fortūnae:** i.e., the present successful turn of events for Caesar's cause. If Caesar showed no faith in the state religion, which he repeatedly used as a political instrument, he did nevertheless express confidence in the workings of *fortūna,* which could be

turned to the advantage of those willing to seize the opportunities offered by it. Of such opportunism he was a master. —**obsecūtus:** sc. *esse.*

9. **causam:** i.e., a "just" cause (Pompey's, in Cicero's eyes). —**secūtus:** sc. *esse vidēberis.*

10. **eadem:** sc. *causa.*

11. **sed meum aliquod factum condemnāvisse:** the point of Caesar's elaborate argument is that, should Cicero join Pompey *now,* his action could not be justified (a) by the conviction that Pompey's cause is the winning cause, since the turn of events has favored Caesar; or (b) by the belief that Pompey's cause is the right cause, since it has undergone no changes from the time when Cicero decided to remain uncommitted to it. Therefore, Caesar reasons, if Cicero joins Pompey *now,* his action will be interpreted only as a condemnation of some deed perpetrated by Caesar himself. —**quō:** abl. of comparison.

12. **Quod:** connecting relative (also in line 15). —**nē faciās:** indirect command governed by *petō* (13). —**prō iūre:** "in view of the obligations." Caesar uses here language which was deeply rooted in the traditional morality of Roman society; the *iūs amīcitiae* was a strong—at times almost sacred—bond uniting men of mutual interests and sympathies, whether the bond be personal or political (or both). So important in this brief letter is the term *amīcitia* that Caesar employs it three times (lines 6, 13, and 17) as well as the attribute *benevolentia* (4).

13. **virō bonō et quiētō et bonō cīvī:** "for a man of principle and peace and a loyal citizen." *bonus vir* refers to a man's personal convictions, whereas *bonus cīvis* refers to his fidelity to his *patria.* By stating that nothing is more fitting for such a man than neutrality, Caesar implicitly vitiates the claim of the *optimātēs* that it was the duty of every *bonus vir* to defend the state.

15. **perīculī causā:** "because of retribution which they feared" (i.e., at the hands of Pompey if they remained neutral). See Caesar's description of the senate meeting in January (section 3.29–32) and Cicero's description of the Pompeians who were behaving like Sulla (section 40.18–19). On the other hand, those who might have feared Caesar have no reason to do so, for he has formulated his policy of *clēmentia, amīcitia,* and *fidēs.*

16. **explōrātō et vītae meae testimōniō et amīcitiae iūdiciō:** "after examining both the evidence supplied by my life and the verdict given by friendship." Caesar's forensic diction is appropriately

addressed to a figure whose career has been glorified by his successes in the courts. By "evidence" Caesar refers to his repeated victories over his opponents and his merciful treatment of them, and by "verdict given by friendship" he means his respect for his friends and for the political position taken by them. Caesar offers Cicero two choices: either to join the winning side or to remain neutral.

19. **ex itinere:** i.e., to Massilia and then to Spain.

52.1. **L. Vibullium Rūfum:** see sections 23.12, 25.4, and 26.6–7. Caesar also seems to refer to him in section 42.15–16 but does not name Vibullius in his account of the incidents at Corfinium and in Spain.

5. **mitteret:** generic subjn. with *idōneum . . . quem* (AG 535f).

9. **prō disciplīnā et praeceptīs:** "as a lesson and a warning."

11. **illum:** = *Pompēium* (sc. *satis magna incommoda accēpisse*).

13. **centum atque xxx:** probably not an exaggeration, for Pompey had lost at least forty cohorts in Italy (see n. 44.3) and sixty in Spain. — **sē:** again sc. *satis magna incommoda accēpisse.* —**morte . . . et dētrīmentō:** abl. of cause. Campaigning in Africa while Caesar was besieging Massilia, Curio blockaded the town of Utica, which was defended by Attius Varus. Juba, the king of the Numidians (see n. 7.10), came to assist Varus and destroyed the army commanded by Curio (see list of personal names and n. 2.25), who himself died fighting.

14. **Curictam:** this town on an island off the coast of Illyricum was the site where the Pompeians inflicted heavy losses upon C. Antonius, Marcus's younger brother, and eventually compelled him to surrender. As one of Caesar's *lēgātī*, C. Antonius had come to reinforce the fleet commanded by Dolabella.

15. **sibi ac reī pūblicae parcerent:** hortatory subjn. (secondary sequence) in an indirect statement (AG 588). Again Caesar aligns himself with the republic (see section 34.14). His rhetoric here recalls the language of Pompey as reported by L. Caesar (section 11.7–13). —**quantum . . . fortūna posset** (16): indirect question implied by *documentō* (17).

16. **incommodīs suīs:** abl. of cause.

17. **documentō:** dat. of purpose.

19. **tribuisset:** for the mood and tense see n. 13.6. The same rule applies to *iūrāvisset* (24).

22. **convenīre:** "to be agreed upon."

175

25. **Dēpositīs:** modifies both *armīs* and *auxiliīs* (26) although in sense it fits only *armīs* (an example of zeugma; see n. 50.30 on *illī*).

26. **necessāriō:** adv.

28. **Pompeiō:** the dat. is regularly used with the pass. of *probō*.

29. **dīmissūrum:** sc. *sē*.

31. **ē rē vīsum est:** the idiom *ē rē vidērī* means "to seem advantageous." The MS. *reversus est* seems to conflict with the return of Vibullius to Pompey in *Bellum Cīvīle* 3.11.1.

32. **Libōne:** see section 44.20 and n. —**Lucceiō et Theophane:** for Lucceius, see list of personal names. Theophanes, a Greek from Mitylene, had been granted Roman citizenship by Pompey and became an advisor to him. Theophanes wrote a history to glorify Pompey's campaigns against Mithridates. Eventually he adopted Cornelius Balbus.

34. **ingressum in sermōnem:** "as he launched into his speech."

35. **Quid mihi . . . opus est** (36): "What need do I have" (*opus est*, "there is need," regularly governs a dat. of person and abl. of the thing needed).

36. **cīvitāte:** "citizenship."

37. **Cuius reī:** objective gen. depending upon *opiniō*. Here again the concern for *dignitās* arises. According to Caesar, Pompey could not tolerate a position which, in the eyes of the public, he would seem to hold by virtue of Caesar's generosity.

40. **tamen nihilō minus:** = *tamen*.

53.1. **Servius:** Servius Sulpicius Rufus (see list of personal names).

2. **obitū:** in mid-February Tullia had died after giving birth to a son. This event took place shortly after her divorce from Dolabella, who had been notoriously unfaithful to her.

3. **sānē quam prō eō ac dēbuī graviter molestēque tulī:** "I was very (*sane quam*) seriously and distressfully upset, as (*prō eō ac*) I should have been." The idiom *ferre molestē* means "to be upset."

4. **istīc:** i.e., in Rome.

7. **Quid est quod:** "Why is it that . . . ?"

8. **nōbīscum ēgerit:** "has dealt with us."

9. **nōbīs:** dat. of separation used especially of persons (AG 381) with verbs of taking away (*ērepta esse*).

11. **honōrēs:** "magistracies." Sulpicius's sentiments here are remarkable in view of his current post as Caesar's governor of the province of Achaea.

13. **rēs:** placed in the relative clause as the antecedent of *quae* and agreeing in case with the relative pronoun. In the independent clause, *rēs* would have been in the acc. case as the direct object of *commemorāre* (AG 307b and n.).

14. **sī:** "(to see) if."

15. **possit:** subjn. in an indirect question (AG 576a). —**versus:** placed after its object, like *causā*.

19. **prōstrāta et dīruta:** "leveled and in ruins." Despite the rhetorical exaggeration here, the sites named by Sulpicius were well-known for the disasters inflicted upon them. In 210, the island of Aegina had been captured by the Roman commander P. Sulpicius, who sold the inhabitants as slaves; Aegina had also suffered from pirates before Pompey cleared the Mediterranean. Megara had been sacked by Demetrius Poliorcetes in 307 and again by the Caesarian Fufius Calenus after Pharsalus. In 86, Sulla had burned the Piraeus to the ground. Corinth, sacked by Mummius in 146, had not yet recovered although Caesar was soon to revive it by establishing a colony there.

21. **quōrum vīta brevior esse dēbet:** "whose lives are destined to be relatively short."

22. **oppidum:** = *oppidōrum*.

24. **nōn mediocriter:** an example of litotes (see n. 2.3).

25. **sī tibi vidētur:** "if you please" (lit., "if it seems best to you"). — **fac ante oculōs tibi prōpōnās:** "I should like you to imagine" (lit., "bring it about that you set forth before your eyes").

26. **tibi:** dat. of reference (AG 376–77). —**interiērunt:** i.e., in the recent civil war.

27. **dēminūtiō:** Sulpicius means that Rome has suffered a loss of *dignitās* after the disgraceful spectacle of her two leading generals fighting for supremacy. Although begun in Italy, the civil war generated shock waves which reached virtually every Roman province and undermined Rome's *auctōritās* abroad.

28. **conquassātae sunt:** Sulpicius suggests a direct parallel between the fate of the ruined Greek cities and that of the Roman world. —**in ūnīus mulierculae animulā:** "in the delicate life of one weak woman." Sulpicius's contrast between *imperiō populī Rōmānī* (27) and *ūnīus* suggests that Cicero's mourning for his personal loss should yield to grief for a more profound bereavement: the death of the *rēs pūblica* as he had known it. Also, the diminutives *mulierculae animulā* convey pathos for the human condition.

31. **homō:** "a human being" (cf. *hominem* in line 23 above).

32. **hīsce:** the suffix *-ce* adds emphasis.

34. **opus fuerit:** *opus est,* "there is need," regularly governs a dat. of person. —**ūnā cum rē pūblicā fuisse:** "(that) she lived as long as the republic" (lit., "(that) she was together [*ūnā*] with the republic").

35. **praetōrem, cōnsulem, augurem:** i.e., in the years 66, 63, and 53 respectively.

36. **prīmāriīs:** before her marriage to Dolabella, Tullia had been the wife of C. Calpurnius Piso (betrothed in 67) and then of Furius Crassipes (betrothed in 56).

38. **Quid est quod:** "What is there which . . . ?" Contrast n. 7 above. —**hōc nōmine:** "on this score."

39. **possītis:** generic subjn. (AG 535).

54.1. **Curiō:** Manius Curius, a Roman *eques* and friend of both Atticus and Cicero, whose secretary Tiro he had attended while Tiro was ill in Greece in the fall of 50 (section 8).

   3. **quīn:** "furthermore." —**ubi . . . audiam** (4): Cicero seems to be quoting from some lost poem. The *Pelopidae,* "sons of Pelops," were Thyestes and Atreus, whose heinous crimes provided the material for much Greek and Latin literature. Cicero's quotation, of which he made repeated use since 46 (*Ad Fam.* 7.28.2; *Ad Att.* 14.12.2; 15.11.3) always occurs, with minor variations, in a context concerned with escaping from the vicinity of Rome. For Cicero, the Roman "Pelopidae" were probably Caesar and his followers. The absence of the original context for the quotation makes it impossible to determine whether *audiam* is subjn. or fut. indic.

   5. **mihi . . . videar:** for the meaning see n. 43.6. —**quī . . . intersim:** relative clause of cause (AG 535e and n. 1). —**Ne:** (affirmative particle) "certainly."

   8. **Campō:** = *Campō Mārtiō.* The *Campus Mārtius,* located outside the *pōmerium,* was originally used for mustering troops and for military exercises. It was still the gathering place for the various *comitia* which elected magistrates.

   9. **hōrā secundā:** i.e., beginning at approximately 8 A.M. in midwinter.

  10. **Q. Maximī:** Quintus Fabius Maximus, a lieutenant of Caesar in the final Spanish campaign. As a reward, Caesar had him and Trebonius elected consuls for the last three months of 45, after he himself had vacated his office as sole consul. —**illī:** i.e., Caesar's partisans.

11. **ille:** = *Caesar*, as so often previously (see n. 19.4; 22.4; 24.10).

12. **quī:** = *cum is* in a relative clause of concession (AG 535e). Apparently Caesar had intended to preside, as *dictātor*, over the *comitia tribūta*, for which he had taken the auspices. When he learned of the death of Fabius Maximus, however, he assumed instead the presidency of the *comitia centuriāta* in order to ensure the election of Caninius Rebilus. —**comitiīs tribūtīs:** "at the comitia tributa" (assembly for electing quaestors and curule aediles). —**centuriāta:** sc. *comitia* (acc.). The *comitia centuriāta* was the assembly for electing the praetors, consuls, and censors (see glossary s.v. "Assemblies").

13. **cōnsulem:** i.e., Caninius Rebilus (see section 44.19 and note). — **hōrā septimā:** i.e., approximately 12 noon to 1 P.M. —**quī ... esset:** relative clause of purpose.

14. **quae:** the antecedent is *K(alendās)* (13).

15. **scītō:** fut. imperative second person sing. (AG 449a). —**prandisse:** the Romans usually took their *prandium* just before noon.

16. **mīrificā vigilantiā:** abl. of description. —**quī ... vīderit** (17): for the construction see n. 5 above on *quī ... intersim*.

18. **Quid, sī cētera scrībam?:** "What's the use of writing more?" (lit., "What, if I shall write the rest?") In this type of rhetorical question, the main clause is sometimes expressed in full (*quid est*).

20. **philosophiae portum:** most of Cicero's philosophical works were written during the period 45–44, partly to provide a "haven" for his troubled mind.

55.1. **Matius:** see section 46 and list of personal names.

2. **enim:** "of course" (transitional use of *enim*). —**quae ... contulerint** (3): i.e., the criticisms which people have aimed (*contulerint*) at Matius. The subjn. is generic (AG 535).

3. **Vitiō ... dant:** the expression *vitiō dare* means "to ascribe as a fault" (*Vitiō:* dat. of purpose). —**quod:** "the fact that."

4. **graviter ferō:** similar to *ferō molestē*, "I am upset." —**dīlēxī:** the indic. within an indirect statement represents the feelings of the writer (AG 583).

6. **vīcerint:** *vincere*, introducing an indirect statement, means "to win one's point."

9. **rē:** i.e., Caesar's act of refusal to give up his command in Gaul.

13. **aequē ac:** "as much as" (AG 384 n. 2).

14. **quī ... voluerim:** generic subjn., here expressing cause (AG 535e).

179

15. **īdem** [= *eīdem*] **hominēs:** i.e., Caesar's assassins.

16. **illī et invidiae et exitiō:** "a cause of both his unpopularity and his death" (double dat.).

20. **lībera:** "unrestricted." —**ut timērent, gaudērent, dolērent:** subst. clause of result (= explanatory *ut* in apposition to *haec*, AG 570; GL 557).

22. **nōbīs:** dat. of separation (AG 381). In section 12.8–9, the same construction appears with *extorquērētur*, used by Caesar to describe the actions by which his enemies attempted to remove his *ratiō absentis*.

29. **prō cīvīlī parte:** "in view of my role as a citizen."

30. **Id quidem mē cupere:** the indirect statement depends upon *vincere* (31). See n. 6 above for the meaning of *vincere*.

31. **probat:** note the sing. form with two sing. subjects, a common occurrence with abstract nouns (AG 317b and n.). —**postulō:** here, with infin., means "expect."

32. **māiōrem in modum:** "earnestly" (lit., "in greater measure"). — **rem potiōrem ōrātiōne:** "that actions speak louder than words" (David Stockton, *Thirty-five Letters of Cicero* [Oxford University Press, 1969], p. 198).

33. **expedīre rectē fierī:** "that the right course of action is expedient" (lit., "for it to be done rightly is useful"). This point is based on a tenet of Stoic philosophy frequent in Cicero's works and often expressed as: *quidquid honestum est, idem ūtile vidētur nec ūtile quicquam, quod nōn honestum* (*Dē Officiīs* 3.20).

34. **improbīs:** Matius pointedly describes the self-styled *optimātēs* with one of their favorite terms of opprobrium for the Caesarians (see sections 8.16 and 21.9–10 and n.).

Julius Caesar. Bust in the Vatican Museum, Rome.

LIST OF
PERSONAL NAMES

Lucius Afranius (d. 46)

Lucius Afranius, Pompey's close confederate, was born in Picenum, a district of Italy where Pompey had inherited from his father many loyal clients. Throughout his career Afranius supported Pompey's interests without deviation, first when he was appointed as his legate in *Hispānia citerior* (75–72) to oppose Sertorius, and then in the east (66–61) to suppress Mithridates. Later, in 55, he returned to *Hispānia citerior* when Pompey was governing that province from Rome and served there until 49 and his defeat by Caesar at Ilerda.

Coming from an obscure and undistinguished Picene family, Afranius needed Pompey's patronage to promote his political career. Through bribery he was elected to the consulship for 60 as a *novus homō*, but failed to have Pompey's legislation enacted because of the obstructive tactics of his colleague Metellus Celer. Furthermore, as a politician he turned out to be inept and indolent, and in Cicero's eyes, a nonentity, so ignorant that he did not even know the value of the land he had bought (*Ad Att.* 1.19.4).

Pardoned by Caesar after Ilerda, he returned to fight against his benefactor at Pharsalus and then at Thapsus. Soon after this defeat he was captured in flight and put to death on Caesar's orders in 46.

183

M. Antonius (d. 30)

Born in c. 83 into a family of the plebeian nobility, Marcus Antonius (Mark Antony) was about seventeen years younger than his mentor Caesar, to whom his mother, a member of the Julian *gēns,* was distantly related. When he was twenty-five, like many prominent Romans, he set out for Greece in order to study rhetoric. While in the east, he joined the staff of Aulus Gabinius, the proconsul of Syria, who made him a cavalry officer. In 55 he left Gabinius for Gaul, where he served intermittently under Caesar until 50. Meanwhile, with the help of Caesar's money and influence, Antonius became quaestor in 52 and both tribune and augur in 50. In running for the augurate, he defeated the prominent optimate L. Domitius Ahenobarbus. As a tribune he immediately showed his partisanship by proposing that the two legions detained in Italy be sent to Syria and that all recruiting cease. After his efforts on the proconsul's behalf were frustrated by the intransigence of the opposition, he joined Caesar for the march into Italy, where he was left in charge while Caesar secured the Spanish provinces. Later in 48, Antonius ably commanded the left wing at Pharsalus. After the battle, Antonius took charge of Italy as Caesar's *magister equitum.* During this period he married Fulvia, the former wife of Curio and, before him, of Clodius. In 44 he shared the consulship with Caesar until the Ides of March.

After Caesar's assassination he vied with Octavian until they became reconciled and formed with Lepidus the "second triumvirate" in late 43. In the proscriptions which followed Cicero was marked out as Antonius's victim (December 43). Next the triumvirate, with Antonius as general, defeated the army of the republicans at Philippi in October 42. Subsequently Antonius, while fulfilling his responsibilities in the east, formed an alliance with Cleopatra of Egypt. Their combined forces were defeated by Octavian at Actium in 31. Antonius fled to Egypt, where he, the hero of Philippi and Cleopatra's lover, committed suicide.

Appius: See **Claudius.**

Atticus: See **Pomponius.**

Balbus: See **Cornelius.**

Quintus Caecilius Metellus Pius Scipio Nasica

A scion of a famous patrician family, Scipio at first bore the name P. Cornelius Scipio Nasica. After Q. Metellus Pius (consul in 80) of noble plebeian status had adopted him through his will, he was known as Quintus Caecilius Metellus Pius Scipio Nasica and combined in his person an illustrious heritage which no other Roman could challenge. Tribune of the plebs in 59 and praetor in 55, Scipio became a candidate for the consulship in 53, a year marred by violence and riots so that no elections could be held. This explosive situation was finally resolved in 52 by the appointment of Pompey as sole consul, who then moved close to the *optimātēs* by marrying Cornelia, the daughter of Scipio, the noblest man in Rome. Not much later, in order to save his father-in-law from prosecution for bribery, Pompey made him his colleague for the remaining five months of the year. Thereafter, Scipio was always associated with those who were in the vanguard of Caesar's adversaries. As proconsul of Syria, he contributed two legions to the republican forces at Pharsalus. Upon Caesar's victory (in 48) he fled to Africa and died after his forces were defeated at Thapsus in 46.

Throughout his career, Scipio's character and achievements never matched his lineage. Neither Caesar nor Cicero cast him in a favorable light. The former describes him as greedy, corrupt, and depraved (*Bellum Cīvīle* 3.31–33), the latter chastises him for his ignorance (*Ad Att.* 6.1.17).

M. Caelius Rufus (82–48)

Marcus Caelius Rufus was born at Interamnia in Picenum, where his father was a thrifty *eques* who owned property in Africa. When Caelius was sixteen, his father brought him to Rome. There he completed his education in public affairs with Cicero and Crassus within three years before entering upon his political career. It was then that Caelius became involved with Catiline, although he seems to have refrained from joining the conspiracy of 63. Two years later, Caelius travelled to Africa, where as a member of the governor's staff he acquired administrative experience and looked after his father's property. Upon his return to Rome, he made his reputation in 59 by successfully prosecuting C. Antonius Hybrida, who was defended by Cicero, his former colleague in the consulship. Caelius's brilliant victory at the expense of his mentor gained for him a formidable reputation and influenced him to leave his father and rent a fashionable house on the Palatine from Publius Clodius, with whose infamous sister Clodia he had an affair. When Caelius later broke with her, she sought revenge by collaborating with his prosecutors in 56. In trouble, Caelius turned for help to Cicero, whose masterly defense resulted in his protégé's acquittal.

Now free to return to politics, Caelius was elected tribune for 52 and became an ardent supporter of Milo and critic of Pompey. He was also one of the ten tribunes who sponsored the law to grant Caesar the right to run for the consulship *in absentiā*. In the following year, before Cicero left for his governorship in Cilicia, he asked Caelius to keep him informed about events in Rome while he was away. The resulting correspondence (e.g. section 1) provides invaluable evidence for the political crises which eventually fomented the civil war of 49. During this period, and when he was curule aedile in 50, Caelius's opportunism made him more than ever partial to Caesar's cause, so that early in the following year, he left Rome for Cisalpine Gaul. Within two years, after becoming dissatisfied with Caesar's policies, he joined a revolt in southern Italy and was killed by Caesar's troops when he was only thirty-four years of age. Caelius died as a man who deserved, in the words of the rhetorician Quintilian, "both a wiser mind and a longer life."

Marcus Calidius (d. 48)

A member of a lesser senatorial family, Marcus Calidius was praetor in 57, when he supported a bill to restore Cicero from exile. He soon earned a reputation as a gifted and fluent orator and used his considerable talents on behalf of Gabinius in 54 and Milo in 52. He also successfully defended himself against a charge of bribery after he had run for the consulship in 51 and lost to his rival C. Marcellus. Cicero, in attesting to his eloquence (*Brūtus* 274–78), goes on to say that in spite of its stylistic charm and penetrating ideas, Calidius's rhetoric often lacked the power to move. During the civil war, Calidius took the side of Caesar, who subsequently appointed him governor of Cisalpine Gaul, where he died in 48.

Lucius Calpurnius Piso Caesoninus

The Calpurnii Pisones were an illustrious family which by 60 could already count eight members who had held the consulship. Sometime in 59, Lucius Calpurnius Piso arranged the marriage of his daughter Calpurnia to Julius Caesar, the consul. This alliance provided Caesar with an aristocratic connection of convenience, for Piso, an ex-praetor, was a man of considerable standing among the oligarchy. In return Piso could use the support of Caesar and Pompey to win the consulship, to which he was elevated in 58. When Piso refused to exert his influence to thwart a sentence of exile for Cicero, the orator never forgot and virulently attacked him for the way in which the proconsul governed his province of Macedonia from 57 to 55. That a prosecution for incompetence or corruption never occurred casts some doubt upon Cicero's allegations. Later in 50, when Piso shared the censorship with Appius Claudius, he pursued an independent course and intervened to check the excesses of his colleague. During the civil war, he urged moderation in trying to bring about a compromise both before and after Caesar's assassination.

Q. Cassius Longinus (d. 47)

Quintus Cassius Longinus was a friend of Titus Pomponius Atticus, Cicero's confidant, and a cousin of the more famous C. Cassius Longinus, who later became one of Caesar's assassins. Ignoring the use of the lot, Pompey appointed Quintus as his quaestor in Spain, probably in 52. This connection, however, did not last long, for, when in 49 both the Cassii were serving as tribunes, Quintus disagreeed with his cousin and supported Caesar's cause in the senate early in January. For the Spanish campaign later in the same year he joined Caesar, who made him propraetor in *Hispānia ulterior*. During his tenure as governor (49–48), his excessive greed and brutal extortions caused such discontent that when Caesar ordered him to prepare for a campaign against King Juba in Numidia, he could not carry out his assignment because of rebellious subjects and mutinous legions. After being relieved of his command, he drowned in the mouth of the Ebro River as he was returning to Rome with his plunder.

Cato: See Porcius.

The Claudii Marcelli

During the final years of the republic, after several generations of failure to attain the highest office, the great plebeian family of the Claudii Marcelli once again became prominent by attaining three successive consulships in 51, 50, and 49.

(a) *Marcus Claudius Marcellus* (d. 45). He was elected to the consulship for 51 after establishing a reputation of persistent opposition to the policies of the so-called *populārēs*. For instance, he helped Cicero suppress the Catilinarian conspiracy in 63 when he imparted valuable information about Catiline's plans, and in 52 he defied the wishes of Pompey by joining Cicero in supporting Milo. Later, as consul, he openly opposed Caesar, while trying to undermine the foundations of his power. In April 51 Marcellus introduced a resolution in the senate to revoke the rights of citizenship which Caesar had granted to the colony of Novum Comum according to the *lēx Vatīnia* of 59. In order to demonstrate his contempt for Caesar and his conviction that Caesar's legislation was not valid, he had a citizen of Novum Comum flogged and humiliated in the Roman forum, a brutal act which Cicero described as scandalous (*Ad Att.* 5.10.2). Even if Marcellus did not believe that the man was a Roman citizen, he was after all a Transpadane.

In the autumn, while presiding over the senate, Marcellus proposed that Caesar be recalled from his province and be replaced with L. Domitius Ahenobarbus on the grounds that the province had been pacified after the defeat of Vercingetorix. When the motion did not pass, discussion of the question was postponed to the following year. With such an attack on the legitimacy of Caesar's command, he initiated the sequence of events that led to Caesar's crossing of the Rubicon.

After the battle of Pharsalus, Marcellus lived in voluntary retirement at Mytilene in Lesbos until in 46 Caesar unexpectedly consented to a senatorial request that Marcellus be pardoned. Caesar's generous and clement act moved Cicero to rise in the senate, and in his speech *Prō Mārcellō* he expressed his gratitude for Caesar's magnanimity and urged him to restore the republican form of government.

Marcellus, who had resisted Cicero's suggestions (*Ad Fam.* 4.7–9) that he ask for a pardon, now agreed to return to Rome from Lesbos. But at Piraeus in May 45 he was assassinated by P. Magius Cilo, a member of his retinue.

(b) *Gaius Claudius Marcellus* (d. 40). Among the few facts known about the early career of Gaius Marcellus is his noteworthy marriage to Octavia, sister of Octavian (the future Augustus). When he became consul in 50, he actively tried to continue the anti-Caesarian policies of his cousin Marcus. After Curio's motion that Caesar and Pompey resign their commands and disband their armies was carried in the senate in December, Gaius disregarded the counsel of a large majority. Spurred on by rumors that Caesar was about to invade Italy, and in the company of the two consuls-elect, his cousin Gaius and L. Cornelius Lentulus Crus, he crossed the *pōmerium* in order to entrust the defense of the city to Pompey and the two legions under Pompey's command. This defiant act was bound to provoke Caesar. After the proconsul crossed the Rubicon, Gaius remained neutral for the rest of the war. In 46 he supported the senate's appeal to Caesar that his cousin Marcus be pardoned.

(c) *Gaius Claudius Marcellus.* Not to be confused with his namesake and cousin, Gaius was the brother of Marcus and, like him, a strong Pompeian supporter during his consulship in 49. He died before the end of the war.

Appius Claudius Pulcher

Appius Claudius Pulcher was the eldest of six children, at least three of whom gained notoriety during the late republic. There was Appius himself, proud, shifty, unscrupulous. After the death of his father in 76, he was responsible for maintaining the status of a family which had seen far better days. Appius's youngest brother, Publius Clodius, was to become infamous for his demagoguery, as was his second sister, Clodia, for her licentiousness. Both had altered the spelling of their names to reflect the plebeian pronunciation for reasons of popular appeal.

On the whole, Appius followed whatever political policy was most effective in promoting the fortunes of his family. During the early fifties, he supported the machinations of Clodius to exile Cicero and seemed in general to favor the objectives of the triumvirate. He was also busy in arranging marriage alliances that would be socially and politically expedient. One of his daughters was married to Marcus Brutus, Cato's nephew, whereas the other was the wife of Pompey's oldest son. After he shared the consulship with Domitius Ahenobarbus in 54, he moved away from his former associates and closer to the *optimātēs*. As proconsul of Cilicia (53–51), he tried to recoup his family fortunes through extortion from the provincials. His excesses are vividly described in the correspondence of his successor Cicero, who was conscientiously trying to repair the damage. Upon returning to Rome, Appius was indicted and acquitted through the intrigues of his influential friends. Election to the censorship followed in the early fall of 50. Armed with the powers of the censor, Appius attacked many of his enemies, such as Caelius and Curio, and in trying to eject them from the senate, unintentionally increased the number of Caesar's adherents. Later he accompanied Pompey to Greece and died there before the battle of Pharsalus.

Lucius Cornelius Balbus

Lucius Cornelius Balbus, a Spaniard, was born in Gades (Cadiz) about 100, the year of Caesar's birth. Early in his career, when he was still in his twenties, he helped Pompey in the war against Sertorius, and for this service was granted Roman citizenship by Pompey. Later in Rome, his reputation for business and finance attracted the attention of

Julius Caesar, who, as propraetor of Spain in 61, appointed Balbus to be one of his administrative assistants with the rank of *praefectus fabrum*. In the following year he displayed his political acumen and sound judgment in the negotiations that produced the formation of the "triumvirate" (60), while all the time becoming more closely associated with Caesar, whom he also served in Gaul in the same capacity as in Spain. During Caesar's tenure in Gaul, Balbus traveled back and forth to Rome, where he became the proconsul's agent and intermediary, for he had contrived to maintain connections with the partisans of Pompey even after the rupture that led to the civil war. During this period, Cicero frequently corresponded with Balbus in the belief that he had access to Caesar and could use his influence to obtain a hearing for Cicero, who in 56 had served Balbus well by successfully defending him against the charge of illegal acquisition of citizenship.

After Caesar's death, Balbus cautiously aligned himself with Octavian and was elected to the praetorship (42), propraetorship in Gaul (41), and consulship (40), the first non-Italian to attain that office.

Publius Cornelius Dolabella (d. 43)

If Appian (*Bella Cīvīlia* 2.129) is to be believed, Publius Cornelius Dolabella was born in about 69, although much of the evidence suggests an earlier date. At the time of the outbreak of the civil war in 49, he was considered to be an unscrupulous, ambitious, dissipated, and profligate young patrician, whom Cicero had twice defended successfully before his departure for Cilicia in 51. During the following year, while conducting the prosecution of Appius Claudius Pulcher (Publius Clodius's older brother and Cicero's predecessor as governor of Cilicia), Dolabella became the proconsul's son-in-law, much to his father-in-law's embarrassment and in spite of his protests.

As a partisan of Caesar (section 19.7 and note; section 24.22 and 24.29), Dolabella was given a command in the Adriatic, where in June (?) 49 Pompey's fleet (note 52.14) defeated him. Subsequently, he fought for Caesar at Pharsalus, Thapsus, and Munda. After the assassination, he became consul in 44 in accordance with Caesar's wishes and was appointed by the senate as proconsul of Syria. While passing through Asia en route to his province, he encountered the republican proconsul Trebonius, whom he captured and executed. For these actions the senate declared (February 43) Dolabella a public enemy. Later in the same year, when besieged by C. Cassius at Laodicaea, he committed suicide to escape capture at the hands of the conspirator.

Lucius Cornelius Lentulus Crus (d. 48)

Lentulus Crus was the sixth member of his family to become a candidate (50) for the consulship in a little more than two decades. As praetor in 58, he interceded with the consul Piso in an effort to block Cicero's exile. In 49, when he was consul, he was firmly committed to the political and military defeat of Caesar. According to Caesar (section 5.3–6) Lentulus was burdened with heavy debts and often boasted of his ambition to rival Cornelius Sulla, his ancestor. Vain, self-indulgent and pretentious, he was criticized by Cicero for his ineffectiveness as an administrator (section 24), although he supported the proconsul's desire for a triumph (section 8.21–23). After Pharsalus, Lentulus escaped to Egypt, where he was assassinated on the day after Pompey's death.

Publius Cornelius Lentulus Spinther

As a member of the Cornelii Lentuli, a patrician family of considerable renown (see Lucius Cornelius Lentulus Crus), Publius Cornelius Lentulus Spinther pursued a successful career through the *cursus honorum*. After his aedileship in 63, when he supported Cicero, and praetorship in 60, he enjoyed the friendship of Caesar, through whose influence he not only became a *pontifex* but also obtained the appointment to a propraetorship in *Hispania citerior* for 59 (section 34.8–9). Enjoying the backing of both Pompey and Caesar, he was elevated to the consulship in 57. (Cicero comments in a letter to Atticus [*Ad Att.* 3.22.2]: *Saepe enim tū ad mē scrīpsistī eum* [Spinther] *tōtum esse in illīus* [Pompey] *potestāte*). As consul he favored in turn both Cicero and Pompey. On the one hand, he actively sponsored the former's recall from exile; on the other, he advocated a commission which would give the latter control of the corn supply for five years. But Spinther was also capable of looking out for his own interests. He moved in the senate that the next governor of Cilicia, already designated as Spinther himself, would be responsible for restoring Ptolemy Auletes to the throne of Egypt. Although the motion was passed, Spinther was prevented from carrying out his assignment, which fell to Gabinius, the governor of Syria. For his campaigns in Cilicia from 56 to 54, he was saluted as *imperātor* and finally granted a triumph in 51. During the civil war, while siding with Pompey, he was captured and pardoned by Caesar at Corfinium. Later he returned to oppose Caesar at Pharsalus and died in Africa in defeat. When evaluating his abilities as an orator, Cicero says (*Brūtus* 268) that he lacked natural talent but tried to compensate for his deficiencies with study and training.

191

Curio: See **Scribonius.**

Dolabella: See **Cornelius.**

Lucius Domitius Ahenobarbus (d. 48)

Born around 97 into one of the noblest plebeian families of Rome, Lucius Domitius Ahenobarbus, in the words of Cicero (*Ad Att.* 4.8B.2), was marked out from the time of his birth as destined for the consulship. His marriage to Cato's sister cemented his relationship with another of the families prominent among the *bonī*. In 66 as quaestor, Domitius predictably resisted Manilius's proposal to grant Pompey an extraordinary command against Mithridates. Throughout his career, his enormous wealth and prestige were exploited to support the interests of the conservative faction in the senate and to oppose, fervently but often in vain, the policies of the "triumvirate" and especially of his bitter enemy Caesar. As praetor in 58, he denounced Caesar's legislation of the previous year and questioned its legality without success. His threats to recall Caesar from Gaul if he should be elected to the consulship of 55 moved the "triumvirs" to confer at Luca and arrange a second consulship for Pompey and Crassus in order to thwart Domitius. When actually elected consul for 54, Domitius persisted in his efforts to embarrass Caesar. Later (in 50), he can undoubtedly be numbered among the twenty-two senators who opposed Curio's motion that both Caesar and Pompey should resign their commands and disband their armies. After the outbreak of civil war in 49, the senate appointed him to replace Caesar in Cisalpine Gaul. Surrounded by Caesar's legions at Corfinium, he capitulated and, although spared, returned to oppose Caesar at Massilia and then at Pharsalus, where he sacrificed his life in the republican cause.

Titus Labienus (d. 45)

In the extant sources, Titus Labienus first rose to prominence as a tribune in 63, when he was aligned with the leaders of the *populārēs*. He was born to an equestrian family in Cingulum of Picenum, where Pompey had strong connections. During his tribunate, he collaborated with Caesar and successfully advocated popular election in the college of pontiffs, which resulted in Caesar's becoming *pontifex maximus*. Labienus also proposed that Pompey be granted certain triumphal honors for his victory over Mithridates in Asia. In another *populāris* move, he was again joined by Caesar in the prosecution of Rabirius, who many years earlier (in 100), had allegedly participated in the slaying of the tribune Saturninus and who was now defended by Cicero, the consul. Labienus, whose uncle had died with Saturninus, was once again posing as a champion of the rights of the people. By 59 he had contrived to be elected to a praetorship. Thereafter he served as *lēgātus prō praetōre* with Caesar in Gaul and became his ablest lieutenant. When civil war erupted, Labienus deserted Caesar for uncertain reasons and later supported the Pompeian cause at Thapsus and Munda, where he died fighting.

Lentulus Crus: See **Cornelius**.

Lentulus Spinther: See **Cornelius**.

Lucius Lucceius

Lucius Lucceius, Pompey's personal friend and political advisor, achieved prominence in two very different endeavors. As a politician he was elected to the praetorship for 67. In 64, after Catiline's defeat at the polls, Lucceius prosecuted him for his involvement in the Sullan proscriptions but lost the case. Later in 60, he entered into negotiations with Caesar which resulted in an agreement that Lucceius would use his great wealth to promote their joint candidacy for the consulship. Whereas Caesar was elected, Lucceius was disappointed with attaining only third place behind the conservative Bibulus. Subsequently Cicero, during his defense of Caelius in 56, describes how the prosecution had tried to implicate Lucceius's slaves in an attempted murder of his guest, the Egyptian ambassador. In the course of his speech (*Prō Caeliō*), Cicero praises Lucceius for his learning and integrity. Although during the civil war Lucceius was closely associated with Pompey, he was later pardoned by Caesar.

As a man of letters, Lucceius had set out to compose a history of the Italian and civil wars. In a famous letter written to Lucceius in 56 (*Ad Fam.* 5.12), Cicero asks him to interrupt his work in order to record for posterity Cicero's memorable achievements during his consulship. Lucceius seems never to have completed the task.

Gaius Matius

Little is known about the life of Gaius Matius other than what can be gleaned from his exchange of letters with Cicero (*Ad Fam.* 11.27 and 28). He was born into the equestrian class and pursued a business career while avoiding politics. Because of his moderation and reliability, he became a firm friend of both Caesar and Cicero and accompanied the former into Gaul as a member of his staff. His unflagging support of his friends and unswerving commitment to the principles which he advocated made even Cicero, who did not endorse Matius's political views, praise him for his devoted loyalty, sound judgment, dignity, charm, and literary tastes (*Ad Fam.* 11.27.6). In 44 Matius presided over the games which Octavian held in Caesar's honor.

Marcellus: See Claudius.

Marcus Petreius (d. 46)

A military man who had served in the army as tribune, prefect, and legate (Sallust, *Catilīna* 59.6), Marcus Petreius possessed such exceptional qualities that by 63, after thirty years of service, he also attained the political office of praetor. As propraetor in northern Italy in 62, he fought for the republic and defeated Catiline at Pistoria. In 59 his republican sympathies were offended by the coercive tactics of the triumvirate, and when Caesar tried to have Cato arrested, Petreius was among those senators who supported Cato, saying that he preferred to accompany Cato to prison rather than to side with Caesar in the senate (Dio 38.1). Petreius's courageous stand and strong convictions forced Caesar to yield before he made Cato a hero. In 55 Petreius became one of Pompey's legates in *Hispānia ulterior* and stubbornly resisted Caesar in 49. After the republican defeat at Pharsalus, Petreius loyally followed Cato to Africa and was killed in the aftermath of Thapsus (in 46). In the triumphal procession for his African victories, Caesar offended the Romans with representations of Cato, Scipio, and Petreius, who were all considered champions of liberty (Appian, *Bella Cīvīlia* 2.420).

Piso: See Calpurnius.

Titus Pomponius Atticus (110–32)

Titus Pomponius Atticus was about three years older than Marcus Tullius Cicero, his close friend and frequent correspondent, although by a quirk of fate no letters from Atticus to Cicero are extant. Both men came from equestrian families, the one of old Roman stock, the other a native of Arpinum. Sometime after 86, in order to avoid the civil wars raging in

Italy, Pomponius moved from Rome to Athens, where he stayed for at least twenty years and from where he acquired his *cognōmen* of Atticus. For six months in 79, Cicero resided in Athens so that the two friends could study philosophy together under various Greek teachers. Some years later, Pomponia, Atticus's sister, married Quintus Cicero, the orator's brother, but the match did not turn out to be successful. Before leaving Greece in the middle 60s, Atticus, a man of considerable wealth, purchased an estate at Buthrotum in Epirus, which thereafter he used for his sojourns abroad.

When Atticus returned to Rome toward the end of 65, he came home to support Cicero's candidacy for the consulship by trying to influence his many connections, especially with the optimate aristocracy, to gain backing for his friend. After Cicero as consul had successfully maneuvered to suppress the Catilinarian conspiracy, he stationed on the road leading from the forum to the Capitoline Hill a garrison of *equitēs* under the leadership of Atticus (*Ad Att.* 2.1.7) to protect the senate while it was meeting in the Temple of Concord on December 5 to decide the fate of the prisoners. This event marks one of the rare occasions when Atticus, who preferred to remain behind the scenes, became directly involved in politics. Ultimately Atticus's role in history was distinguished not by his political influence and achievements but by the services which he offered to Cicero as a prudent and honest advisor and as a critic and publisher, using his slaves to copy Cicero's works for circulation. During the various crises in Cicero's career, Atticus always tried to maintain his friend's morale and encourage him, counseling moderation and steadfastness. In the civil war of 49, Atticus remained behind in Rome, preserving his independence and neutrality while keeping his friends and refraining from making enemies. Later, although he, like Cicero, took no part in Caesar's assassination, he tacitly approved of what the "liberators" had done in the name of the republic but still avoided any active involvement. True to his instincts for living safely in times of turbulence, Atticus befriended Antony's wife Fulvia after her husband's defeat at Mutina and thus was spared during the proscriptions which followed the formation of the "second" triumvirate in 43 and took the life of Cicero. During the next decade (in 37), Atticus's daughter Caecilia married Agrippa, Octavian's lieutenant, and their daughter, Vipsania Agrippina, was betrothed to the future emperor Tiberius. Atticus died as quietly as he had lived on March 31, 32, not surviving to witness Octavian's decisive victory at Actium in the following year.

Marcus Porcius Cato (95–46)

The great-grandson of Cato the Censor, Marcus Porcius Cato resembled his ancestor for his integrity, conservatism, and respect for venerable Roman traditions. As a practicing Stoic, the younger Cato applied the tenets of his creed to the performance of his public duties. He first came into prominence as quaestor in 64, when he became the guardian of the treasury and forcefully reformed the financial system to eliminate the corruption of the clerks and scribes who had become accustomed to tampering with the public accounts in their own interest. Because of Cato's efforts, their activities were hereafter scrutinized and regulated by the state. No one, it was said, had done so much for the quaestorship, which was now made equal to the dignity of a consulship (Plutarch, *Cato* 16.2–3; 17.1–2). Through force of character, Cato earned such respect from his contemporaries that when others of his junior status would not dare to challenge the rules of seniority, he would ask for recognition to deliver a moving and compelling speech. Such was the case when, as tribune-elect in 63, he persuaded the senate to take advantage of the extreme decree to execute the Catilinarian conspirators, opposing Caesar's argument that no Roman citizen should be condemned to death without a trial. This was the first of many confrontations that were to occur between Cato and Caesar throughout the ensuing decade, the one a leader of the *optimātēs,* the other of the *populārēs.*

During his tribunate, Cato proposed a decree in the senate to allocate state funds for purchasing grain for the people. This was a popular move designed to attract support from the partisans of Caesar. He also vetoed the bill to recall Pompey and give him a command to dispose of Catiline. Throughout the rest of his career in the senate, Cato was a member of the opposition as he assumed an uncompromising stand against any challenges to the status quo. Aligned with him were L. Domitius Ahenobarbus, who was married to his sister, and M. Calpurnius Bibulus, his son-in-law. He opposed the policies of the triumvirate to give land to Pompey's veterans and to ratify his eastern settlement, using Bibulus, Caesar's consular colleague in 59, as his instrument. In 58 his opponents succeeded in having him removed to Cyprus to administer the new territory, where he acquitted himself with distinction. Upon his return to Rome in 56, Cato campaigned unsuccessfully for the praetorship of 55. In the same year, he became a candidate again and was elected for 54. Later he failed to win the consulship for 51 because he refused to resort to bribery.

At the time of the civil war, he served Pompey and the *optimātēs* first in Sicily and then in Asia Minor. During the conflict in Greece, he was in charge of Dyrrachium. After the defeat of Pompey at Pharsalus, Cato joined the republican forces in Africa. A few days after Caesar won his decisive African victory at Thapsus on April 6, 46, Cato committed suicide to avoid witnessing the demise of the republic and the supremacy of Caesar. "I do not wish," he said, "to be indebted to the tyrant for his illegal actions: for he is acting against the laws when he pardons men over whom he has no sovereignty as if he were their master" (Plutarch, *Cato* 66). So died the man who had already become a symbol of the republic and now was a martyr in the republican cause. As Cicero observed (*Ad Att.* 12.4.2), "Cato foresaw what has happened and will be; he strove to prevent it and left this life to avoid witnessing it."

Scipio: See Caecilius.

C. Scribonius Curio (d. 49)

Like his father of the same name, C. Scribonius Curio pursued the career of the opportunist par excellence. The elder Curio was Sulla's supporter and sharer in his proscriptions, optimate consul in 76, Verres's friend, partisan of Pompey in 66, counsel for the defense at the trial of Clodius in 61, Cicero's ally during his exile, and opponent of Pompey and Caesar at the time of the triumvirate. The younger Curio's change of allegiance in 50 and his support of Caesar with brilliant propaganda seemed to many observers to be the most provocative of the acts that precipitated the civil war of 49.

At the beginning of his career, we often find Curio acting in conjunction with his father and following his lead. In 59, during Caesar's consulship, he alone dared to speak out against the triumvirate (*Ad Att.* 2.18), and at the games of Apollo he was applauded whereas silence greeted the appearance of Caesar (*Ad Att.* 2.19). When he informed his father of a scheme concocted by a certain L. Vettius to murder Pompey, the plot collapsed, and Vettius ended his life in prison (*Ad Att.* 2.24).

In the course of his political career, Curio developed a reputation for being a shrewd politician who possessed a natural talent for oratory. A man of shifting principles, he was known to be unrestrained in his partisanship and willing to use any strategy and any means to accomplish his goals. As quaestor in 53, he served in Asia Minor under Appius Claudius, was elected pontifex in 52, and ran successfully for the tribunate in 51 as an enthusiastic supporter of the *optimātēs*.

Early in his term of office, Curio posed as an independent, proposing agrarian and grain laws which were intended to irritate the *optimātēs,* and after March 1, 50, vetoing any legislation designed to abbreviate or terminate Caesar's command in Gaul. Whatever the motives may have been for his change of allegiance, he is alleged to have received an enormous bribe from Caesar with which to pay the debts incurred by his extravagant ways. Furthermore, his marriage to Fulvia after the death, in 52, of her former husband Clodius may help to explain his new attachment to Caesar as well as his sense that a crisis was at hand which he could use to promote his own career. To the end of his tribunate, he remained the effective champion of Caesar's interests, especially when he surprised the opposition by proposing to the senate shortly before the end of his term that both Pompey and Caesar resign their commands, a motion which passed by a vote of 370 to 22 and which motivated Marcellus, the presiding consul, to dismiss the senate and entrust the defense of Rome to Pompey. Soon after, Curio left Rome to join Caesar.

After performing various commissions for Caesar early in 49, he was entrusted with the task of taking Africa from the Pompeians. When his campaign failed and his army was annihilated by Pompey's ally, the Numidian king Juba, Caesar wrote (*Bellum Cīvīle* 2.42) that Curio stayed at his post to die honorably: *Hortātur Curiōnem Cn. Domitius, praefectus equitum, cum paucīs equitibus circumsistēns, ut fugā salūtem petat atque in castra contendat, et sē ab eō nōn discessūrum pollicētur. At Curiō numquam sē āmissō exercitū, quem ā Caesare fideī commissum accepērit, in eius cōnspectum reversūrum cōnfirmat atque ita proeliāns interficitur* ("Cn. Domitius, commander of the cavalry, surrounding Curio with a few horsemen, urged him to seek safety in flight and to hasten into camp, and he promised that he would not desert him. But Curio declared that he would never return to Caesar's sight after losing his army, which he had received from Caesar and which had been entrusted to his charge. And so he was killed while fighting.")

Curio's success in the forum had eluded him on the battlefield.

Spinther: See Cornelius Lentulus.

Servius Sulpicius Rufus (d. 43)

Servius Sulpicius Rufus, whom the poet Byron describes as "the Roman friend of Rome's least mortal mind" (*Childe Harold* 4.44), studied rhetoric and law on Rhodes with Cicero. Whereas Cicero intended to learn as much of the law as was necessary for an orator, Sulpicius aimed to acquire as much eloquence as he needed to become a guardian of the civil law (*Brūtus* 150). He succeeded so well that, like Cicero in his vocation, he excelled all those who had preceded him.

Unsurpassed in his knowledge of Roman jurisprudence and dedicated to upholding the ideals of the republican form of government, Sulpicius set out upon a political career. After attaining the quaestorship in 74, the curule aedileship in 69, and the praetorship in 65, he became a candidate for the consulship in 63, and like Catiline suffered defeat at the hands of Silanus and Murena. At once Sulpicius, supported by Cato, prosecuted Murena on a charge of bribery, hoping that a conviction would gain him the office which he had been denied in the elections. Cicero, Sulpicius's old friend, successfully defended Murena with the argument that what Rome needed to cope with the threats of Catiline was a practical politician, not an erudite jurisconsult. After his defeat in 63, Sulpicius did not realize his ambition to become consul until 51, when he was elected along with the arch-conservative M. Claudius Marcellus. When Marcellus proposed that Caesar's command in Gaul be terminated on March 1, 50, his learned colleague successfully opposed the motion on the grounds that it was both premature and illegal.

Upon the outbreak of civil war, Sulpicius left Rome but soon returned to the city, where he was one of only two senators with consular rank to attend a meeting of the senate summoned by Caesar on April 1. After the battle of Pharsalus, Sulpicius retired to Samos to devote himself to the study of law until Caesar appointed him, as a man of moderation, to be proconsul of Achaea in 46. He performed his last service to the state when he agreed, though ill, to participate in an embassy to Antonius, who was encamped before Mutina in January, 43. There he died, succumbing to the harshness of the wintry climate. In a subsequent meeting of the senate, when the consul Pansa asked the senators to consider conferring honors upon Sulpicius, Cicero rose to deliver his friend's eulogy, known as the ninth Philippic, in which he supported Pansa's motion of a public funeral and a statue to be erected on the Rostra. The motion was carried.

Gaius Trebonius (d. 43)

The son of a Roman *eques*, Gaius Trebonius first appeared in politics as quaestor (60) when he opposed the transition to plebeian status of P. Clodius and aligned himself with Cicero and the *bonī*.

Sometime later in the fifties, he changed his mind and supported the policies of the triumvirate. As tribune in 55, he sponsored a bill, which became known as the *lēx Trebōnia,* to grant Spain to Pompey and Syria to Crassus for a tenure of five years after their consulship. From 54 he was one of Caesar's *lēgātī* in Gaul and was stationed with three legions among the Belgians (*Bellum Gallicum* 5.24). In the spring of 49, when Caesar was besieging Massilia, after several weeks he handed over the operation to Trebonius, who with the help of Decimus Brutus overcame the resistance of the Massiliotes and concluded a truce with them. Although Caesar made him consul in October 45 and promised him the province of Asia, he turned against his leader and joined the assassins in 44. After arriving in Asia, he was murdered by Dolabella in January of the next year, presumably for treason.

GLOSSARY OF
KEY TERMS

Aedile

Among other municipal duties, the aediles supervised the corn supply and public games. There were two curule aediles elected by the *comitia tribūta* and two plebeian aediles elected by the *concilium plēbis*. They had to be at least thirty-seven years of age. The office of aedile was not an essential part of the *cursus honōrum*. Like other magistrates (except the censors) the aediles held office for one year.

Assemblies

An assembly, called a *comitia* (*-ōrum*, n. pl.), was a meeting of Roman citizens summoned by a Roman magistrate and always divided into voting groups, each group casting a single vote. The assemblies met in Rome, where Italian citizens would have to travel if they wished to vote, since a representative system was never introduced during the republic. Only those who were asked by the presiding magistrate could speak on a given proposal (*rogātiō*), and although discussion often did precede the voting, no amendments to a proposal were permitted. Such an assembly, where freedom of speech was limited and where attendance was denied to those without the means for traveling, could hardly be called democratic, as the connotations of that word are understood today.

The following assemblies still played an influential role in the Roman system of government in the late republic:

(a) *comitia centuriāta*. This assembly, originally organized in military units, had in the course of time assumed a political character. The centuries, comprising the *comitia centuriāta,* were divided into classes according to wealth, and those with the greater wealth not only contained the majority of the one hundred ninety-three voting units if they voted together, but they also voted first. Whenever a majority was reached, the voting ceased so that often the lower centuries, where most of the eligible voters were assigned, were not even allowed to vote. Hence the voting in this assembly was strictly controlled by those centuries in which only wealthy citizens were enrolled. In Cicero's time the *comitia centuriāta* was chiefly responsible for electing the consuls, praetors, and censors when a consul or praetor presided. For the most part, its legislative functions had been transferred earlier to the *comitia tribūta.*

(b) *comitia tribūta*. The tribal assembly or *comitia tribūta* was composed of all the citizens distributed among thirty-five tribes (four urban and thirty-one rural). A consul or praetor usually presided. Since its voting machinery, using the tribal unit, was less cumbersome and more democratic than that of the *comitia centuriāta*, it was here that most laws were passed in the middle and late republic. Because citizens who had migrated to Rome from the country were still registered in their rural tribes and often voted with the urban *plēbs,* the *nōbilēs* could not influence the outcome as effectively as in the *comitia centuriāta.* The tribal assembly elected the curule aediles, quaestors, and certain lesser magistrates.

(c) *concilium plēbis*. The composition of the *concilium plēbis* consisted of the same thirty-five tribes as the *comitia tribūta,* but only plebeians could attend and vote. A tribune usually presided. After 287 B.C. the decrees of this assembly, called *plēbiscīta,* although passed by only a part of the citizens, applied as *lēgēs* to all. As an elective body, the *concilium plēbis* chose the tribunes and plebeian aediles.

Calendar

The Romans divided their year into twelve months, designated by the adjectives *Iānuārius, Februārius, Mārtius, Aprīlis, Māius, Iūnius, Quintīlis* (later *Iūlius*), *Sextīlis* (later *Augustus*), *September, October, November,* and *December.* The fact that before 153 B.C. the Romans began the year with the month of March explains the numerical names of *Quintīlis* (the fifth month) through *December* (the tenth month).

Each month had three fixed points: the Kalends (*Kalendae*), the Nones (*Nōnae*), and the Ides (*Īdūs, -uum,* f. pl.). The Kalends always fell

202

on the first of the month. The Nones were the seventh day of March, May, July and October, but the fifth day of the other months. The Ides always occurred eight days after the Nones (hence the fifteenth or thirteenth). Before Caesar's adjustment of the calendar in 46, the year consisted of three hundred fifty-five days, distributed as follows: March, May, July, and October had thirty-one days each, February had twenty-eight, and each of the rest twenty-nine. Since this year of 355 days was shorter than the solar year of 365 days, the Romans, at the discretion of the *pontificēs,* added an intercalary "month" of varying length to compensate for the difference. After Caesar's revision this correction was no longer necessary.

When specifying a particular day of the month, the Romans calculated back from the nearest of the three fixed points, counting inclusively (i.e. including the days at either end). Hence the rules for converting are as follows:

For days preceding the Nones or Ides, add one to the fixed date and subtract the modern date. Thus February 2, in the Roman calendar, would be: 5 (for the Nones) + 1 = 6 − 2 = the fourth day before the Nones, expressed in Latin as *ante diem quartum Nōnās Februāriās* (adj.), commonly abbreviated to *a. d. iv Nōn. Feb.,* or as *quartō diē ante Nōnās Februāriās* (abbr. *iv Nōn. Feb.*).

For days preceding the Kalends, add two to the number of days in the specified month (one for the last day of that month and one for the first, or Kalends, of the next month), and subtract the given date. Thus August 19 would be: 29 + 2 = 31 − 19 = the twelfth day before the Kalends of September, expressed as *ante diem duodecimum Kalendās Septembrēs* (abbr. *a. d. xii Kal. Sept.*) or as *duodecimō diē ante Kalendās Septembrēs* (abbr. *xii Kal. Sept.*). The first of these alternatives is more common, and since it is considered to be an indeclinable substantive the propositions *ad, ex,* and *in* may be used before it (e.g. *ex a. d. iii Īd. Nov.* = "from November 11"). The day before the three fixed points is always expressed with *prīdiē: prīdiē Īdūs Mārtiās* (abbr. *pr. Īd. Mārt.*) = March 14.

Censor

Two censors were elected every five years from Roman citizens of consular rank to revise the rolls of citizens and review the lists of senators. They also auctioned to the *equitēs* (*pūblicānī*) the contracts for public works and for collection of provincial taxes. The censors held office for eighteen months.

Clientēs

In Roman society, a client was a citizen of dependent status for whom a citizen of greater standing (his *patrōnus*) performed certain services (*beneficia*), legal, political, or economic. Because the client incurred obligations (*officia*) to his patron, he was expected to show his gratitude and return the favor. For example, when a patron gave legal counsel to his client, he would expect in return the vote of the client in the next election. Many of the prominent patrician and plebeian families and their leaders could boast of numerous clients not only in Rome and Italy but also in the provinces. The more numerous their clients, the greater their prestige.

Cohort

In Caesar's army, the cohort was the standard tactical unit. There were six centuries to a cohort, and ten cohorts (each consisting of some 400–500 men) comprised a legion. Although Caesar appointed *lēgātī* to command individual legions, he placed his greatest trust in the centurions because they were often the only professional officers with extensive combat experience. The six centurions of the tenth cohort were lowest in rank, whereas the centurions of the first cohort (the *prīmī ōrdinēs*) were ranked above all the others. The highest ranking centurion of the first cohort was called the *prīmus pīlus*.

Consul

The two consuls, who had to be at least forty-three, were elected for one year by the *comitia centuriāta* and possessed the *imperium*. They were the supreme magistrates in Rome, who formulated and executed state policy. Like the praetors, they were often assigned to provinces as proconsuls.

Cursus Honōrum

Four magistracies—the quaestorship, aedileship, praetorship, consulship—comprised the *cursus honōrum* or sequence of offices. An ambitious politican was expected to hold these offices in succession, except for the aedileship, which could be passed over. Election to all of the offices was for one year only.

Equitēs

In the late republic, citizens who possessed more than four hundred thousand *sestertiī* but who were not yet eligible to enter the senate were granted a public horse. These *equitēs* formed a second class of citizens below those of senatorial rank. They can be divided into three categories: (1) sons of senators who had not yet attained the quaestorship which carried admission to the senate; (2) wealthy businessmen and financiers, who chose not to pursue a career in the senate and of whom many were involved in purchasing contracts to collect provincial taxes; (3) the landed gentry (*domī nōbilēs*), leaders in their own communities, from those municipalities of Italy which had been granted the privilege of citizenship.

Imperium

Imperium was the supreme civil and military power (right to command) which a superior magistrate (consul, proconsul, praetor, propraetor) exercised at home (*domī*) and abroad (*mīlitiae*) within certain limitations as specified by law. For example, a proconsul was required to relinquish his *imperium* if he were to leave his province.

Mūnicipium

In the late republic, a *mūnicipium* was an Italian community which enjoyed full Roman citizenship and was self-governing (i.e., it had its own duly elected magistrates). In all cases, however, Rome expressly forbade an independent foreign policy.

Names

Most Roman males had three names: the *praenōmen*, *nōmen*, and *cognōmen* (e.g. Gaius Julius Caesar). The *praenōmen* indicated the individual (our "first name"); the *nōmen* showed the *gēns* or clan, a group of families sharing a common ancestor; and the *cognōmen* was an additional name of a family or individual, which often originally referred to a personal peculiarity (e.g. *cicer,* "chick-pea"). A second *cognōmen,* called an *agnōmen,* was sometimes added to commemorate a personal achievement (e.g. Publius Cornelius Scipio Africanus). The *agnōmen* Africanus was granted to Scipio for his victories over the Carthaginians in Africa.

205

Nōbilēs

This term is applied to the direct male descendants of consuls, and some scholars include descendants of praetors and curule aediles.

Novus Homō

A man who had attained a curule magistracy (consulship, praetorship, aedileship) and who could boast of no ancestors from among the nobility was known as a *novus homō*. Rarely was such a man promoted to the consulship.

Optimātēs

The *optimātēs*, or *bonī*, were those citizens (usually of senatorial or equestrian rank) who wanted to preserve the status quo and, in particular, the dominant position of the senate. They did not form a party or faction but were drawn together by a common way of thinking (see n. 21.10 and n. 32.13).

Praetor

The eight praetors, who had to be at least forty years of age, were elected for one year by the *comitia centuriāta*. Like the consuls, they possessed the *imperium* and therefore had the right to command armies and summon meetings of the assemblies and senate. Their primary responsibilities, however, were to exercise the civil jurisdiction and preside over the standing criminal courts (*quaestiōnēs perpetuae*). After their year of office, most praetors were assigned by the senate to govern provinces as propraetors.

Populārēs

The term *populārēs* refers to those politicians who, in order to achieve their ends, disregarded the senate and appealed directly to the popular assemblies. They were, or were thought to be, champions of the rights of the people (see n. 21.10).

Prōvincia

Originally the word *prōvincia* denoted the sphere of activity of a Roman magistrate. For example, financial matters were the "province" of the quaestor, and judicial affairs the "province" of the praetor. Later it designated a district, usually overseas, which had been acquired by

Rome and was administered by a governor (proconsul or propraetor) assigned by the senate. In comparison with the urban magistrate, the provincial governor was almost omnipotent. In his person he combined military, administrative, financial, and judicial functions. There were no public meetings, no senate, no right of appeal to constrain him.

Of the twelve provinces which Rome had acquired before the final days of the republic, Cisalpine Gaul (*Gallia citerior*) demands special mention because of its importance in Caesar's narrative of the civil war. This province, which extended from the Alps in north Italy to the Rubicon River, was probably created some time after the Social War (90–88 B.C.), possibly by Sulla. It was unique among the Roman provinces in that it contained cities (*mūnicipia*) which had been granted the rights of full citizenship even before Caesar, as governor of Cisalpine Gaul, made the *Trānspadānī* (those living across the Po River) citizens.

Quaestor

This office was open to all those male citizens who had reached the age of thirty. Of the twenty quaestors elected by the *comitia tribūta*, two were in charge of the treasury (*aerārium*) in Rome, whereas the rest served as assistants to provincial governors. Election to this office, which was held for one year, resulted in entry into the senate as a junior senator (*pedārius;* see below).

Senate

The senate was composed of about six hundred members, who, upon becoming quaestors, had been enrolled for life, unless they were to be removed by the censors for misconduct. It was their function to advise the magistrates on domestic matters and especially on foreign policy. Their decrees did not have the force of law. The presiding magistrate (consul, praetor, or tribune, in order of precedence) called upon senators to speak according to rank. Those who voted but did not speak were the *senātōrēs pedāriī*. They had held, or were holding, only the magistracies of lower rank (quaestorship, aedileship). They and the other senators voted by moving to either side of the chamber.

Senātūs Cōnsultum ("decree of the senate")

Decrees passed by the senate were merely advisory. They were not legally binding, but they did provide the magistrates with the moral support of the senate. In times of crisis, the *senātūs cōnsultum ultimum* was passed. It declared a state of emergency, instructing the consuls and other magistrates "to see to it that the state suffer no harm." Like other senatorial decrees, it had no binding legal force.

Consuls, praetors, and tribunes, in order of precedence, could convene and consult the senate. The presiding magistrate, who did not normally put a motion of his own, had the right to select which motion was to be voted upon. If the motion was passed, it was recorded as a *senātūs cōnsultum*.

Tribune

The office of the tribune of the plebs (*tribūnus plēbis*), which was not part of the *cursus honōrum*, was established in the first half of the fifth century B.C. for the purpose of upholding the rights of the plebeians in their strife with the patricians. The person of each of the ten tribunes was considered sacrosanct, and if they suffered any act of violence, the plebeians were under oath to come to their defense. The tribunes had the right to propose legislation to the *concilium plēbis* and the power of veto (*intercessiō*) over all legislative motions and almost all *senātūs cōnsulta* (see n. 3.34). Like all other Roman magistrates except the censors, tribunes were elected for an annual term. Of course, they had to be citizens of plebeian status. Unlike the other magistrates, who took office on January 1, they assumed their duties on December 10.

Tribūnī Aerāriī

"The *lēx Aurēlia* of 70 created three panels of *iūdicēs*, senators, Equites, and *tribūnī aerāriī;* the second class undoubtedly consisted only of holders of the public horse, but Cicero himself could describe the third too as Equites, and this is only explicable on the basis that by property and birth they too were of equestrian standing." (P. A. Brunt, *The Fall of the Roman Republic* [Oxford: Clarendon Press, 1988], p. 146).

LATIN-ENGLISH VOCABULARY

ā, ab (+ abl.) from, away from; by

abdicō (1) resign

abdūcō, -cere, -xī, -ctum lead away, remove

abhorreō, -ēre, -uī shrink from, have no taste for

abiciō, -icere, -iēcī, -iectum throw, throw to the ground

absēns, -ntis absent

absum, abesse, āfuī, āfutūrus be away, be absent

accēdō, -dere, -ssī, -ssum go to, approach; be an additional factor

accidō, -ere, -ī happen

accipiō, -ipere, -ēpī, -eptum receive

acerbus, -a, -um bitter, harsh, distressing

acūtus, -a, -um sharp, shrewd

ad (+ acc.) to; for; near; in respect to

addō, -ere, -idī, -itum add

addūcō, -cere, -xī, -ctum lead to, influence, convince

adeō (adv.) so, to such an extent; in fact

adferō, -rre, attulī, allātum bring, report

adfīnitās, -ātis, f. relationship (by marriage)

adflīgō, -gere, -xī, -ctum damage, injure, batter

adhibeō, -ēre, -uī, -itum bring to, apply; call in

adhūc (adv.) up to this point, still

adimō, -imere, -ēmī, -emptum take away, remove

aditus, -ūs, m. approach, access

adiungō, -gere, -xī, -ctum attach

adiūtor, -ōris, m. supporter

adiuvō, -iuvare, -iūvī, -iūtum abet, promote, help

administrātiō, -ōnis, f. operation, control

administrō (1) conduct, direct

admīrābilis, -e remarkable

admīror (1) be surprised, wonder

admoneō, -ēre, -uī, -itum remind

adoptō (1) adopt

adsentor (1) flatter

adsum, -esse, -fuī, -futūrus be present

adulēscēns, -ntis, m. a youth

advehō, -here, -xī, -ctum bring

adveniō, -īre, -vēnī, -ventum arrive

adventō (1) arrive, draw near

adventus, -ūs, m. arrival

adversārius, -ī, m. opponent, antagonist

adversus (+ acc.) against

adversus, -a, -um unfavorable; opposed

aedificō (1) build

aegrē (adv.) scarcely; with difficulty

aēneātor, -ōris, m. trumpeter

aequitās, -ātis, f. fairness

aequus, -a, -um just, right, fair, reasonable

aerārium, -ī, n. treasury

aes aliēnum, aeris aliēnī, n. debt

aetās, -ātis, f. age, time

agmen, -inis, n. infantry, army

agō, agere, ēgī, āctum do, act; discuss, plead; (of time) spend

āiō say

aliēnus, -a, -um another's; disloyal; improper

aliquandō (adv.) at last

aliquis (-quī), -qua, -quid (-quod) someone, something; some

aliquō (adv.) somewhere, anywhere

aliquot (indecl. adj.) several, numerous, many

aliter (adv.) otherwise

alius, -a, -ud other, another

alō, -ere, -uī, -tum support, promote (the interests of)

alter, -era, -erum the other (of two), the second

alter . . . alter the one . . . the other

ambō, -ae, -ō both

āmēns, -ntis mad, insane

āmentia, -ae, f. madness, insanity

amīcitia, -ae, f. friendship

amīcus, -a, -um friendly

amīcus, -ī, m. friend, supporter

āmittō, -ere, -mīsī, -missum
lose, let go

amō (1) like, love

amplius (adv.) more

amplus, -a, -um distinguished,
impressive, important

an (conj.) or

angustus, -a, -um narrow

anima, -ae, f. loved one

animadvertō, -tere, -tī, -sum
notice

animus, -ī, m. mind; courage,
morale, disposition, attitude

annus, -ī, m. year

ante (+ acc.) before; (adv.)
before, formerly, previously

anteā (adv.) before, formerly,
previously

antecēdō, -dere, -ssi, -ssum
arrive before, arrive first

antecursōrēs, -um, m. pl.
vanguard

antepōnō, -ere, -osuī, -ositum
prefer

antequam (conj.) before

aperiō, -īre, -uī, -tum open;
reveal

appāreō, -ēre, -uī, -itum appear

appellō (1) call, name

appetō, -ere, -īvī (-iī), -itum
seek, aim at

appropinquō (1) approach

apud (+ acc.) among, at the
house of, in the presence of

arbitrātus, -ūs, m. choice;
arbitrātū (+ gen. or
pronominal adj.) at the

discretion (of), in the
judgment (of)

arbitrium, -ī, n. discretion,
direction

arbitror (1) think

arcānō (adv.) secretly

arcessō, -ere, -īvī, -ītum
summon

ardeō, -dēre, -sī, -sum burn, be
on fire

arma, -ōrum, n. pl. arms

armō (1) arm, equip

artificium, -ī, n. device,
contrivance, stratagem

asservō (1) guard

astūtē (adv.) cleverly, cunningly

atque, ac (conj.) and

atquī (conj.) and yet

attingō, -tingere, -tigī, -tāctum
touch, undertake; move,
affect

attribuō, -uere, -uī, -ūtum
grant

auctor, -ōris, m. proposer,
initiator, advocate, supporter,
champion

auctōritās, -ātis, f. authority,
prestige, influence

audācia, -ae, f. boldness, daring,
effrontery, impudence

audāx, -ācis bold

audeō, -dēre, -sus sum dare,
presume, have the courage

audiō, -īre, -īvī (-iī), -ītum
hear

auferō, -ferre, abstulī, ablātum
take away, remove

augeō, -gēre, -xī, -ctum
increase (in military power),
advance (in dignity)

augur, -uris, m. augur

auguror (1) predict, judge,
interpret

auspicium, -ī, n. omen

auspicor (1) take the auspices,
seek omens

aut (conj.) or

autem (conj.) however;
moreover

auxilium, -ī, n. help, aid; (pl.)
reinforcements, reserves

āvertō, -tere, -tī, -sum turn
away, divert, alienate

āvocō (1) call away, divert

barbarus, -a, -um foreign

beātus, -a, -um healthy, blessed;
wealthy

belligerō (1) wage war

bellum, -ī, n. war

bene (adv.) well

beneficium, -ī, n. a favor,
kindness, benefit, service

benevolentia, -ae, f. goodwill

bis (adv.) twice

bonum, -ī, n. benefit, privilege,
blessing

bonus, -a, -um good, honorable

brevī (adv.) briefly, in a few
words; soon

brevis, -e short

brevitās, -ātis, f. conciseness,
brevity

cadāver, -eris, n. corpse

cadō, -ere, cecidī, cāsum fall

calamitōsus, -a, -um disastrous

capiō, -ere, cēpī, -tum take,
seize, capture; (with
cōnsilium) form a plan

careō, -ēre, -uī, -itum (+ abl.)
be deprived of, lack

castellum, -ī, n. bastion,
bulwark

castīgō (1) criticize, chide

castra, -ōrum, n. pl. camp;
(with *facere*) take the field

cāsus, -ūs, m. misfortune,
predicament

causa, -ae, f. cause, reason;
objective

causā (+ gen.) for the sake of

caveō, -ēre, cāvī, cautum
beware of; (with *ab* + abl.)
guard against; (with subjn.)
take care

cēdō, -dere, -ssī, -ssum yield; go

celeriter (adv.) quickly

cēnseō, -ēre, -uī, -um propose,
think, recommend, decree

centuriō, -ōnis, m. centurion

certē (adv.) certainly, surely

certō (1) compete, contend

certus, -a, -um sure; particular,
specific

circā (+ acc.) around, about

circiter (adv.) about

circum (+ acc.) around, about

circumcircā (adv.) round about

**circummittō, -ittere, -īsī,
-issum** send around

212

circummūnitiō, -ōnis, f. siege-work, encirclement

circumsistō, -sistere, -titī, -titum surround

circumveniō, -īre, -vēnī, -ventum surround

citerior, -us nearer

citrā (+ acc.) on this side of

cīvīlis, -e civil, of a citizen

cīvis, -is, m. citizen

cīvitās, -ātis, f. state; citizenship

clam (adv.) secretly

clāmō (1) shout

clārus, -a, -um clear, bright, famous

coepī, -isse, -tum began

cōgitātiō, -ōnis, f. thought

cōgitō (1) think, contemplate

cognitus, -a, -um known

cognōscō, -ōscere, -ōvī, -itum learn

cōgō, -ere, coēgī, coāctum force; collect

cohibeō, -ēre, -uī, -itum restrain

cohors, -rtis, f. cohort

cohortātiō, -ōnis, f. exhortation, encouragement

cohortor (1) urge, encourage

collaudō (1) praise to the skies, commend

collēga, -ae, m. colleague

colligō, -igere, -ēgī, -ectum collect

collocō (1) station

colloquium, -ī, n. conference

colloquor, -ī, -locūtus sum confer

colō, -ere, -uī, cultum honor, worship; cultivate

colōnus, -ī, m. colonist, settler

comes, -itis, m. or f. companion

comitātus, -ūs, m. company, escort, retinue

comitium, -ī, n. meeting place; (pl.) assembly, election

commemorō (1) mention

committō, -ere, -mīsī, -missum entrust; begin (a contest)

commodē (adv.) well, adequately

commodum, -ī, n. advantage, convenience

commodus, -a, -um favorable, suitable, agreeable

commoror (1) delay

commōtus, -a, -um upset, annoyed

commūnicō (1) share information, plan together

commūniō, -ōnis, f. association

commūnis, -e common, mutual, joint; public

commūtātiō, -ōnis, f. change, reversal

comparō (1) prepare; muster, raise

compleō, -ēre, -ēvī, -ētum fill, complete

complūrēs, -a several

compōnō, -ōnere, -osuī, -ositum settle

comportō (1) bring together, collect

compositiō, -ōnis, f. settlement, agreement

concēdō, -dere, -ssī, -ssum grant

conciliō (1) win over, obtain

concilium, -ī, n. meeting

concitō (1) arouse

conclāmō (1) shout, applaud

concordia, -ae, f. peace, harmony

concupiō, -ere, -īvī, -ītum covet, desire greatly

concurrō, -rere, -rī, -sum run together, assemble, gather

concursō (1) scurry about, run around

condemnō (1) condemn

condiciō, -ōnis, f. condition, compromise; (pl.) terms

condūcō, -ere, -xī, -ctum bring together, collect, unite

cōnferō, -rre, contulī, collātum compare; (with reflexive) go; direct (hostile feelings against)

cōnfestim (adv.) immediately

cōnficiō, -icere, -ēcī, -ectum accomplish, finish, complete; muster

cōnfīdō, -dere, -sus sum (+ dat.) trust, rely on

cōnfiō, -fierī be done, be accomplished

cōnfirmātiō, -ōnis, f. strengthening, encouragement

cōnfirmō (1) strengthen, encourage; say

cōnflictō (1) better, beset

cōnfugiō, -ere, -fūgī flee

coniungō, -gere, -xī, -ctum join, coordinate

cōnor (1) try

conquassō (1) shake violently

conquiescō, -escere, -ēvī sleep, go to sleep, relax

conquīrō, -rere, -sīvī, -sītum search out, round up

conquīsītor, -ōris, m. recruiting officer

cōnscendō, -dere, -dī, -sum board, embark on

cōnscientia, -ae, f. conscience

cōnscrībō, -bere, -psī, -ptum enroll; write

cōnsensiō, -ōnis, f. coalition

cōnsentiō, -tīre, -sī, -sum agree, concur; be consistent

cōnsequor, -quī, -cūtus sum follow, overtake, obtain

cōnservō (1) preserve, keep, save

cōnsīderō (1) think about, examine

cōnsilior (1) deliberate, consult, seek advice

cōnsilium, -ī, n. advice, plan, decision, policy, strategy, counsel; meeting

cōnsistō, -istere, -titī, -titum stop, halt, stand, make a stand

cōnsōlātiō, -ōnis, f. solace

cōnspicor (1) catch sight of, spot, see

cōnstantia, -ae, f. steadfastness

cōnstat, -āre, -itit it is plain, it is evident

cōnstituō, -uere, -uī, -ūtum decide; establish

cōnsuēscō, -ēscere, -ēvī, -ētum become accustomed

cōnsuētūdō, -inis, f. custom, habit

cōnsul, -is, m. consul

cōnsulāris, -e consular, of consular rank

cōnsulātus, -ūs, m. consulship

cōnsulō, -ere, -uī, -tum (+ dat.) look out for, look after; (+ acc.) consult, ask the advice of

cōnsultum, -ī, n. decree

cōnsūmō, -ere, -psī, -ptum spend

contendō, -dere, -dī, -tum hasten, march; struggle; demand

contentiō, -ōnis, f. conflict, dispute

contentus, -a, -um (+ abl.) satisfied

continēns, -ntis restrained, moderate

contineō, -ēre, -uī, -entum hold in, restrain, enclose

contingō, -ingere, -igī, -āctum touch, be in contact with; (impers.) it happens, it comes about

continuō (adv.) immediately

contiō, -ōnis, f. meeting; speech

contiōnor (1) deliver a speech, address a meeting

contrā (+ acc.) against; (adv.) on the other hand

contrahō, -here, -xī, -ctum assemble, muster

contrōversia, -ae, f. dispute

contumēlia, -ae, f. abuse, insult

conturbō (1) blur, confuse

conveniō, -īre, -vēnī, -ventum come together, assemble; meet

convenit, -ire, it (+ dat.) it is fitting, it is consistent

conventus, -ūs, m. assembly

convertō, -tere, -tī, -sum turn, divert, shift, change

convīcium, -ī, n. abuse, reproach, mockery

cōpia, -ae, f. abundance, supply; (pl.) forces, troops; resources

cōram (adv. *or* + abl.) in person, face-to-face

crēbrō (adv.) frequently

crēdō, -ere, -idī, -itum (+ dat.) believe

cruciō (1) torture

crudēlis, -e cruel, relentless

crudēlitās, -ātis, f. cruelty

cum (+ abl.) with

cum (conj.) when, since, although

cum prīmum (conj.) as soon as

cum ... tum not only ... but also

cūnctor (1) delay, hesitate

cūnctus, -a, -um all

cupiditās, -ātis, f. desire, ambition

cupidus, -a, -um (+ gen.) eager, desirous

cupiō, -ere, -īvī, -ītum desire, want, wish

cūra, -ae, f. concern, worry

cūrō (1) take care, care for

cursus, -ūs, m. course, voyage

custōdia, -ae, f. protection, safe-keeping, confinement

custōdiō, -īre, -īvī, -itum guard

custōs, -ōdis, m. guard, sentry

damnō (1) condemn

dē (+ abl.) down from, from; concerning, about

dēbeō, -ēre, -uī, -itum ought; owe

dēcēdō, -dere, -ssī, -ssum go away, depart, leave, stray

decem (indeclinable adj.) ten

dēcernō, -ernere, -rēvī, -rētum decide, decree

decet, -ēre, decuit (+ acc.) it is right, it is proper

dēclārō (1) express

dēdecus, -oris, n. disgrace, infamy

dēditiō, -ōnis, f. surrender

dēdūcō, -cere, -xī, -ctum lead away, lead on, transfer, remove; (with *rem*) bring (the matter)

dēfendō, -dere, -dī, -sum defend, protect, repulse, ward off

dēfensor, -ōris, m. defender, protector

dēferō, -rre, dētulī, dēlātum report

dēficiō, -icere, -ēcī, -ectum fail

dēfīniō, -īre, -īvī (-iī), -ītum specify, indicate

dēiciō, -icere, -iēcī, -iectum throw down, drop; (with reflexive) jump down

deinde *or* dein (adv.) then, next

dēlectō (1) please, delight

dēlīberātiō, -ōnis, f. issue, question, dilemma, consideration

dēlīberō (1) consider, think over

dēligō, -igere, -ēgī, -ēctum choose, select

dēminūtiō, -ōnis, f. weakening, depletion

dēmonstrō (1) show, point out

dēnique (adv.) at last, finally, in short

dēplōrō (1) lament

dēpōnō, -ere, -osuī, -ositum put down, deposit, lay down, lay aside

dēportō (1) bring, carry

dēprāvō (1) corrupt

dēprecor (1) ward off, beg off, avert (by entreaty)

dēpr(eh)endō, -dere, -dī, -sum seize, take by surprise

dēscīscō, -īscere, -īvī, -ītum
deviate, turn away

dēscrībō, -bere, -psī, -ptum
copy

dēserō, -ere, uī, -tum abandon,
desert

dēsinō, -inere, -iī, -itum cease

dēsistō, -istere, -titī, -titum
cease

dēspērātiō, -ōnis, f. despair

dēspērō (1) despair, give up
hope

dēsum, -esse, -fuī, -futūrus
(+ dat.) fail, be lacking, be
unavailable

dētrahō, -here, -xī, -ctum
remove, detach

dētrīmentum, -ī, n. harm; loss

deus, -ī, m. god

dēvinciō, -cīre, -xī, -ctum bind,
obligate

dexter, -ra, -rum right

dīcō, -cere, -xī, -ctum say, tell

dictitō (1) say repeatedly

diēs, -ēī, m. *or* **f.** day

difficilis, -e difficult

diffīdō, -dere, -sus sum (+ dat.)
lack confidence in

dignitās, -ātis, f. self-esteem,
prestige, good standing

dignus, -a, -um worthy

dīgredior, -dī, -ssus sum depart

dīlectus, -ūs, m. recruitment,
levy

dīligens, -ntis careful

dīligentia, -ae, f. care, energy

dīligō, -igere, -exī, -ectum
esteem, like

dīmicō (1) fight

dīmidius, -a, -um half

dīmittō, -ere, -mīsī, -missum
send away, disband; abandon

dīripiō, -ipere, -ipuī, -eptum
plunder

discēdō, -dere, -ssī, -ssum
leave, depart, withdraw

disceptō (1) debate, argue

discessus, -ūs, m. departure

discindō, -ndere, -dī, -ssum
tear, tear apart

discordia, -ae, f. disagreement,
strife

discrībō, -bere, -psī, -ptum
assign

discrīmen, -inis, n. crisis,
danger, turning point

disiciō, -icere, -iēcī, -iectum
break up, scatter

dispergō, -gere, -sī, -sum
scatter, split up

dispōnō, -ōnere, -osuī, -ositum
place at intervals, deploy

disputātiō, -ōnis, f. discussion,
debate, argument

dissēnsiō, -ōnis, f.
disagreement, feud, quarrel

dissentiō, -tīre, -sī, -sum (with
ab **+ abl.)** disagree (with)

dissimilis, -e unlike

dissimulō (1) conceal, disguise

distinguō, -guere, -xī, -ctum
differentiate, distinguish

distrahō, -here, -xī, -ctum
separate

distribuō, -uere, -uī, -ūtum
share out, allot, assign;
scatter

diū (adv.) for a long time, long

diuturnus, -a, -um long-lasting

dīvīnus, -a, -um divine

dīvulgō (1) make public,
publicize, divulge

dō, dare, dedī, datum give;
(with *litterās* or *epistulam*)
post

doceō, -ēre, -uī, -tum inform,
tell, teach

documentum, -ī, n. example,
evidence, proof

doleō, -ēre, -uī, -itum be upset,
grieve, hurt, ache

dolor, -ōris, m. pain, sorrow,
grief, resentment, distress

domesticus, -a, -um personal,
family, internal

dominātiō, -ōnis, f. absolute
power, authority

dominātus, -ūs, m. control,
power

domus, -ūs, f. house, home

dubitō (1) hesitate; doubt

dubius, -a, -um doubtful,
wavering, faint

dūcō, -cere, -xī, -ctum lead;
consider

dum (conj.) while; until;
provided that

duo, -ae, -o two

dux, -cis, m. leader, guide

ē, ex (+ abl.) from, out of; in
accordance with

ecce (interj.) look! mark this!

ēditus, -a, -um high

ēdūcō, -cere, -xī, -ctum lead out

efficiō, -icere, -ēcī, -ectum
complete; bring about

effugiō, -ere, -fūgī escape

ego I

ēgredior, -dī, -ssus sum put
out, disembark, leave

ēlābor, -bī, -psus sum slip away

ēligō, -igere, -ēgī, -ectum
choose, select

ēmānō (1) arise

enim (conj.) for

eō (adv.) there, to that place

eō, īre, iī (īvī), itum go

eōdem (adv.) to the same place,
to the same person

epistula, -ae, f. letter

eques, -itis, m. horseman; (pl.)
cavalry

equitātus, -ūs, m. cavalry

ergā (+ acc.) toward

ergō (adv.) therefore

ēripiō, -ipere, -ipuī, -eptum
snatch away, take away,
rescue

errābundus, -a, -um wandering

**ērumpō, -umpere, -ūpī,
-uptum** break out;
disintegrate

ēruptiō, -ōnis, f. break out,
sally

etiam (adv.) even, also; in fact;
still

etsī (conj.) even if, although

ēvādō, -dere, -sī, -sum make one's way, pass

ēveniō, -enīre, -ēnī, -entum happen, come about

ēventus, -ūs, m. outcome; fate

ēvertō, -tere, -tī, -sum overturn

ēvocātus, -ī, m. veteran (soldier)

ēvocō (1) call out, summon, mobilize

ēvolō (1) fly away

exaedificō (1) build

excēdō, -dere, -ssī, -ssum leave, depart, withdraw

excipiō, -ipere, -ēpī, -eptum exclude; catch, overtake; receive

exclūdō, -dere, -sī, -sum cut off, separate

excūsātiō, -ōnis, f. justification, exoneration

exemplum, -ī, n. precedent; copy

exeō, -īre, -iī, -itum go out, leave, depart

exercitus, -ūs, m. army

exigō, -igere, -ēgī, -āctum force out, demand, exact

eximius, -a, -um remarkable, extraordinary

existimātiō, -ōnis, f. reputation, credit; judgment

existimō (1) think

exitiābilis, -e destructive, ruinous

exitiōsus, -a, -um destructive, deadly

exitium, -ī, n. destruction, death

exitus, -ūs, m. departure; outlet, way out

expediō, -īre, -īvī, itum free, extricate

expeditus, -a, -um free from difficulty, unobstructed

expellō, -ellere, -ulsī, -ulsum drive out

expers, -rtis (+ gen.) uninvolved in, taking no part in

expleō, -ēre, -ēvī, -ētum fill up, cover

explicō (1) extricate; clarify

explōrō (1) ascertain, investigate

expōnō, -ōnere, -osuī, -ositum set forth, describe, display

exprimō, -imere, -essī, -essum portray, depict

exquīrō, -rere, -sīvī, -sītum ask for

exsistō, -ere, exstitī arise, emerge

exspectātiō, -ōnis, f. anticipation, apprehension, expectation

exspectō (1) wait for, expect

exspoliō (1) rob, strip

ex(s)tinguō, -guere, -xī, -ctum extinguish, put out

exsurgō, -gere, -rēxī rise, rise up, take action

extorqueō, -quere, -sī, -tum
remove, wrench away

extrā (+ acc.) outside of

extrēmus, -a, -um most
important; final

facilis, -e easy

facinus, -oris, n. deed, act;
misdeed, crime

faciō, -ere, fēcī, factum do,
make; bring it about; (with
castra) take the field

factiō, -ōnis, f. clique, group

factum, -ī, n. deed

facultās, -ātis, f. opportunity

fallō, -lere, fefellī, -sum deceive

falsō (adv.) erroneously,
wrongly, mistakenly

falsus, -a, -um erroneous,
untrue

fāma, -ae, f. rumor, talk, gossip;
reputation

famēs, -is, f. lack of food,
famine, hunger

familiāris, -is, m. (close) friend

familiāritās, -ātis, f. close
friendship

fānum, -ī, n. temple, shrine

fateor, -ērī, fassus sum confess,
admit, concede

fautor, -ōris, m. supporter

faveō, -ēre, fāvī, fautum
(+ dat.) favor

fēlīx, -īcis successful, fortunate,
happy

fēmina, -ae, f. woman, wife

ferē (adv.) almost

ferō, -rre, tulī, lātum carry;
endure; say; (with *condiciōnēs*)
offer

ferōx, -ōcis fierce, defiant,
fanatic

ferrum, -ī, n. iron, sword

ferus, -a, -um savage

festinātiō, -ōnis, f. haste

fidēs, -eī, f. loyalty; pledge;
trust, trustworthiness

fīlius, -ī, m. son

fīnis, -is, m. end, boundary;
(pl.) territory

fīnitimus, -a, -um neighboring

fiō, fierī, factus sum be made,
become; be done, happen

firmus, -a, -um strong,
powerful, secure

flāgitiōsus, -a, -um shocking,
disgraceful, outrageous,
scandalous

flāgitō (1) demand

flamma, -ae, f. flame, fire,
conflagration

fleō, -ēre, -ēvī, -ētum weep

flōrēns, -ntis flourishing

flūmen, -inis, n. river

foedus, -a, -um disgraceful,
shocking

fōrma, -ae, f. appearance

fortasse (adv.) perhaps

forte (adv.) by chance

fortis, -e brave

fortūna, -ae, f. good *or* bad
luck, destiny; (pl.) wealth,
property

frāter, -ris, m. brother

frequēns, -ntis numerous, in throngs, crowded

fretum, -ī, n. strait

frūmentum, -ī, n. grain

frustrā (adv.) in vain

fuga, -ae, f. flight, retreat

fugiō, -ere, fūgī flee, escape, retreat; avoid

furor, -ōris, m. rage, frenzy, anger

gaudeō, -dēre, gāvīsus sum rejoice, be glad, be happy

gener, -ī, m. son-in-law

genus, -eris, n. kind, class

gerō, -rere, -ssī, -stum carry, carry on, wage; do

gladiātor, -ōris, m. gladiator

gladiātōrius, -a, -um of gladiators, for gladiators

glōria, -ae, f. glory, renown, distinction

glōrior (1) boast, exult

gradus, -ūs, m. step, stage, degree

grātia, -ae, f. influence, gratitude, favor; *grātiam habēre* feel grateful; *grātiās agere* give thanks

grātulor (1) congratulate

grātus, -a, -um pleasing; grateful

gravis, -e severe, serious

gravor (1) refuse, be reluctant, object

gubernāculum, -ī, n. rudder

gubernātor, -ōris, m. helmsman

habeō, -ēre, -uī, -itum have; hold; consider; (with *grātiam*) feel grateful; (with *iter*) make one's way

haud (adv.) by no means

hem (interj.) alas!

hercule (interj.) by Hercules!

hiberna, -ōrum, n. pl. winter quarters

hic, haec, hoc this

hīc (adv.) here, in this place

hinc (adv.) from here

hodiē (adv.) today

homō, -inis, m. man, mankind, human being

homunculus, -ī, m. mere man, insignificant man

honestās, -ātis, f. honor, integrity

honestē (adv.) with honor, honorably

honestus, -a, -um honorable, reputable, regarded with respect

honor, -ōris, m. esteem, dignity, distinction; office

hortor (1) urge, encourage

hūmānitās, -ātis, f. compassion

hūmānus, -a, -um human, proper to man

iaceō, -ēre, -uī lie

iaciō, -ere, iēcī, -tum throw, cast

iactūra, -ae, f. loss

iam (adv.) already, now; soon

iam pridem (adv.) for a long time

ibi (adv.) there, in that place

idcircō (adv.) for this reason

īdem, eadem, idem the same

idōneus, -a, -um suitable

Īdūs, -uum, f. pl. Ides

igitur (adv.) therefore, then

ignōrātiō, -ōnis, f. ignorance

ignōrō (1) be ignorant, not know

ignōscō, -ōscere, -ōvī, -ōtum (+ dat.) pardon, forgive

ille, illa, illud that

illūc (adv.) there, to that place

imitō (1) imitate, emulate

impedimentum, -ī, n. hindrance; (pl.) baggage

impediō, -īre, -īvī, -ītum hinder, block; veto

impedītus, -a, -um inconvenient, difficult

impellō, -ellere, -ulī, -ulsum urge on, stimulate, motivate

impendeō, -dēre (+ dat.) hang over, threaten

imperātor, -ōris, m. general

imperium, -ī, n. command, power

imperō (1) [+ dat.] order; (+ acc.) levy

impertiō, -īre, -īvī, -ītum devote, bestow

impetrō (1) obtain one's request

impetus, -ūs, m. attack, onslaught, thrust

implicō (1) hem in, envelop, enfold, entangle

implōrō (1) ask for, appeal to

impōnō, -ere, -osuī, -ositum impose, inflict

improbō (1) criticize, disapprove of

improbus, -a, -um disloyal, unprincipled; remorseless, relentless, heartless

imprūdenter (adv.) thoughtlessly

impudēns, -ntis shameless, brazen

impūnītē (adv.) without punishment

in (+ abl.) in, on, among; (+ acc.) into, against; among; toward

inānis, -e deserted, empty

inaudītus, -a, -um unheard of

incautus, -a, -um thoughtless, reckless

incendium, -ī, n. burning, conflagration

incertus, -a, -um uncertain

incidō, -ere, -ī, incāsum happen upon, fall

incipiō, -ipere, -ēpī, -eptum begin

incitō (1) arouse, provoke, stir up

incolumis, -e unharmed, safe

incommodum, -ī, n. loss, disadvantage

incrēdibilis, -e unbelievable

inde (adv.) from there

indignor (1) be resentful

ineō, -īre, -iī, -itum enter (upon)

inexplicābilis, -e insoluble, baffling

īnfāmia, -ae, f. scandal

īnferō, -rre, intulī, illātum bring in; (with *bellum* + dat.) make war on

īnfirmus, -a, -um weak, irresolute

īnflammō (1) set on fire

ingravēscō, -ere grow worse

ingredior, -dī, -ssus sum go into, enter (upon), begin

inimīcitia, -ae, f. hostility, enmity

inimīcus, -ī, m. (personal) enemy

inīquitās, -ātis, f. unfairness, injustice

inīquus, -a, -um unfair, unjust

initium, -ī, n. beginning

iniūria, -ae, f. injustice, wrong

iniūstus, -a, -um unjust

innumerābilis, -e countless

inopia, -ae, f. lack

inquam say

inrideō, -ēre, -sī, -sum mock, make fun of

īnsāniō, -īre, -īvī, -ītum be insane, be mad, be out of one's mind

īnsequor, -quī, -cūtus sum pursue

īnsidiōsē (adv.) treacherously, deceitfully

īnstar (+ gen.) like

īnstituō, -uere, -uī, -ūtum decide; begin; establish

īnstitūtum, -ī, n. established practice, custom

intellegō, -gere, -xī, -ctum understand, realize

inter (+ acc.) among, between

intercēdō, -dere, -ssī, -ssum veto; occur

intercessiō, -ōnis, f. veto

interclūdō, -dere, -sī, -sum cut off, prevent

interdum (adv.) at times

intereā (adv.) meanwhile, in the meantime

intereō, -īre, -iī, -itum die, perish

interest, -esse, -fuit (+ gen.) it is of importance, it is in the interest of, it is to the advantage of

interim (adv.) meanwhile, in the meantime

intermittō, -ere, -mīsī, -missum stop, discontinue; let pass

internūntius, -ī, m. mediator, go-between

interpellō (1) interrupt

interpōnō, -pōnere, -posuī, -positum insert, introduce

intersum, -esse, -fuī, futūrus be present, take part in

intervāllum, -ī, n. space

intestīnus, -a, -um personal, private

intrōdūcō, -cere, -xī, -ctum introduce, bring in

introeō, -īre, -iī, -itum enter

introitus, -ūs, m. entry

invādō, -dere, -sī, -sum seize upon, take control of, grip

inveniō, -venīre, -vēnī, -ventum come upon, find, discover

invidia, -ae, f. envy, hatred, unpopularity

invidiōsus, -a, -um unpopular

invidus, -a, -um envious, malevolent

invidus, -ī, m. detractor

invītus, -a, -um unwilling

invocō (1) call upon

ipse, ipsa, ipsum -self

īrācundia, -ae, f. resentment, anger

īrāscor, -ī, īrātus sum (+ dat.) be angry (with)

is, ea, id this that; he, she, it

iste, ista, istud that

istīc (adv.) there, over there

ita (adv.) so; as follows

itaque (adv.) and so, therefore

item (adv.) likewise

iter, -ineris, n. journey, march, route; (with *habēre*) make one's way

iterum (adv.) again

iubeō, -bēre, -ssī, -ssum order

iūcundus, -a, -um pleasant, pleasing

iūdicium, -ī, n. trial, judgment, decision

iūdicō (1) judge, decide, try (a case)

iūgerum, -ī, n. parcel of land (= ⅝ acre)

iūmentum, -ī, n. pack animal

iungō, -gere, -xī, -ctum join

iūrō (1) swear an oath

iūs, iūris, n. legal procedure, right, justice

iūs iūrandum, iūris iūrandī, n. oath

iuvō, iuvāre, iūvī, iūtum help, aid

iuxtā (+ acc.) near

Kalendae, -ārum, f. pl. Kalends

labor, -ōris, m. work, effort

labōrō (1) work, take pains, exert oneself

lacrima, -ae, f. tear

laetus, -a, -um happy, glad

languidus, -a, -um listless, idle, apathetic

largitiō, -ōnis, f. bribe

laureātus, -a, -um wearing laurel

laus, -dis, f. praise, reputation, renown, esteem

lēgātiō, -ōnis, f. embassy

lēgātus, -ī, m. lieutenant, ambassador

legiō, -ōnis, f. legion

legō, -ere, lēgī, lēctum collect, enroll; choose; read

lēnis, -e soft, gentle, mild, moderate

levis, -e light; trivial

levō (1) relieve, reduce

lēx, lēgis, f. law

libēns, -ntis glad, cheerful, willing

līber, -era, -erum free

liber, -brī, m. book

līberālitās, -ātis, f. generosity

līberī, -ōrum, m. pl. children

līberō (1) free, set free

lībertās, -ātis, f. freedom

lībrārius, -ī, m. secretary

licentia, -ae, f. disorderliness, freedom

licet, -ēre, -uit (impers. + dat.) may, be allowed

lictor, -ōris, m. lictor, attendant

litterae, -ārum, f. pl. letter, dispatch, correspondence

locuplēs, -ētis rich

locus, -ī, m. place; loca, -ōrum, (n. pl.) places, region

longinquitās, -ātis, f. length

longinquus, -a, -um distant

loquor, -ī, locūtus sum speak

lūcet, -ēre, lūxit it is light, day dawns

lūdus, -ī, m. game; school

lūmen, -inis, n. light, lamp, torch

lūx, lūcis, f. light

magistrātus, -ūs, m. magistrate; magistracy

magnitūdō, -inis, f. size

magnopere (adv.) greatly, earnestly

magnus, -a, -um large, great

māior, -us larger, greater

maleficium, -ī, n. wrongdoing, misdeed

mālō, -lle, -luī prefer

malum, -ī, n. trouble

malus, -a, -um bad

mandātum, -ī, n. instruction, order

mandō (1) [+ dat.] give instructions, order

māne (adv.) in the morning

maneō, -ēre, -sī, -sum remain, stay; (with in + abl.) abide (by), persist (in)

manus, -ūs, f. hand; band, forces

mare, -is, n. sea

māter, -tris, f. mother

maximus, -a, -um largest, greatest

medicus, -ī, m. doctor

mediocris, -e little, small, slight

mēhercule (interj.) by Hercules!

melior, -us better

meminī, -inisse remember

memor, -ōris (+ gen.) mindful

memorō (1) recall, mention, quote

mēns, mentis, f. mind

mereor, -ērī, -itus sum (with adv. and dē + abl.) deserve, be deserving (of a person)

meritum, -ī, n. service, meritorious action

metuō, -ere, -ī fear

metus, -ūs, m. fear, intimidation

mīles, -itis, m. soldier

mīlia, -ium, n. pl. thousands; **mīlia passuum** miles

mīliēns (adv.) a thousand times

minae, -ārum, f. pl. threats

minimē (adv.) by no means, not at all, least of all

minimus, -a, -um very little, smallest

minuō, -uere, -uī, -ūtum reduce, lessen

mīrificus, -a, -um amazing

mīror (1) be surprised, wonder

mīrus, -a, -um extraordinary, astonishing, remarkable

miser, -era, -erum unhappy, unfortunate, pitiful, contemptible

misericordia, -ae, f. compassion, mercy

mittō, -ere, mīsī, missum send; pass over; let go

moderātiō, -ōnis, f. restraint, control

modestē (adv.) with restraint

modicus, -a, -um small, slight

modo (adv.) just, just now, recently; only

modus, -ī, m. kind, sort, way

moenia, -um, n. pl. fortifications

molestia, -ae, f. worry, trouble, distress

mōlior, -īrī, -ītus sum build, undertake

moneō, -ēre, -uī, -itum advise, warn

mora, -ae, f. delay

morior, -ī, -tuus sum die

moror (1) delay

moveō, -ēre, mōvī, mōtum move, motivate, influence, affect, arouse

multī, -ae, -a many

multō (adv.) much

mūlus, -ī, m. mule

mūniceps, -ipis, m. citizen of a *mūnicipium*

mūnicipium, -ī, n. town, community

mūniō, -īre, -īvī, -ītum fortify

mūnitiō, -ōnis, f. fortification

mūnītus, -a, -um well-fortified, secure

mūrus, -ī, m. wall

mūtō (1) change

nam (conj.) for

nancīscor, -ī, nactus sum find, obtain; overtake

nāscor, -ī, nātus sum be born, come into existence; start

nātūra, -ae, f. nature, temperament, disposition

nāvigō (1) sail, make a voyage

nāvis, -is, f. ship

necessāriō (adv.) of necessity, without an option

necessārius, -a, -um necessary, obligatory

necessārius, -ī, m. close friend, adherent

necesse (indecl. adj.) necessary

necessitūdō, -inis, f. close relationship, bond

negō (1) say . . . not, deny, refuse

negōtium, -ī, n. business, task, responsibility; trouble

nēmō, -inis, m. no one

nē . . . quidem not even

neque, nec (conj.) and not, nor

neque . . . neque neither . . . nor

nequeō, -īre, -īvī be unable

nequīquam (adv.) in vain

nesciō, -īre, -īvī, -ītum not know

neuter, -ra, -rum neither

nihil (indeclinable), n. nothing; (adv.) not at all

nisi (conj.) unless, if not, except

nītor, -tī, -sus sum struggle

noceō, -ēre, -uī, -itum (+ dat.) harm

nōlō, -lle, -luī be unwilling

nōmen, -inis, n. name, reputation

Nōnae, -ārum, f. pl. Nones

nōndum (adv.) not yet

nōn modo or nōn sōlum . . . sed etiam or vērum etiam not only . . . but also

nōnnūllī, -ae, -a some

noster, -ra, -rum our

nōtus, -a, -um famous, well-known, familiar

novus, -a, -um new, strange, unusual, unfamiliar

nūbō, -bere, -psī, -ptum (+dat.) marry

nūdō (1) strip

nūdus, -a, -um stripped

nūllus, -a, -um no; (as pronoun) no one

numerus, -ī, m. number

numquam (adv.) never

nunc (adv.) now

nūntiō (1) report, announce

nūntius, -ī, m. message, news; messenger

nusquam (adv.) nowhere

obeō, -īre, -iī, -itum meet; (with *diem*) die

obitus, -ūs, m. death

oblivīscor, -vīscī, -tus sum forget

obscūrus, -a, -um uncertain, dark, covered

obsecrō (1) beg, implore

obsequor, -quī, -cūtus sum (+ dat.) give in to, submit to

obsideō, -ēre, -ēdī, -essum besiege, blockade

obsidiō, -ōnis, f. siege

obstringō, -ngere, -nxī, -ctum constrain, bind

obtemperō (1) [+ dat.] obey, comply with

obtestor (1) implore

obtineō, -ēre, -uī, -tentum hold on to, retain

obtingō, -ngere, -gī fall (to) by lot

obveniō, -ire, -vēnī, -ventum
(+ dat.) fall to the lot of,
happen, occur

obviam īre *or* prōdīre (+ dat.)
go to meet

obvius, -a, -um in the way of,
to meet

occīdō, -dere, -dī, -sum kill

occultus, -a, -um hidden,
secret, unseen

occupō (1) seize; preoccupy,
engage

octo (indeclinable adj.) eight

oculus, -ī, m. eye

ōdī, -isse hate, dislike

odium, -ī, n. hate, hatred

offendō, -dere, -dī, -sum upset,
displease, annoy

officium, -ī, n. obligation, duty

omittō, -ere, -mīsī, -missum
pass by, leave out, omit

omnīnō (adv.) on the whole,
altogether, to sum up, in
short

omnis, -e complete, entire; all

operam dare pay attention, see
to it

opīniō, -ōnis, f. belief, idea,
opinion

opīnor (1) think

oportet, -ēre, -uit (impers.)
ought, should

oppetō, -ere, -īvī, -itum
encounter, meet prematurely

oppidānī, -ōrum, m. pl.
townspeople

oppidum, -i, n. town

oppōnō, -ōnere, -osuī, -ositum
(+ dat.) oppose

opportūnitās, -ātis, f.
advantage, convenience

opprimō, -imere, -essī, -essum
overwhelm, suppress

ops, opis, f. help; (pl.) wealth,
resources, influence

optimus, -a, -um best,
excellent, very fine, very loyal

optō (1) desire, long for

opus, -eris, n. work; siegework,
fortification

opus est (+ dat. of person,
abl. of thing needed) there
is need; it is essential

ōra, -ae, f. shore, coast

ōrātiō, -ōnis, f. speech, manner
of speaking, language

ōrdō, -inis, m. rank, order,
century

ōs, ōris, n. mouth, face

ostentum, -ī, n. sign, portent

ōtium, -ī, n. leisure, peace,
tranquillity, comfort, security

pācō (1) subdue

pāctiō, -ōnis, f. agreement

paene (adv.) almost

paenitet, -ēre, -uit regret

pār, paris equal

parātus, -a, -um ready, prepared

parcō, -ere, pepercī, parsum
(+ dat.) spare

parō (1) prepare

pars, -tis, f. part, side,
direction, portion

particeps, -cipis (+ gen.) sharing (in)

partim (adv.) partly

partior, -īrī, -ītus sum share, divide, distribute

parvus, -a, -um small, little

passus, -ūs, m. pace

pastor, -ōris, m. shepherd

patefaciō, -facere, -fēcī, -factum open, open up

pater, -tris, m. father

patior, -tī, -ssus sum allow, suffer

patria, -ae, f. country, fatherland

paucī, -ae, -a few, a few

pauculī, -ae, -a just a few, only a few

paulō (adv.) a little

paulum (adv.) a little

pāx, pācis, f. peace

peccātum, -ī, n. error, mistake

peccō (1) err, blunder, do wrong

pectus, -oris, n. chest

pecūnia, -ae, f. money

pēior, -us worse

pellō, -ere, pepulī, pulsum drive, drive out, rout

per (+ acc.) through

peragō, -agere, -ēgī, -āctum, complete

percurrō, -rere, -rī, -sum overrun

perditus, -a, -um corrupt, depraved, ruined

pereō, -īre, -iī, -itum die, perish

perfector, -ōris, m. achiever, creator

perferō, -rre, -tulī, -lātum report

perficiō, -icere, -ēcī, -ectum complete

perfidia, -ae, f. treachery

perfungor, -gī, -ctus sum (+ abl.) experience fully, enjoy

perīclitor (1) test

perīculum, -ī, n. danger, risk

perītus, -a, -um (+ gen.) skilled (in), familiar (with)

perlegō, -ere, -ēgī, -ēctum read through, scan

permisceō, -scēre, -scuī, -xtum throw into confusion, confound

permoveō, -ēre, -mōvī, -mōtum distrub, alarm, influence

perniciōsus, -a, -um destructive

perpetuus, -a, -um continuous, continual

perscrībō, -bere, -psī, -ptum record

persevērō (1) persist

persōna, -ae, f. position, character

perspectus, -a, -um clearly understood

persuādeō, -dēre, -sī, -sum (+ dat.) persuade

pertendō, -dere, -dī, -tum proceed, push on

perterreō, -ēre, -uī, -itum
frighten, intimidate

pertimēscō, -ēscere, -uī become
alarmed

pertinācia, -ae, f. obstinacy,
stubbornness

pertineō, -ēre, -uī pertain,
relate

perturbātiō, -ōnis, f. confusion,
disorder

perturbō (1) upset, trouble,
throw into confusion

**perveniō, -venīre, -vēnī,
-ventum (with _ad_ + acc.)**
reach, arrive at, obtain

pervulgō (1) circulate

pēs, pedis, m. foot

petitiō, -ōnis, f. candidacy

petō, -ere, -īvī, -ītum seek, seek
to obtain; ask for; stand for
election

philosophia, -ae, f. philosophy

pistrīnum, -ī, n. bakery, mill

pius, -a, -um loyal, righteous

**placeō, -ēre, -uī, -itum
(+ dat.)** please; **(impers. +
dat.)** it is pleasing, it is
approved (by)

plāga, -ae, f. blow, stroke,
wound

plānē (adv.) clearly, obviously

plēbs, -bis, f. the common
people

plectō, -ere punish

plēnus, -a, -um full

plērīque, -aeque, -aque most
of, the majority

polleō, -ēre exert power, exert
influence, be strong

polliceor, -ērī, -itus sum
promise

pōnō, -ere, -osuī, -ositum
place, put; (with _castra_) pitch

pōns, -ntis, m. bridge

ponticulum, -ī, n. little bridge

pontifex, -icis, m. priest

populus, -ī, m. people

porta, -ae, f. gate

portus, -ūs, m. harbor, port

possessiō, -ōnis, f. holding,
possession

possum, posse, potuī be able,
can

post (+ acc.) after, behind;
(adv.) later

posteā (adv.) afterward, later

posteāquam (conj.) after

posterior, -us later; less
important, inferior

posterus, -a, -um following

postrēmō (adv.) finally, at last

postrīdiē (adv.) on the
following day, on the day
after

postulātum, -ī, n. demand

postulō (1) ask, demand

postquam (conj.) after

potēns, -ntis powerful

potentia, -ae, f. power

potestās, -ātis, f. opportunity,
power

potior, -īrī, -ītus sum (+ abl.)
get possession of

potior, -us more important, preferable

potius (adv.) rather

praebeō, -ēre, -uī, -itum provide, show, present

praecipuē (adv.) especially

praeclārus, -a, -um famous, illustrious

praeda, -ae, f. booty, spoils

praedium, -ī, n. estate, property

praeditus, -a, -um endowed

praefectus, -ī, m. officer

praeficiō, -icere, -ēcī, -ectum put in command of

praemittō, -ere, -mīsī, -missum send ahead

praemium, -ī, n. reward, bonus

praemoneō, -ēre, -uī, -itum predict, foretell

praepōnō, -ere, -osuī, -ositum intend; prefer

praescrībō, -bere, -psī, -ptum dictate, prescribe

praesēns, -ntis present, in person; available; immediate

praesertim (adv.) especially

praesidium, -ī, n. garrison; guard, protection

praestō (adv.) available, ready

praestō, -āre, -itī, -itum (+ dat.) surpass; (+ acc.) furnish, provide; be preferable

praesum, -esse, -fuī, -futūrus (+ dat.) be in command of

praeter (+ acc.) except; past; contrary to

praetereā (adv.) besides

praetereō, -īre, -iī, -itum pass by (an opportunity), neglect

praetor, -ōris, m. praetor

praetōrius, -a, -um of praetorian rank

prandeō, -dēre, -dī, -sum eat a midday meal

prex, -ecis, f. entreaty; prayer

prīdiē (adv.) on the day before

prīmārius, -a, -um of the highest standing

prīmō (adv.) at first

prīmum (adv.) first, above all

prīmus, -a, -um first, foremost

prior, -us first, former, earlier

pristinus, -a, -um former

prius (adv.) first, beforehand

priusquam (conj.) before

prō (+ abl.) before; in return for; in view of

probō (1) approve of, prove; regard it as right

procul (adv.) at a distance

prōdūcō, -ere, -xī, -ctum bring forth, present

profectiō, -ōnis, f. departure

prōferō, -rre, -tulī, -lātum bring forth

prōficiō, -icere, -ēcī, -ectum achieve, accomplish; advance

proficīscor, -icīscī, -ectus sum set out

prōfugiō, -ere, -fūgī flee

prōgredior, -dī, -ssus sum advance, go

prohibeō, -ēre, -uī, -itum keep away, prevent

prōicī, -icere, -iēcī, -iectum abandon, forsake

prōiectus, -a, -um neglected

proinde (adv.) accordingly, likewise

proinde ac sī just as if

prōmissum, -ī, n. promise

prōmittō, -ere, -mīsī, -missum promise

promptus, -a, -um responsive

prōnūntiō (1) announce publicly

prope (adv.) almost

propensus, -a, -um inclined, partial, disposed

properē (adv.) hastily, quickly

properō (1) hasten, hurry

propius (adv.) nearer

prōpōnō, -ōnere, -osuī, -ositum set before, propose

prōpositum, -ī, n. point, issue, theme

propter (+ acc.) because of, on account of

prōsiliō, -īre, -īvī rush forward

prōspiciō, -icere, -exī, -ectum foresee; view, gaze upon, see in the distance

prōsum, -desse, -fuī, -futūrus (+ dat.) benefit, help

prōtinus (adv.) at once, immediately

prōvideō, -idēre, -īdī, -īsum foresee; provide for, see to

prōvincia, -ae, f. province

proximus, -a, -um next, following, nearby, nearest

pūblicus, -a, -um public, of the people, for the people

puer, -ī, m. boy; slave

pugnō (1) fight

putō (1) think

quaerō, -rere, -sīvī, -sītum look for, ask, seek

quaestiō, -ōnis, f. debate, issue

quaestor, -ōris, m. quaestor

quaestōrius, -a, -um for a quaestor, of a quaestor

quam (adv.) how

quam (conj.) than

quam diū as long as; how long

quam ob rem *or* **quamobrem** for this reason; why

quam prīmum as soon as possible

quamquam (conj.) although; and yet

quandō (interrogative adv.) when; **sī quandō** if ever

quantus, -a, -um how great, how much

quā rē therefore, for this reason; why

quartus, -a, -um fourth

quasi (conj. *and* adv.) just as if, just as; as it were

quattuor (indeclinable adj.) four

quem ad modum as; how

queror, -rī, -stus sum complain, complain about

quī, quae, quod who, which, that

quid what? why?

quīdam, quaedam, quoddam a certain

quidem (adv.) at any rate, at least, admittedly, in fact

quīn (conj.) [with subjn.] that . . . not, that; [with indic.] why not?

quinque (indeclinable adj.) five

quintus, -a, -um fifth

quintus, -a, -um decimus, -a, -um fifteenth

quis who?

quisquam, quidquam (quicquam) anyone, anything

quisque, quidque each, every one

quīvīs, quaevīs, quodvīs (quidvīs) anyone at all, anything at all, any at all

quō (adv.) where, to what place

quoad (conj.) as long as, until

quod (conj.) because; the fact that, namely that

quodsī (conj.) but if

quō modō as; how

quondam (adv.) once

quoniam (conj.) since

quoque (adv.) also

quotiēnscumque (conj.) as often as

rapiō, -ere, -uī, -tum seize, take away

ratiō, -ōnis, f. way, reason, consideration; plan (of action)

ratus, -a, -um fixed, established

recēdō, -dere, -ssī, -ssum withdraw

reciperō (1) recover

recipiō, -ipere, -ēpī, -eptum take, receive; **(with reflexive)** return, retreat

recitō (1) read aloud

recognōscō, -ōscere, -ōvī, -itum acknowledge, recall

reconciliō (1) win back, reconcile

rectē (adv.) correctly, rightly

recūsō (1) refuse

reddō, -ere, -idī, -itum give back, return, deliver

redeō, -īre, -iī, -itum go back, return

redūcō, -cere, -xī, -ctum lead back, bring

referō, -rre, rettulī, relātum bring back, return, report; make a proposal, open a debate; ascribe

refertus, -a, -um loaded, crammed, packed

regiō, -ōnis, f. region, area

rēgnō (1) rule, be a king, reign

rēgnum, -ī, n. rule, regime

regredior, -dī, -ssus sum return

relātor, -ōris, m. proposer (of a motion in the senate)

relinquō, -inquere, -īquī, -ictum leave, leave behind, abandon reliquus, -a, -um rest of

remaneō, -ēre, -sī, -sum stay, remain

reminīscor (1) recall

remissus, -a, -um lax, casual

remittō, -ere, -mīsī, -missum send back, return

remōtus, -a, -um distant

removeō, -ēre, -mōvī, -mōtum move back, remove

renūntiō (1) report, announce

repellō, -ellere, -ulī, -ulsum drive back

repente (adv.) suddenly

repentīnus, -a, -um sudden

reperiō, -īre, repperī, -tum find, find out, learn, know

reprehendō, -dere, -dī, -sum blame

reputō (1) reflect

rēs, reī, f. matter; activity; exploit

rescrībō, -bere, -psī, -ptum write back

reservō (1) keep, withhold

rēs frūmentāria, reī frūmentāriae, f. grain supply

rēs gestae, rērum gestārum, f. pl. achievements, accomplishments, exploits

resistō, -istere, -titī (+ dat.) resist

respiciō, -icere, -exī, -ectum look back, regard, have regard for

respondeō, -dēre, -dī, -sum answer, reply

respōnsum, -ī, n. answer, reply

rēs pūblica, reī pūblicae, f. state, republic

restituō, -uere, -uī, -ūtum restore

restō, -āre, -itī stay, linger

retineō, -ēre, -uī, -entum hold back, detain

retrahō, -here, -xī, -ctum bring back by force, summon back

revertor, -tī, -sus sum (or pf. act. *revertī*) return

rēx, rēgis, m. king

rīdiculus, -a, -um funny, laughable

ruō, -ere run wild, rush

rursus (adv.) back; again

sacerdōtium, -ī, n. priesthood

sacrāmentum, -ī, n. oath

saepe (adv.) often

salūs, -ūtis, f. safety, salvation, welfare, health

salvus, -a, -um safe

sānē (adv.) certainly

sānē quam assuredly, decidedly

sanguis, -inis, m. blood

sapiēns, -ntis wise, intelligent

sapientia, -ae, f. wisdom, intelligence, common sense

satis (adv. or indeclinable noun) enough

scālae, -ārum, f. pl. scaling ladder (*or* scaling ladders)

scelerātus, -a, -um criminal, scandalous

scelus, -eris, n. crime, scandal

scīlicet (adv.) to be sure, evidently

sciō, -īre, -īvī, -ītum know

scīscitor (1) inquire

scrībō, -bere, -psī, -ptum write

sēcessiō, -ōnis, f. withdrawal, mutiny

sēcrētō (adv.) individually, separately, in private

secundus, -a, -um favorable, propitious; second

sed (conj.) but

sēdātus, -a, -um calm, untroubled

sedeō, -ēre, sēdī, sessum sit

sēdēs, -is, f. seat, position, base, rendezvous

sēdō (1) bring to order, assuage; (pass.) calm down, subside

sēdulō (adv.) diligently, earnestly

sēgnis, -e sluggish, slothful, inactive

sella, -ae, f. chair, seat

semel (adv.) once

semper (adv.) always

senātor, -ōris, m. senator

senātōrius, -a, -um of a senator

senātus, -ūs, m. senate; senātūs cōnsultum decree of the senate

sēnsus, -ūs, m. character, disposition

sententia, -ae, f. opinion, idea

sentiō, -tīre, -sī, -sum feel, think

septimus, -a, -um seventh

sequor, -quī, -cūtus sum follow

sermō, -ōnis, m. talk, conversation, discourse

sērō (adv.) late

serviō, -īre, -īvī, -ītum (+ dat.) serve

servō (1) save

servus, -ī, m. slave

sex (indeclinable adj.) six

sī (conj.) if

sī quandō if ever

sīc (adv.) thus, so

sīcut, sīcutī (conj.) as, just as

significō (1) indicate, show, mean; signal

signum, -ī, n. standard, sign, signal

silentium, -ī, n. silence

sileō, -ēre, -uī be silent, be silent about, be quiet

similis, -e like

simul (adv.) at the same time

simulātiō, -ōnis, f. pretense, pretext

simul atque (conj.) as soon as

sīn (conj.) but if

sine (+ abl.) without

singulāris, -e exceptional, outstanding

singulī, -ae, -a one each

sinister, -ra, -rum left

sīn minus but if not

sinō, -ere, sīvī, sītum allow

sīve . . . sīve whether . . . or

socer, -ī, m. father-in-law

societās, -ātis, f. partnership

socius, -ī, m. ally, partner, companion

sōl, sōlis, m. sun; **sōlis occāsus** sunset

sōlācium, -ī, n. consolation, comfort

sollicitūdō, -inis, f. anxiety, concern, worry

somnus, -ī, m. sleep

soror, -ōris, f. sister

sors, -rtis, f. lot, chance

spatium, -ī, n. space, distance; period (of time)

spectāculum, -ī, n. entertainment, show

spectō (1) look at, watch; consider; aim at

spērō (1) hope

spēs, -eī, f. hope, expectation, promise

sponte voluntarily; **meā sponte** of my own accord

statim (adv.) at once, immediately

statiō, -ōnis, f. post, picket, military garrison

statuō, -uere, -uī, -ūtum decide; establish

status, -ūs, m. situation, condition

stō, stāre, stetī, statum stand

strātus, -a, -um prostrate

studeō, -ēre, -uī (+ dat. or inf.) be eager

studium, -ī, n. enthusiasm, partisan spirit; energy; study

stultus, -a, -um foolish, stupid

suādeō, -dēre, -sī, -sum (+ dat.) persuade, counsel

suāvis, -e sweet, charming, pleasant

sub (+ abl.) under, at the foot of; **(+ acc.)** under, up to; (with expressions of time) just before

subeō, -īre, -iī, -itum undergo

subitō (adv.) suddenly

sublevō (1) support, promote; raise up, lift up

subsequor, -quī, -cūtus sum follow closely, follow immediately

subsidium, -ī, n. relief, support, reinforcement

subsistō, -istere, -titī, -titum stop

subveniō, -venīre, -vēnī, -ventum (+ dat.) come to the aid of

summa, -ae, f. gist, substance; outcome

summē (adv.) intensely

summus, -a, -um (of time) last; **(of place)** highest, top of; **(of quality)** greatest

sūmō, -mere, -mpsī, -mptum take, assume

superbia, -ae, f. arrogance

superior, -us former, previous; higher; greater

superveniō, -venīre, -vēnī, -ventum arrive (on the scene)

suscēnseō, -ēre, -uī (+ dat.) be angry, be indignant

suscipiō, -ipere, -ēpī, -eptum take up, undertake

suspiciō, -ōnis, f. suspicion

suspicor (1) suspect, infer

sustentō (1) support

tālis, -e such, of such a kind

tam (adv.) so

tamen (adv.) nevertheless, yet; at least

tametsī (conj.) even if, although

tamquam (conj.) as though; just as

tandem (adv.) finally, at last

tantōpere *or* **tantō opere (adv.)** to such a great degree

tantum (adv.) only

tantus, -a, -um so great, such great

tardō (1) hamper, delay

tardus, -a, -um slow, slow to act

tēctum, -ī, n. building, house

tegō, -gere, -xī, -ctum cover, cover up

temere (adv.) rashly, recklessly

temeritās, -ātis, f. rashness, recklessness

tempestās, -ātis, f. storm

templum, -ī, n. temple

temptō (1) try, tamper with

tempus, -oris, n. time

tenebrae, -ārum, f. pl. darkness

teneō, -ēre, -uī, -tum hold, hold back

terra, -ae, f. land, earth

terreō, -ēre, -uī, -itum frighten, intimidate

terrestris, -e on land

terror, -ōris, m. alarm, extreme fear, intimidation, threat

tertius, -a, -um third

tertius, -a, -um decimus, -a, -um thirteenth

testātus, -a, -um well-documented

testificor (1) declare solemnly

testis, -is, m. witness

timeō, -ēre, -uī fear, be afraid

timidus, -a, -um cowardly, apprehensive, nervous

timor, -ōris, m. fear

tolerābilis, -e bearable

tollō, -ere, sustulī, sublātum raise; remove

tormentum, -ī, n. catapult

tot (indeclinable adj.) so many

totidem (indeclinable adj.) just as many

tōtus, -a, -um all, the whole

trādō, -ere, -idī, itum surrender, hand over

trādūcō, -cere, -xī, -ctum lead across

trāiciō, -icere, -iēcī, -iectum transport

trāmes, -itis, m. path

trāmittō, -ere, -mīsī, -missum cross, cross over

trānseō, -īre, -iī, -itum go across, cross; desert

trānsferō, -rre, -tulī, -lātum hand over, transfer

trānsmarīnus, -a, -um overseas, from across the sea

trānsportō (1) convey, transport

trepidē (adv.) hurriedly

trēs, tria three

tribūnicius, -a, -um of a tribune, tribunitial

tribūnus, -ī, m. tribune

tribuō, -uere, -uī, -ūtum attribute, grant

trīduum, -ī, n. period of three days

trīgintā (indeclinable adj.) thirty

triumphō (1) exult

triumphus, -ī, m. triumph

tuba, -ae, f. trumpet

tueor, -ērī, tūtus sum watch over, protect

tum (adv.) then, at that time

tumultus, -ūs, m. upheaval, disorder

tunc (adv.) then, at that time

turba, -ae, f. disorder, confusion; crowd

turpis, -e disgraceful, shameful, base

tūtus, -a, -um safe

tuus, -a, -um your

tyrannus, -ī, m. tyrant, despot

ubi (conj.) when **(adv.)** where, in what place

ubi prīmum (conj.) as soon as

ubīque (adv.) everywhere

ūllus, -a, -um any

ulterior, -us further, more distant

ultimus, -a, -um last, final; furthermost

ultrō citrōque (adv.) back and forth

umbra, -ae, f. shadow

umquam (adv.) ever

ūnā (adv.) together

undique (adv.) from all sides, on all sides

ūniversus, -a, -um whole, entire, all

ūnus, -a, -um one

urbs, urbis, f. city

usquam (adv.) anywhere

usque (adv.) all the way, right up

ūsus, -ūs, m. use, advantage

ut (+ indic.) as, when

uterque, utraque, utrumque each (of two)

ūtilis, -e useful, expedient

ūtor, -ī, ūsus sum (+ abl.) use, experience, take advantage of; abide by

utrimque (adv.) on both sides

valdē (adv.) exceedingly, strongly, quite

valeō, -ēre, -uī, -itum be well, be strong, be able; *plūrimum valēre* be most powerful, have very great influence; *valē* **(imperative)** farewell

vāllum, -ī, n. wall, rampart

varietās, -ātis, f. diversity

vehementer (adv.) strongly, tremendously

vehiculum, -ī, n. cart, wagon

vel (conj.) or; **vel . . . vel** either . . . or

veniō, -īre, vēnī, ventum come

verbum, -ī, n. word

verbōsus, -a, -um wordy, prolix

vereor, -ērī, -itus sum fear

vērō (adv.) but; certainly; what is more

versus (+ acc.) towards

vērus, -a, -um true, accurate

vester, -ra, -rum your

vestis, -is, f. clothing, clothes

veterānus, -a, -um veteran

vetus, -eris old, long-standing; veteran, experienced

victōria, -ae, f. victory

videō, -ēre, vīdī, vīsum see; know, realize; foresee; **(pass.)** seem, appear; **(impers. pass.)** seem best, seem right

vigilāns, -ntis alert

vigilantia, -ae, f. wakefulness

vigilia, -ae, f. watch, night-watch, picket

vīlla, -ae, f. country house, villa

vincō, -ere, vīcī, victum conquer, prevail, win; prove

vindicō (1) claim, lay claim to; restore

violō (1) dishonor, outrage

vir, -ī, m. man

virtūs, -ūtis, f. courage, excellence

vīs, vīs, f. force, violence; (pl.) *vīrēs, vīrium* strength, energy

vīta, -ae, f. life

vitium, -ī, n. fault, flaw

vīvō, -ere, -xī, -ctum live, be alive

vīvus, -a, -um alive, living

vocō (1) call

volō, velle, voluī be willing, wish, want

volūmen, -inis, n. scroll, book

voluntās, -ātis, f. will, good will, intention, attitude

voluptās, -ātis, f. pleasure

vōtum, -ī, n. vow

vōx, vōcis, f. voice; word

vulgō (adv.) far and wide, publicly

vultus, -ūs, m. face, expression

Selected Bibliography

Balsdon, J. P. V. D. "The Veracity of Caesar." *Greece and Rome* 4 (1957): 19–27.

Beard, Mary and Michael Crawford. *Rome in the Late Republic*. Ithaca, NY: Cornell University Press, 1985.

Broughton, T. Robert S. *The Magistrates of the Roman Republic*. 2 vols. New York: American Philological Association, 1951–1952.

Brunt, P. A. *The Fall of the Roman Republic*. Oxford: Clarendon Press, 1988.

Burns, A. "Pompey's Strategy and Domitius' Stand at Corfinium." *Historia* 15 (1966): 74–95.

Carter, J. M., ed. *Julius Caesar: The Civil War, Books I and II.* Warminster: Aris & Phillips, 1991.

Gelzer, M. *Caesar: Politician and Statesman*. Cambridge, MA: Harvard University Press, 1968.

———. *The Roman Nobility*. Oxford: Basil Blackwell, 1969.

Gruen, Erich S. *The Last Generation of the Roman Republic*. Berkeley, CA: University of California Press, 1974.

Habicht, Christian. *Cicero the Politician*. Baltimore: Johns Hopkins University Press, 1990.

How, W. W., ed. *Cicero: Select Letters*. 2 vols. Oxford: Clarendon Press, 1959.

Lacey, W. K. "The Tribunate of Curio." *Historia* 10 (1961): 318–29.

Leach, John. *Pompey The Great*. London: Croom Helm Ltd., 1978.

Perrine, B., ed. *Caesar's Civil War*. Boston: D. C. Heath, 1882.

Peskett, A. G., ed. *Gai Iuli Caesaris Commentariorum De Bello Gallico Liber Primus*. Cambridge: Cambridge University Press, 1896.

Pocock, L. G. "What Made Pompeius Fight in 49 B.C.?" *Greece and Rome* 6 (1959): 68–81.

Sabben-Clare, James. *Caesar and Roman Politics: 60–50 B.C.* Oxford: Oxford University Press, 1971.

Seager, Robin. *Pompey: A Political Biography.* Berkeley: University of California Press, 1979.

Shackleton Bailey, D. R. "The Credentials of L. Caesar and L. Roscius," *Journal of Roman Studies* 50 (1960): 80–83.

———, ed. *Cicero: Epistulae ad Familiares.* 2 vols. Cambridge: Cambridge University Press, 1977.

———. *Cicero's Letters to Atticus.* 7 vols. Cambridge: Cambridge University Press, 1965–1970.

Sherwin-White, A. N. "Violence in Roman Politics." *Journal of Roman Studies* 46 (1956): 1–9.

Stockton, David. *Cicero: A Political Biography.* Oxford: Oxford University Press, 1971.

———, ed. *Thirty-five Letters of Cicero.* Oxford: Oxford University Press, 1969.

Syme, Ronald. *The Roman Revolution.* Oxford: Oxford University Press, 1985.

Taylor, Lily Ross. *Party Politics in the Age of Caesar.* Berkeley, CA: University of California Press, 1975.

Tyrrell, R. Y. and L. C. Purser, eds. *The Correspondence of M. Tullius Cicero.* 6 vols. 2nd edition. Dublin: Hodges, Foster, & Figgis, 1885–1899.

Tyrrell, W. B. "Labienus' Departure from Caesar in January 49 B.C." *Historia* 21 (1972): 424–40.

von Fritz, Kurt. "Emergency Powers in the Last Centuries of the Roman Republic." *Annual Report of the American Historical Association* (1942): 221–37.

———. "Pompey's Policy before and after the Outbreak of the Civil War of 49 B.C." *Transactions of the American Philological Association* 73 (1942): 145–80.

———. "The Mission of L. Caesar and L. Roscius in January 49 B.C." *Transactions of the American Philological Association* 72 (1941): 125–56.

Wirszubski, Ch. *Libertas as a Political Idea at Rome during the Late Republic and Early Principate.* Cambridge: Cambridge University Press, 1968.

Wistrand, Erik. *Caesar and Contemporary Roman Society.* Göteborg: Kungl. Vetenskaps-och Vitterhets-Samhället, 1978.

Yavetz, Zwi. *Julius Caesar and His Public Image.* Ithaca, NY: Cornell University Press, 1983.